Desert Frontier

Desert Frontier

*Ecological and Economic Change
along the Western Sahel, 1600–1850*

James L. A. Webb, Jr.

The University of Wisconsin Press

The University of Wisconsin Press
2537 Daniels Street
Madison, Wisconsin 53718

3 Henrietta Street
London WC2E 8LU, England

Printed in the United States of America

Library of Congress Cataloging-in-Publication Data
Webb, James L. A.
  Desert frontier : ecological and economic change along the western
    sahel, 1600–1850 / James L. A. Webb, Jr.
  Includes bibliographical references and index.
  ISBN 0-299-14330-9   ISBN 0-299-14334-1 (paper)
  1. Sahel—Economic conditions. 2. Environmental degradation—
    Sahel—History. I. Title.
HC1002.W43   1995
330.966—dc20   94-10506

To Alison Jones Webb

Contents

Illustrations

Figure and Maps

Tables

Preface

This book is concerned with the ecological and economic history of the southern frontier of the western Sahara known as the western sahel. Beginning in about 1600, the climate of this transitional ecological zone situated between the arid expanses of the full desert and the open grasslands of the western African savanna began a long-term and dramatic shift toward increasing aridity, and over the course of the period 1600–1850 the desert frontier moved 200–300 kilometers to the south. As this movement progressed, desert-edge pastoral nomads were forced to shift their zones of pasturage farther to the south. Agricultural communities either had to abandon their villages or had to face subjugation by the nomads. Along this desert frontier new patterns of regional economy were forged, based in part on the new specialized systems of production and exchange which came to characterize the broader region.

This movement of the desert frontier was facilitated by a transformation in the political geography of the savanna immediately before the period under study. Following the Moroccan conquest of Timbuktu in 1591, Songhai, the last great empire of the West African savanna, collapsed. In its wake, the rulers of the former provinces of Songhai attempted to consolidate their authority in the savanna. With the increasing political competition came an increasing demand for North African- and sahelian-bred horses, and as the northern grasslands became desiccated and the threat from trypanosomiasis (sleeping sickness) retreated, new crossbred horses saw their rate of survival improve. This brought about a cavalry revolution in the western savanna, and with it a marked increase in political violence. The savanna began to export an overall greater number of slaves to North African, sahelian, savanna, and Atlantic markets.

For the pastoral nomadic communities of the sahel, the savanna lands held special economic promise and risk. The northern savanna lands offered more abundant pasturage and the possibility to trade animal products, salt, and other desert goods for agricultural produce. But the sahelian nomads' contact with the rainfed agricultural lands was in general only seasonal. The transhumant herders were obliged to remove their herds to the central and northern range of the sahel during the rainy season. The disease of trypanosomiasis endemic to the southern lands could decimate not only the imported horses but also the desert-edge herds of cattle and camels. Malaria and other tropical fevers could strike down the herders themselves.

Over the period 1600–1850, the agriculturalists along the northern edge of the retreating savanna experienced a series of disasters resulting from the deterioration in ecological conditions and the collapse of a centralized state structure. Subject to predatory raiding from across the desert frontier, many Black African communities picked up and moved south. Along the south-western frontier, few went farther south than the Senegal River. This river, which meandered through the flatlands of the savanna, offered broad flood-plains inundated by river waters which had originated far to the south in the rainy mountains of Guinea. In this sense, the Senegal River was a magnet which prevented the further retreat of the agricultural communities. Along the south-eastern frontier, agricultural communities moved south and southeast from the Tagant into the Assaba and Gidimaxa regions. Farming communities in the Hawd withdrew to the south.

In a broad sense, the desiccation of the desert edge strengthened the position of the desert peoples relative to the agriculturalists. Desert peoples became increasingly able to enforce their claims to part of the agricultural production of sedentary farmers. Agricultural populations were drawn into desert slavery and walked across the Sahara to slave markets in North Africa. The agricultural frontier was rolled back through political violence. The advance of the desert frontier exacted a high toll in human suffering. A sizable slave system began to take shape in the western sahel and in the western Sahara itself.

Along this shifting desert frontier, distinguished by new systems of pastoral and agricultural production and a marked increase in political violence, a new ethnic identity began to emerge early in our period of study. It drew from Arab, Berber, Soninke, Fuulbe, and Wolof traditions, although the Arab and Berber features were dominant and the invocation of a Muslim identity required that the non-Arabo-Berber features be largely ignored. The pastoralists along the western sahel would come to call themselves Bidan, or "Whites," and in some areas to juxtapose their claims to identity in opposition to those of the "Blacks" of the savanna. The mixing of peoples that accompanied the south-ward movement of the sahel meant that those who were Whites had roots in diverse ethnic heritages. This was true even for noble Whites—the timeless "racial" identity conferred on the Whites by the contemporary proponents of a racialist interpretation of the history of the Islamic Republic of Mauritania notwithstanding. But with the changing balance of power at the desert edge and in an environment of intense competition for scarce resources, the desert-edge pastoralists came to invoke the older oppositions of Black and White deeply embedded in the Arab conception of world geography. And this invocation of ethnic identity created its own reality.

The year 1850, which marks the end of our period of study, like the beginning date in 1600, is only approximate. This ending point was chosen because, along the southwestern frontier of the desert, in the decade of the 1850s there was a sharp military and political discontinuity in the ongoing historical process. From the Afro-European town of Saint-Louis du Sénégal at the mouth of the Senegal River, on the heels of a commercial crisis in the gum arabic trade, the French in 1854 began the military conquest of the lower Senegal River valley. This campaign anticipated the military conquest of the western savanna farther to the east, although this would not take place until later in the nineteenth century. Along the southwestern frontier, the gum trade continued apace, even as the economic center of the region shifted south and as the gum trade lost its preeminent importance owing to the explosive growth in the peanut trade.

A similar discontinuity in historical patterns took place along the southeastern frontier. The 1850s marked the jihad of Umar Tall, which once again transformed the political geography of the western savanna, disrupted the lives of hundreds of thousands, and sent large numbers of Black Africans into slavery in the desert and desert edge and across the desert into North Africa. This marked increase in political violence in the second half of the nineteenth century in the western savanna harkened back to the massive disruption caused by the Moroccan plundering expeditions of the late seventeenth and early eighteenth centuries. Also in the 1850s, the gum arabic boom, which previously had been of real importance only along the lower and middle valleys of the Senegal River, reached the desert-edge populations along the upper valley of the Senegal (although on a smaller scale than that along the lower and middle Senegal).

This book is organized in five chapters. The first discusses the evidence of the shift in climate and the emergence of the desert frontier. The second and third chapters analyze the major patterns of migration, trade, and political violence across different regions of the desert edge and how and why these patterns changed over time. I have defined the (shifting) southwestern frontier as the Gibla and the lower and middle portions of the Senegal River valley. I have defined the (shifting) southeastern frontier as the Tagant, Hawd, and the region from the upper portion of the Senegal River valley eastward up to and including Kaarta. Because the historical patterns along the southwestern and southeastern frontiers are discrete, I have treated these regions in separate chapters. The fourth and fifth chapters examine the two major sectors of trade from the western sahel. The horse and slave trade between the desert edge and the savanna underwrote the political violence along the desert frontier and within the savanna. Gum arabic was the most valuable good exported from the western sahel into the Atlantic sector for most of the period under study.

This research focus on regional ecological and economic change has produced a body of data which allow some comparisons between the Atlantic, North African, and sahelian markets for the peoples of the western savanna. These data suggest that for most of the period under study the larger and most significant markets were those in North Africa and within the sahelian region itself, not those which lay across the ocean. The study concludes that the dominant historical forces which shaped the patterns of economic and ecological change along the western sahel were regional rather than European or North African. This allows for a revision of earlier interpretations which stressed the importance of the Atlantic sector—particularly the Atlantic slave trade—in understanding the economic history of the western sahel.

Sources

This book is based principally upon European archival sources and African oral traditions. The principal funds of relevant European archival materials are stored in Dakar at the Archives Nationales du Sénégal, in Paris at the Archives Nationales de France, in Aix-en-Provence at the Archives Nationales de France Section Outre-Mer, and in London at the Public Record Office at Kew Gardens. The European documentary materials were, for the most part, generated by the commercial community which resided at Saint-Louis du Sénégal. These materials contain valuable information about the evolution of the desert frontier, but this information is largely incidental to their overriding preoccupation with European commerce, which was focussed largely on the Atlantic slave trade and, to a lesser degree, on the export of African agricultural goods, particularly gum arabic.

African oral traditions are embedded in a variety of materials. Some Black and White oral traditions found their ways into Arabic manuscripts, which in turn were translated into European languages or into documents written by Europeans or Afro-Europeans at Saint-Louis du Sénégal. Other Black and White traditions were collected by earlier generations of researchers, published as formal historical works, or made available to researchers in special archives. But many White, as opposed to Black, oral traditions remained part of an ongoing oral tradition. Most historians of Senegambia and western Mali during these centuries chose to delimit their investigations at the desert edge, as it was located at the time of their research. With the assistance of desert interpreters I was able to recover some of this White tradition relating to the Black African world and desert-savanna relations.

The archival evidence in European languages is characterized by a strong regional bias. Most information about the African interior which can be gleaned from the archives concerns the southwestern frontier. This was the region with which the Europeans and Afro-Europeans at Saint-Louis du Sénégal had the most familiarity. The oral data gleaned from interviews in the desert in the early 1980s are likewise richer for the southwestern frontier. For the southeastern frontier, the European-language materials are not extensive. Yet when supplemented by oral traditions, the two sources permit the description of broad processes of historical change. All translations are my own unless they are otherwise attributed.

Research for this book began during the summer of 1979 with a visit to Dakar, Sénégal. There, I began to consult the documentary holdings of the Archives Nationales du Sénégal. I also made an initial visit to the Islamic Republic of Mauritania. The following year I was fortunate to receive a generous research grant, which allowed me to return to Mauritania (and Senegal and the Gambia) for a period of 21 months and which funded additional archival research in London and Paris. In Nouakchott, the U.S. chargé d'affaires Stanley Schrager intervened with the Peace Corps to allow me to receive language training in Hassaniyya with the U.S. volunteers. Gerald Hanisch, a U.S. Foreign Service officer, kindly allowed me the use of an apartment. Later in my sojourn, John and Mary Grayzel graciously extended to me their warm hospitality. My research affiliation with the Institut Mauritanien de Recherche Scientifique in Nouakchott facilitated my research in Mauritania.

After receiving my Ph.D. from The Johns Hopkins University, during the mid-1980s I accepted a position as a consultant to the Organisation pour la Mise en Valeur du fleuve Gambie, a regional West African development organization composed of the member states of Senegal, the Gambia, Guinea, and Guinea-Bissau. Over the course of more than two and one-half years, I worked as part of an multidisciplinary team of natural and social scientists, evaluating the probable social, economic, and environmental impacts of the construction of large dams proposed for the Gambia River basin. Later, I was able to bring this research experience in environmental impact analysis to bear on the historical problem of ecological change along the western sahel.

Acknowledgments

In writing this book, I have accumulated numerous debts to other scholars. I owe a special intellectual debt to Professor Philip D. Curtin, who served as my undergraduate and graduate advisor at The Johns Hopkins University and whose pathbreaking work on Senegambian economic history first stimulated my interest in the desert frontier. Over the years of my association with Professor Curtin, he has been a model of academic professionalism and excellence.

I owe a special debt of gratitude to the Mauritanian historian Mokhtar Wuld Hamidun at the IMRS. Mokhtar Wuld Hamidun facilitated my introduction to other Bidan historians, and he graciously shared his own wealth of knowledge of desert oral tradition.

Many colleagues have been generous enough to read earlier versions of separate chapters or of the entire manuscript and to share their criticisms with me. In particular I would like to thank George E. Brooks, David C. Conrad, Henry A. Gemery, Jan S. Hogendorn, Samba Ka, Robin Law, François Manchuelle, E. Ann McDougall, Roderick S. McIntosh, Abdel Wedoud Ould Cheikh, and James F. Searing. Richard L. Roberts made helpful suggestions for the improvement of the book's organization. David Robinson and Martin A. Klein each read an earlier draft and the penultimate revision of the manuscript and provided detailed commentaries and suggestions. The generosity of all these scholars is most appreciated. These readers have suggested useful lines of inquiry and have saved me from a multitude of errors. The errors that remain are, of course, mine alone.

This work would not have been possible without the dedicated assistance of the library staffs of The Johns Hopkins University and, in more recent years, of Colby College. On research trips, the archival and library staffs of the Archives Nationales de France, the Archives Nationales de France Section Outre-Mer, the Bibliothèque Nationale de France, the British Museum Library, the Public Record Office at Kew Gardens, the Library of Congress, and the Smithsonian Museum of African Art did much to facilitate my research.

The research for this book was funded by a predissertation summer travel grant from The Johns Hopkins University (1979), a Fulbright Research grant (1980–82), and financial support from the Social Science Grants Committee and the Interdisciplinary Studies Council of Colby College (1990–92). I would also like to express my appreciation to Colby College for funding summer research assistance (1989 and 1990) and for its enlightened policy of granting pretenure sabbaticals to assistant professors.

The Cambridge University Press graciously granted permission to reprint two of my articles. A shorter version of chapter 5 was published as "The Trade in Gum Arabic: Prelude to French Conquest in Senegal" in the *Journal of African History* 26 (1985), 149–168, and an abridged version of chapter 4 appeared as "The Horse and Slave Trade between the Western Sahara and Senegambia" in the *Journal of African History* 34 (1993), 221–246.

The illustrations, with the exception of 3.1, are reproductions of water-colored engravings which illustrate Frederic Shoberl (ed.), *The World in Miniature. Africa, Containing a Description of the Manners and Customs with Some of the Historical Particulars of the Moors of the Zahara, and of the Negro Nations between the Rivers Senegal and Gambia*, 4 vols. (London, 1821–27). I would like to thank the reference librarians and staff of the Rare Books Collection of the John J. Burns Library of Boston College for their permission to photograph these images and to reproduce them in this text.

Abbreviations

ANF	Archives Nationales de France
ANFSOM	Archives Nationales de France, Section Outre-Mer
ANS	Archives Nationales du Sénégal
BCEHSAOF	*Bulletin du Comité des études historiques et scientifiques de l'Afrique occidentale française*
BSG	*Bulletin de la Société de géographie (de Paris)*
Bull. IFAN	*Bulletin de l'Institut fondamental de l'Afrique noire*
Bull. SOAS	*Bulletin of the School of Oriental and African Studies*
CHEAM	Centre des Hautes Études d'Administration Musulmane
CO	Colonial Office Series, Public Record Office, London
IFAN	Institut Fondamental d'Afrique Noire
IJAHS	*International Journal of African Historical Studies*
IMRS	Institut Mauritanien de Recherche Scientifique
JAH	*Journal of African History*
NAG	National Archives of the Gambia
PRO	Public Record Office, London
RC	*Revue coloniale*
RMM	*Revue du monde musulman*
T	Treasury Series, Public Record Office, London

Note on Orthography and Terminology

In rendering the terms and proper names from West African languages which appear in this book, I have used spellings currently accepted by most Senegambian scholars. These spellings differ from those employed by some earlier generations of scholars, principally in the preference for the expression of the geminate vowel: to write Fuuta instead of Futa and Waalo instead of Walo. In transcribing terms and proper names from Hassaniyya, an admixture of Berber and Arabic for which there is no generally accepted system of transliteration, I have employed a simple, Anglicized approach which omits diacritical marks.[1] The effort here has been to avoid unnecessarily burdening the general reader. Toward this same goal, wherever possible, I have preferred translations of sahelian terms to transliterations.

The terms "White" and "Black" are regional cultural constructs which refer to the cultural identities of groups on the northern and southern sides of the desert frontier, respectively, rather than to skin color, although individuals affiliated with White groups were in general lighter in complexion (that is, more olive) than those who were Black (more brown). There were, however, numerous exceptions to this generalization; some of the most noble Whites were as deep brown as the darkest Blacks. Desert people referred to themselves as Whites (generally using the term "Bidan," which means "White"), and the Arabic-speaking world has long referred to sub-Saharan Africa as the Land of the Blacks (Sudan). Desert people also used the term "Kwar" (possibly derived from a classical Arabic term for villager or alternatively from a Twareg term for the color black) to refer to Blacks.[2] To the north of the desert frontier, Europeans were generally referred to as Christians (Nasrani: people of Nazareth).

1. For the sake of consistency, it has been occasionally necessary to render a desert individual's name in two different forms: to respect the French system of transcription, when the individual has published using this form, and otherwise to use the simplified (Anglicized) spelling.
2. For a discussion of the linguistic roots of these terms, see Catherine Taine-Cheikh, "La Mauritanie en noir et blanc. Petite promenade linguistique en Hassāniyya," *Revue du monde musulman et de la Méditerranée* 54, no. 4 (1989), 90–105.

On the Black side of the frontier, the Black African peoples of Senegambia did not employ a broad term of cultural identity to refer to all (Black) sedentary peoples in the region (in juxtaposition to the nomadic populations). This was probably due to the fact that these nonliterate cultures did not have a broader sense of the historical processes in which they were then engaged. Today, however, the non-Arabic-speaking peoples of Senegambia who have had significant contact with European culture refer to themselves as Black Africans. They have assimilated a cultural designation first created in the premodern Arab world and then passed on to Europeans who later reintroduced it to sub-Saharan Africa during the era of European colonialism. Desert people (as well as other Arabic-speaking peoples from the wider world) were generally referred to as Naar, which signified "Arabic speaker." The folk etymology of the term "Naar" is contested: some Black Senegambians contend that it means "liar" (thus underscoring the perceived unreliability of desert people); some White Mauritanians insist that it is derived from the Arabic word for fire (thus indicating that desert people are dangerous like fire). In Senegambia, those whose behavior and outlook are identified with general European culture are referred to as Tubab (probably derived from the Arabic word for doctor: *tabib*) regardless of their skin color.

The terms "White" and "Black" are thus deeply inscribed in the history of the sahel of western Africa. These terms have not been borrowed from the cultural constructs of European-American and African-American identities in the Western world, which have been based, in part, upon the cultural perception of skin color. On the contrary, the usage in the Western world of the cultural terms "White" and "Black" to refer, in part, to skin color (pink and brown, respectively) seems to be a distant and refracted borrowing from the Arabo-African past.

Desert Frontier

1

Ecological Change and the Emergence of the Desert Frontier, 1600–1850

The western sahel is a transitional ecozone of approximately 300 kilometers in width which runs laterally along the southern frontier of the vast expanse of the western Sahara. In an ecological sense, the western sahel is rich: it is the region in which the flora and fauna of the Sahara are found mixed with the flora and fauna of the more humid West African savanna. And although the absolute size of the plant and animal populations is not large, the high ratio of species to total population—the high biodiversity index—accounts for the great resiliency of the natural environment. But because biological productivity in the western sahel is governed principally by the precipitation which falls during a single short and unpredictable annual rainy season, the high biodiversity index is not matched by a high level of biological productivity.

The mixing of the animal and plant species of the desert and savanna ecozones has been, in part, the result of long centuries of selective human land use practices whereby livestock herding and agricultural regimes have produced a derived natural environment. Indeed, this is true even for the great expanses of the western Sahara itself. But this mixing has also been shaped by dramatic shifts in climate which have brought about transformations in sahelian lifestyles. During long periods of increasing aridity, agricultural communities have been forced south while transhumant pastoralists have been drawn into the zones of abandoned, once-cultivated lands. Similarly, during long periods of increasing humidity, herders have been forced northward by rising risks from trypanosomiasis and malaria while farmers have been tempted to expand to the north by the increased possibilities for rainfed agriculture.

The climate of the southern frontier of the western Sahara has been determined principally by the interaction of two separate systems of wind. The air mass that dominates the Sahara for much of the year is known as the Tropical Continental. It is hot and dry because it subsides from higher levels and because

3

of the nature of the surface of the desert itself. Far to the south is an extremely moist wind system known as the Tropical Maritime, which is centered over the Bight of Benin and draws humidity from the southern Atlantic Ocean.[1]

The turbulent interface between the Tropical Continental and the Tropical Maritime systems is known as the Inter-Tropical Convergence Zone, or more recently as the Inter-Tropical Discontinuity (ITD). This ITD moves north into the western savanna and western sahel with the rotation of the northern hemisphere of the earth toward the sun during the summer months and then retreats south. The annual cycle of advance and retreat creates the short rainy season and the lengthy dry season characteristic of the sahel and savanna grasslands. Rainfall decreases markedly as the ITD moves north, and the great annual movement of the life-giving rains explains in good measure the narrow, lateral ecological zones which have had such a profound influence on styles of life in West Africa.[2]

Dramatic shifts in sahelian climate over deep historical time have been studied by both natural and social scientists.[3] For the more distant periods, scholars have been able to identify long phases that persisted over many centuries. The relatively more abundant data available for more recent centuries have permitted the definition of shorter climatic phases. But the periodization of climate history for the more recent past has remained tentative because of the fragmentary nature of the evidence developed to date and because of methodological problems of data interpretation. Surprisingly, the authors of the two major assessments of historical climate in western Africa have arrived at nearly opposite conclusions about the climate of the western sahel during the seventeenth and eighteenth centuries.

Sharon E. Nicholson, a meteorologist, made the first attempt to assemble a climatic chronology for Africa and drew upon diverse materials assembled by historians, including historical journals and chronicles with qualitative observations about weather and ecological conditions. She argued that the climatic history of the western sahel over the past five centuries was defined by a humid phase that began in the late fifteenth century and lasted through the eighteenth century (although the eighteenth century was marked by droughts) and, in turn, a dry phase which continues up to the present day.[4] George Brooks, an historian, has suggested that over the long period from c. 1100 C.E. to c. 1860 C.E., the western sahel experienced two dry epochs, separated only by a long century of increased humidity from c. 1500 to c. 1630.[5] Thus for the critical seventeenth and eighteenth centuries, Nicholson and Brooks have taken diametrically opposed positions and have argued for "wet" and "dry" periods, respectively (see Table 1.1).

Table 1.1. Periodization of climatic phases in western Africa, 1100 C.E. to the present

	Nicholson	Brooks
Wet	c. 800 to c. 1300s	
Dry	c. 1300s to c. 1450	c. 1100 to c. 1500
Wet	late fifteenth to late eighteenth century	c. 1500 to c. 1630
Dry	late eighteenth to late nineteenth century	c. 1630 to c. 1860
Wet	late nineteenth century	c. 1860 to c. 1900
Dry	late nineteenth century to the present	early 1900s
Moderate		1930–60
Sporadic drought		1960 to the present

Sources: Nicholson, "A Climatic Chronology for Africa," esp. 75–81, 251–254, and "Climatic Variations in the Sahel," 3–24; Brooks, *Landlords and Strangers,* chapter 1.

The Long-term Trend toward Increasing Aridity

The apparent discrepancies between these periodizations of sahelian climate can be resolved by abandoning the somewhat artificial construct of wet and dry periods. The evidence presented below on sahelian and savanna climate in the seventeenth and eighteenth centuries does suggest that these centuries were more humid than the nineteenth or twentieth century. But the evidence also strongly suggests that a long-term trend toward increasing aridity, or desertification, began in the late sixteenth or early seventeenth century and continued through our period of study. The experience of increasing aridity was undoubtedly uneven across the sahel and northern savanna. At the northern extremes of the annual movement of the ITD, rain falls extremely unevenly and unpredictably, and thus it is not surprising that the early droughts chronicled in the sahel and savanna were not coordinated. Over time, however, the experience of the marked trend toward increasing aridity was common to the wider region.

Evidence from historical maps and travellers' accounts is strongly suggestive of a wetter climate at the beginning of our period of study. An early sixteenth-century Portuguese observer recorded the existence of lakes in the western Sahara.[6] Late seventeenth-century and early eighteenth century maps depict a prominent river at Cap Timiris as the R. de St. Anthoine or Riviere St. Jean and represent lakes connected to this river by streams. Thereafter, these bodies of water evaporate from the cartographic record. The early maps further depict a settled village of "Moors" at a distance of 200–300 kilometers east of the coast at the approximate latitude of Arguin (near Cap Blanc). This settlement site was perhaps 250 kilometers to the north of the northernmost extent of settlement by the middle of the nineteenth century. These early maps also depict the gum groves of the western sahel as far north as the St. John

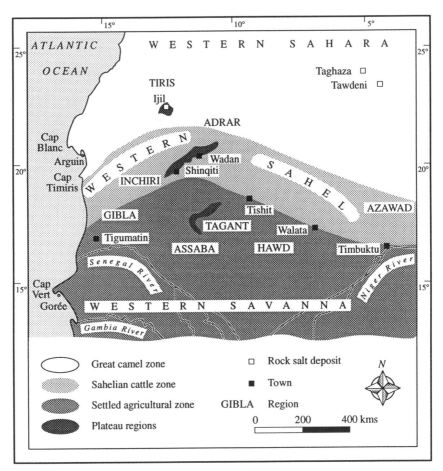

Map. 1.1. Approximate location of ecological zones, c. 1600.

River (Riviere St. Jean). Beginning in the 1740s the groves begin their carto-graphic descent toward the south.[7]

Further indirect evidence of this northern extension of settlement comes from the accounts of European observers. In 1591, Melchior Petoney, writing from the island of Arguin close to the western Saharan coast, mentioned the names of towns in the interior in the kingdom of Darha and commented: "One city there is called Couton, another Xanigeton, as also the cities of Tubguer, Azegue, Amader, Quaherque, and the town of Faroo. The which townes and cities are very great and fairely built, being inhabited by rich Moores, and abounding with all kinde of cattell, Barley, and Dates."[8] Harry T. Norris has proposed tentative identifications of these towns (with the exception of Faroo) mentioned by Petoney. All are in the Adrar.[9] If these identifications are indeed correct, Petoney's late sixteenth-century account might be interpreted to place the Adrar within the sahelian cattle zone.

In the early seventeenth century the French traveller Claude Jannequin de Rochefort stopped at Cap Blanc on his way to Senegal. Jannequin, like the map-makers many decades later, described the coast near Cap Blanc and Arguin as a desert; but he provided further details which suggest that the fisher community that he encountered was located at the utmost extreme of the ecological zone in which cultivation was possible. He noted: ". . . they [the fisherfolk] have nothing for food in this cursed country except the fish that they dry in the sun, and some grain and some tobacco . . ."[10] Departing from Cap Blanc, Jannequin visited the Senegal River valley in the 1630s. There, he was struck by the density of the forests along the middle valley. He wrote of the difficulty of walking in the forests even if well-shod and remarked poetically that the forests were full of beautiful echoes, not because of concavity of the caverns, but owing to the length and thickness of the forest solitude.[11]

Additionally striking are the observations of the mid-eighteenth-century naturalist Michel Adanson. In the course of his botanical studies he made numerous trips on the Senegal River, and the flora and fauna he described there belong to an ecosystem markedly different from that of the late nineteenth and twentieth centuries. In the 1750s there were still deep woods along the length of the Senegal River. The desert herders, in order to bring their animals down to the river region, were obliged to burn sections of the woods to eliminate local tse-tse fly infestation and to encourage the growth of vegetation beneficial to their herds. Adanson himself set ablaze a wooded region and learned that the fire was still burning eight days later.[12]

Another important observation, dating from the first half of the nineteenth century, concerns ecological change along the northern edge of the western sahel. At this period, it was apparently common knowledge that increasing aridity had transformed the patterns of land use there. As one desert writer noted about 1830:

> The abundance of habitation between Wadan and Timbuctu was likewise found between Wadan and Tichit. One could always pass the night or take a siesta in a habitation and in huts between these towns. I have observed this to be true, since one does not pass by a spot without seeing broken pots. That is the evidence of my shaykh—may God sanctify his spirit and illumine his sepulcre—and the testimony of everybody, both intelligent and unintelligent. Nowadays, the routes are deserted between Wadan and Timbuctu. There is no inhabited locality, nor anything smaller in size. It is a desert wilderness in our present time.[13]

In addition to these qualitative observations, there are quantitative data from which one can adduce evidence of climatic change. During Adanson's sojourn in northern Senegambia from 1749 to 1753, he kept a record of the number of rainfall events, the dates on which they occurred, and their intensity. His work was continued by an engineer named Andriot. The series of observations made at Saint-Louis du Sénégal by Andriot are of especial interest because they are complete for the year 1754 and run from January through October for the year 1755. They were made in the midst of a period of general famine in the sahel, which lasted from 1747 to 1758, although 1754 and 1755 were apparently somewhat better than the immediately preceding years of more abject drought.[14]

Andriot measured total annual rainfalls of approximately 520 millimeters and 400 millimeters in 1754 and 1755, respectively.[15] The significance of these two rainfall totals, when compared with nineteenth- and twentieth-century data, is apparent. For the nineteenth century, complete observations at Saint-Louis du Sénégal are available for the years 1861–64, 1868–70, 1873–82, and 1892–99; the mean annual rainfall over these years was 408 millimeters. In the period 1951–60, the decade with the highest average rainfall in the northern parts of West Africa in the twentieth century, the mean annual rainfall for Saint-Louis du Sénégal was below 400 millimeters. Thus, what appear to be below-average rainfalls in 1754 and 1755, which occurred in a period of general drought and famine, were equivalent to or greater than average rainfalls in the late nineteenth century and were in excess of above-average rainfalls in the mid-twentieth century.[16]

Additional evidence for environmental change comes from observations of the agricultural regimes along the Senegal River valley. Over time, the low-yielding cultivated crops such as millet and sorghum, familiar to nineteenth-century observers, replaced the higher-yielding maize, which had been introduced by the Portuguese either during the more humid sixteenth century or during the seventeenth century itself. Père Jean-Baptiste Labat, writing in the early eighteenth century and drawing on the notes of the French company directors André Brüe and La Courbe, is explicit on the fact that maize was a dominant crop of the late seventeenth and early eighteenth centuries.[17] At least by the middle of the eighteenth century, however, the agricultural regime had begun to change. The principal harvests were described as mixed, being composed of millet and sorghum and maize.[18] And by the mid-nineteenth century, the cultivation of maize in Waalo had ceased, and even in Kajoor, to the south, the cultivation of maize had become a minor affair.[19] This is another significant piece of evidence, because the cultivation of maize requires at least 600 millimeters of annual rainfall (or the equivalent in humidity retained in flooded soils). Maize produces higher yields than millets or sorghums during average or good years of rainfall, but disastrously lower yields during years of poor rainfall. The fact that maize was a staple of the Senegal River valley suggests that total annual rainfall there in the late seventeenth and early eighteenth centuries may have been in excess of total annual rainfall today in the Casamance area of southern Senegal, which receives approximately 50–75 percent more precipitation than the Senegal River valley and the rest of northern Senegal.[20]

The twentieth-century droughts in Mauritania and in Senegal have involved annual pluviometric deficits on the order of 50 percent or more of expected annual rainfall. This degree of shortfall was probably characteristic of the droughts of the mid-eighteenth century, and if so it would go far toward explaining how droughts in northern Senegal could occur in years in which 520 and 400 millimeters of rain fell. The famines of the seventeenth and eighteenth centuries in the western sahel were the result of the failure of specific production regimes which were adapted to more humid conditions.

Other evidence of the changing climatic regime can be discerned from comparing historical observations concerning the seasonality of the rains with more recent observations. Research on the changing pattern of rainfall events in the West African savanna under the conditions of increasing aridity observed in the second half of the twentieth century indicates that, as annual rainfall totals diminish, the rainfall events become fewer in number and increase in intensity. This means the rain that does fall has a greater erosive impact, is not absorbed as thoroughly by the soil, and thus is less available to nourish agriculture.[21] Likewise, as annual rainfall totals diminish, the length of the rainfall season has been shortening, beginning later and ending earlier, and in the middle of the summer rainy season, a minidrought (a period of four to six weeks without precipitation) may occur, which can reduce yields of non-drought-resistant crops such as maize by more than 50 percent.[22]

The same patterns may be discerned in the period under study. In the late seventeenth century, the dry season along the Senegal River was said to last from October to March.[23] By the first quarter of the eighteenth century, the rains were said to begin in June (rather than April or May).[24] Francis Moore, writing of his experiences in the Gambia in the 1730s, observed a rainy season of four months' duration, also beginning in June.[25] Adanson, in Senegal during the drought of 1747–58, observed a rainy season which began at the end of June and lasted for three months.[26]

Finally, yet another striking feature of the current rainfall regime of the West African sahel under conditions of increasing aridity in the post-1960s period is the great variability in annual rainfall totals.[27] It is probable that this variability was part of the statistical profile of the western sahel during the period under study. Put another way, sharp and drastic declines in total annual rainfall (i.e., droughts) appear to accompany shifts toward a drier climate. The droughts and subsequent famines that appear in the historical record for seventeenth- and eighteenth-century Senegambia thus themselves stand as evidence of a marked trend toward increasing aridity.

Ecological Zones

In the year 1600 the major ecological zones of camel herding, cattle herding, and rainfed agriculture were approximately 200–300 kilometers to the north of their positions some 250 years later. The floodplains of the Senegal River used for flood-recession agriculture were still banded by a belt of wooded lands that to the north accommodated rainfed agriculture and cattle herding and extended into the Adrar (Berber: mountain) and Tagant (Berber: forest) plateau regions, the Assaba (Hassaniyya: mountain which encircles), the Gibla (Hassaniyya: west), and the Hawd (Hassaniyya: basin). To the north and west of the Adrar were regions so arid that only camel nomads could survive there. To the east was a region desiccated to the point that it was not possible to cross it, save at extreme risk.

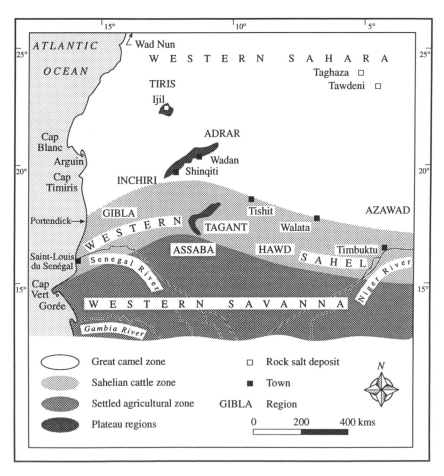

Map 1.2. Approximate location of ecological zones, c. 1850.

By 1850 the climatological trend toward increasing aridity had pushed the sahelian cattle zone out of the Adrar and out of the Inchiri (Hassaniyya: the tent in camp [during transhumance]). These desert pastures had been given over to camel herding. The sahelian cattle zone had descended into lands once used for rainfed agriculture, and new desert settlements had grown up that were in part dependent upon the importation of cereals from the south. The increasingly arid conditions had pushed rainfed agriculture south to within 100 kilometers of the Senegal River.

The Great Camel Zone

Over long centuries desert people extended the zone of camel herding into marginal and submarginal lands in response to changes in the ecology of the desert and the play of the trans-Saharan trade.[28] In difficult arid conditions, the camel was ideally suited as a transport animal. It had several advantages over its closest competitors: the camel could survive without water or fresh grazing for 8–10 days, or twice as long as a donkey;[29] the strongest draft camels could carry 200 kilograms of freight, or one-third more than the donkey or the draft ox; fewer men were required to tend camels than donkeys, and thus long-distance transport costs, figured in ton-kilometers, were lower;[30] and the camel could negotiate the hazardous footing of the full sand desert, which no other domesticated desert animal could do.[31]

All domesticated desert animals were able to tolerate greater salinity in water than human beings could, and the camel was able to tolerate higher concentrations of salt than any other domesticated animal. In addition, the camel had a further advantage over other desert herd animals in that the milch camel's lactation was not dependent upon the availability of fresh pasture, as was the lactation of cattle, sheep, and goats. Milch camels normally lactated for 11 months out of 12, and the camel's ability to turn salty water into sweet milk for almost the entire year allowed desert people to exploit lands which otherwise would have remained submarginal.[32]

By the end of the period under study, the great camel zone, by far the largest of the two great zones of livestock production in the western Sahara, had grown considerably. By 1850 it extended in an unbroken expanse from the Maghrib south to well below the Adrar plateau region. In this zone the camel was the principal herding animal, and human dependence upon the camel was profound.

Several features of the camel allowed its efficient exploitation of the sparse terrain of the arid desert. The camel had the highest ratio of leg length to torso length, and the camel's long legs allowed it more mobility and consequently a wider range reach than other domesticated animals. For example, during a season of ample pasturage, camels could range up to 25 kilometers a day compared with 15–20 kilometers for goats or sheep, although this advantage was modified somewhat by the fact that camels have no territorial instincts and this often forced herdsmen to hobble their camels to prevent them from straying. But during the dry months, camels would voluntarily return to the well for water, and during these months they were herded on terrain with such sparse pasture that it was unable to support other domesticated desert species.

The camel browsed rather than grazed. It ate the foliage of desert trees, shrubs, and low-lying plants, but owing to the physiognomic structure of its mouth, the camel could not eat the small grasses which were the prime forage of grazing animals like sheep. Goats were also a browsing animal, but because of their smaller size they had access only to foliage at lower heights. In order to maximize the use of the biomass on desert terrain, a common strategy was to mix herds of camels with sheep and goats where possible. But for desert herders to take full advantage of the vast tracts where the terrain was so poor that sheep and goats could not survive, they often herded camels alone. The general principle was: the poorer the terrain, the stricter the human dependence upon the camel.

The great camel zone did not define the geographic limits of camel herding; for example, camels were found as far south as the Senegal River and, in the dry season, in the lands beyond. During the eighteenth century, because camels were deeply identified with Arabo-Berber culture and, by extension, with Islam, some Black African rulers kept some camels to signify the prestige which came from their affiliation with the Muslim desert world.[33] But to the south of the great camel zone, the density of camels per square kilometer was far below that which could thrive on the pasturelands. There were two reasons for this. First, the decreasing density of camels in relation to the carrying capacity of the biomass was not due to a lack of pasturage or water but, on the contrary, to their relative abundance. Herders allocated better pastureland and more abundant water resources to animals which could produce more value—measured in meat, milk, and hides—than camels could. Second, camels were by far the most expensive of all herding animals, and they were highly susceptible to disease in the moister zone near the river. Thus, the more sparing investment in camels as one approached the river strategically minimized their potential loss to disease.

The Sahelian Cattle Zone

In the larger region of western Africa, herders raised two varieties of cattle—the *Bos taurus*, or taurin, and the *Bos indicus*, or zebu. Taurin are thought to have been originally introduced into western Africa by the Berbers of southern Morocco because of the deep similarities shared by the cattle of those two areas. The separation between the taurin of North Africa and those of sub-Saharan West Africa can likely be explained by an earlier period of desiccation which effectively split the taurin zone in two, when the great central regions of the desert became too dry for cattle herding and were given over to camel nomads.

The zebu cattle, by contrast, seem to have been introduced from the east,[34] probably in a recent period and perhaps as recently as a century or two before the period under study.[35] The zebu carried no immunity to trypanosomiasis and were able to insinuate themselves only into the sahelian ecozone, above the zone of trypanosomiasis in the savanna. Over the course of several centuries, the zebu gradually expanded south into the new lands created by the movement of the desert frontier. By the mid-nineteenth century, the zebu had evolved into two distinct sub-breeds: the *zebu gobra*, considered the draft animal par excellence of northern Senegambia, and the *zebu moor* herded at the desert edge.[36]

The sahelian cattle zone was in fact a zone of mixed herding of cattle, camels, sheep, goats, donkeys and, from the eighteenth century in the Tagant and the Hawd, of horses. But in the sahelian cattle zone, herders generally measured their wealth in numbers of cattle. The cattle herds needed to be watered daily, and this meant that, for long stretches of the year, pasture had to be found within a half day's journey from the wellhead. This also meant that desert groups measured their own territorial requirements in terms of their cattle's needs. In this respect, the water and pasturage requirements of the cattle herds played a central role in the organization of desert life.

The Pattern of Transhumance

At least by the second half of the eighteenth century, under conditions of increasing aridity, new patterns in the search for pasturage developed. In the western part of the sahelian cattle zone, seasonal rainfall and the annual flooding of the Senegal River were strong determinants of a transhumant cycle. This rainfall and flooding were not directly linked: the waters of the Senegal River swelled from heavy rains falling in the Fuuta Jalon highlands in distant Guinea, 1,000 kilometers or so to the southeast, rather than from local rainfall in the middle and lower valleys of the river. The rainfall and flooding together, however, did result in clear choices for the desert herders. In early winter, after the recession of the floodwaters from the floodplain of the Senegal, they took their animals from the north of the cattle zone down to the river where good pasture flourished. Many herders continued this southward movement past the river into Waalo and Kajoor, directly to the south of the Trarza, where good pasture could also be found. This southward movement did not continue far to the south of the Brakna region, because beyond Fuuta, which straddled the river, lay the expanse of the Ferlo. The Ferlo would support livestock herding (it was in fact nearly a continuous extension of the desert steppe into the savanna) but it was not rich enough to attract herders from the north of the river, and water in the dry season was in short supply there. Many Brakna herdsmen instead travelled southeast to find better pasture in the Gorgol region. This pattern of southward movement repeated itself in the eastern part of the sahelian cattle zone. There, herdsmen from the Hawd took their animals into western Mali and to the floodplains of the Niger.

There were direct costs associated with transhumance. The onset of the rainy season brought increased danger from disease to the herds at pasture in the south. The rainy season also brought a worsening of the disease environment for the desert herders, particularly an increased incidence of malaria. A desert proverb summed up the situation: "The lives of camels and Whites are short in the land of the Blacks where the trees grow tall."[37] To avoid the worst of these dangers during the rainy season, most herders moved their animals back into the northern range of the sahelian cattle zone. By then, the summer rains had replenished the steppe pasture there, and the range was usually sufficient to maintain the herds for several months, until the southward movement began again. In the event that the pasture was insufficient, herdsmen moved some of their camels, goats, and sheep farther to the north, to the pasturelands of the Inchiri and the Tiris.[38] Along the eastern range of the sahelian cattle zone, herders generally sought their pasture in the Hawd, the large basin of pastureland renowned for its biomass. In the central plateau regions, Tagant herders moved south into the Gorgol and Gidimaxa regions if conditions forced them to, but many managed to find adequate pasture in the Tagant itself, often in the area of the Tamurt en Naaj, the largest temporary lake in the western Sahara which formed after the summer rains.

At least by the mid-eighteenth century, the transhumant cycle along the western sahel was linked to the grain harvests along the Senegal River and even farther to the south. In the Gibla, desert slaves and freed slaves continued to cultivate the flooded lakeshores and streambeds in the steppe, but by mid-century the desert people received their grain in good measure from Wolof farmers along the lower Senegal River valley and in Kajoor and in Bawol and from Tukulor farmers along the middle Senegal River valley. Behind the floodplain and along the Atlantic coast was the *jeeri* land. Here, farmers planted with the first rains and harvested following the summer rains. In the floodplain itself, in the *waalo* land, farmers planted their cereals after the recession of the floodwaters, a month or so after the ending of the rainy season. In the waalo, the residual water in the earth was sufficient for the winter crop to come to fruition near the end of the long dry season. Along the eastern range of the sahelian cattle zone, herders from the Hawd moved south into Soninke and Bambara rainfed and stream-flooded agricultural lands seeking grain.

THE EMERGENCE OF THE DESERT FRONTIER

In the fourteenth century C.E., Arab nomads from the Maghrib began to migrate south into the western Sahara. These Arab immigrations altered the balance of political power between the autochthonous Berber herders and the

Sudanic states along the western sahel and were central to the new societies that emerged there, with cultural features distinct from those in the surrounding regions. Sometime in the course of these conflicts, between the fourteenth and seventeenth centuries, for example, the Berber custom of veiling the male face disappeared from the western Sahara, although it lived on in the central Sahara. And during these centuries the Berber peoples of the western Sahara gave up elements of their matrilineal kinship system, which they had held in common with the Black African groups in the savanna, and came to adopt a more patrilineally oriented, Arab system. This process of cultural change and assimilation is sometimes called Arabization as shorthand for the ethnic and cultural change that took place both within the desert and at the desert frontier. But because Black African populations were also assimilated into the newly emerging desert ethnicity and the contribution of Black African culture has been largely submerged in desert peoples' historical reconstructions, the notion of Arabization glosses over a complex process of cultural selection from Black African, Berber, and Arab sources.[39]

The forging of this new ethnic identity along the desert edge was probably only the most recent example of a deep and ongoing historical process associated with climatic change, but our understanding of the earlier transformations in identities is rudimentary. Centuries before the period under study, an ethnic group known as the Bafur had been agriculturalists along the desert edge, with settlements in the Adrar and Inchiri. And during the Songhai Empire (1492–1591) and perhaps even earlier, ethnic interactions between Berbers and Soninke had produced a new Soninke dialect, Azayr, that had an important admixture of Berber.

It is clear, however, that at least by the late seventeenth century a new ethnic identity with Arab, Berber, and Black African features had begun to develop. And by dint of their proximity to and their interrelatedness with the Black African world below the Sahara, sahelian pastoral people at some point came to refer to themselves as Bidan, which means, in desert Arabic, "the Whites."[40] This slowly unfolding redefinition of ethnic identity along the western sahel was neither uniform nor complete. In the Adrar, a few communities of Whites continued to speak Azayr into the twentieth century.[41] And groups of Berber-speakers continued to speak Berber into the early twentieth century, even though Hassaniyya, the language of the Arab immigrants, became the lingua franca of the western Sahara.[42]

The creation of the new sahelian ethnicity was partly a response to the Arab immigrants' pressures toward assimilation and partly a response to rapid ecological change. The period of increasing humidity from c. 1450 or 1500 to c. 1600 encouraged agriculturalists and savanna pastoralists to push northward. In the period which followed, the desiccation of the western sahel and northern savanna confronted farmers with a choice to retreat southward or to adopt a different lifestyle, and herding peoples who moved south found themselves dominant in what had been principally agricultural lands. Along this shifting sahelian frontier, the Arabo-Berber people, and at least some of the non-Arab and non-Berber groups who had been assimilated into the new sahelian ethnicity, came to think of themselves as Whites in relation to the Blacks.[43]

These desert-edge constructions of White and Black identities were accompanied by the reconstruction of White histories that stressed either the historical reality of the immigration of Arabs into the western Sahara or a Berber heritage to the near exclusion of other elements. Bidan oral group histories, some of which would find their way into script, would "document" their immigration into more southern desert-edge lands. In the more northern regions of the western Sahara, in what is today the disputed territory of the former colony of Spanish Sahara and southernmost Morocco, desert identities would have a different inflection. Desert people there had less direct contact with the Black African agricultural societies below the Sahara, and thus were less prone to invoke a White identity. To the east, along the border between the western and central areas of the Sahara was a dangerous, virtually uninhabited region, the Majabat al-Kubra, which loosely enforced a linguistic boundary between the Berber-speaking groups of the Malian Sahara, or Twareg, and the Bidan of the western Sahara.

The new White ethnicity grew up on the periphery of a trans-Saharan trade system, which had earlier shifted from the western Sahara farther to the east. Kumbi Saleh, the presumed capital of Ghana and a center of long-distance trade located in the Tagant region of Mauritania, probably declined in the thirteenth century, as did Awdaghust, another caravan town and oasis in the same region. A center of commercial exchange then began to flourish in the Niger bend region, as Timbuktu grew from a community of 10,000 persons in 1325 to an estimated 30,000–50,000 at its apex in the sixteenth century. Thereafter, during its period of decline from the early seventeenth century, some of the Berber populations associated with Timbuktu dispersed into the western Sahara, in particular to Walata, and later to Tishit and the Adrar.[44]

The new ethnicity also grew up in a context of political turbulence. In 1591 the Moroccan conquest of the Niger bend region destabilized the political arrangement of savanna states under the aegis of the Songhai Empire, centered in Timbuktu. Jolof, one of the semiautonomous constituent states of Songhai which had ruled the areas of northern Senegambia, began to come apart even earlier in the mid-sixteenth century, when aristocracies of the former provinces of Jolof established their own states.[45] And in the late sixteenth century and well into the first half of the seventeenth century, a Fuutanke state known as Grand Fulo, which emerged from Fuuta along the middle Senegal River valley came to dominate the savanna region far to the north of the Senegal River above Fuuta and Waalo and east toward Timbuktu.[46]

The historical record contains numerous references to the earlier Black African occupation of desert regions that came under the control of the Whites, although the dating of this Black occupation remains problematic. For example, two fragments of Black African oral traditions have passed into the written White accounts on the other side of the desert frontier. One recounts the journey of a Bidan caravanner who encountered a Tukulor elder in Fuuta who claimed that the people of Fuuta, the ancestors of the present-day Tukulor, were once resident in the Adrar and in the Tiris.[47] Another White account, again drawing on the oral tradition of Fuuta, makes a similar claim to earlier settlement in the Adrar, as well as what are today the southern portions of the Trarza and Brakna regions in southwestern Mauritania.[48] Additionally, linguistic analysis of topographic names throughout the Tagant and Brakna regions has established the presence of early Tukulor settlements in those regions.[49] Indeed, even today among the Pulaar-speakers of the middle Senegal River valley, the Tagant is referred to as Jeeri Fuuta, the rainfed agricultural lands of Fuuta, even though it has been centuries since the effective occupation of those lands by the Fuutanke.

Some desert tribal oral traditions that concern the founding of White settlements in the Tagant and the Hawd also refer to the southward retraction of Black Africans. In the Hawd at Walata, for example, the White group the Limhajib today hold that their ancestors displaced a Black African Bambara village on this site.[50] And in the Tagant, at Rashid, the Kunta hold that Blacks from the Sudan shared the secret of the wadi with the settlement's founder and thereby facilitated the establishment of the Whites there.[51] From the Tagant and the Assaba regions, Soninke began to withdraw to the south, perhaps as early as the fifteenth century.[52] From the Assaba, the final retraction of the Soninke was completed only in the last third of the nineteenth century.[53]

Although the grand lines of the formation of these new cultural frontiers are sometimes fashioned in oral tradition as the immigration of the Arabo-Berber herders and the withdrawal of Black African cultivators, Blacks' and Whites' social histories were, in fact, deeply intertwined. Black and White oral traditions provide windows into the variety and complexity of the new ethnic identities and relations of production that emerged along the desert edge. Over time there was a series of disparate ethnic transformations in the desert frontier zones. Wolof, Tukulor, Soninke, and Bambara families were incorporated into the White world, and occasionally Arabo-Berber groups merged their ethnic identity with those of Black groups on the other side of the frontier.[54]

The Common Culture of Frontier Societies

For the pastoralists and villagers of the western sahel, the interaction between Arab and Berber and Black African groups generated over time a world of shared assumptions and understandings. These common cultural features persisted, even as the lifestyles of nomadic pastoralism and agriculture emerged ever more distinctly and even as the Azayr language of the Sahara died out and was replaced by an Arabo-Berber language zone to the north of the desert frontier and a West African language zone to the south.

Both White and Black African societies, for example, recognized a fundamental distinction between warriors and clerics, a cultural division foreign to the societies of North Africa. The pattern of accommodations reached between the two cultural models, however, showed considerable variation. In the Gibla, the southwestern corner of the western sahel, at least by the late seventeenth century, desert society had sorted itself out into two ways of life: one headed by warriors, or *hassani*, and the other headed by clerical nomads, or *zwaya*. Here the successful warrior groups were largely of Arab descent, and the clerical groups, largely of Berber descent. Elsewhere the distinctions between warriors and clerics were less sharply drawn. In the Tagant, for example, Berber and Bedouin (largely Arab) groups were both militarized and in competition with one another until, in the two middle quarters of the eighteenth century, a Berber group was able to defeat the reigning Bedouin group and became the dominant warrior group in the Tagant and the Assaba, restricting the influence of the Bedouin to the Hawd.[55] Other variations appeared farther to the southeast. In some cases Bedouin and Berber groups sorted themselves out into dual hierarchies of zwaya and hassani, but some clerical groups combined the two cultures and were highly armed zwaya.[56] Farther to the north, in the Adrar, a Bedouin warrior group had established itself as the dominant hassani group by the middle of the eighteenth century and had begun to exercise some regional authority. Thus by the third quarter of the eighteenth century, there were what we might loosely term emirates in the plateau regions and the Hawd as well as in the Gibla.[57] In the Tiris a large and stable confederation known as the Ulad Barikallah held sway.

In many respects these arrangements were not unlike the spheres of tribal and confederate influence in earlier periods of desert history, but there were some significant differences. Within an emirate, both zwaya and hassani groups recognized the emir's territorial authority, which included the collection of taxes. And additionally, from the establishment of the European coastal entrepôts, from the mid-fifteenth century at Arguin and from the mid-seventeenth century at Saint-Louis du Sénégal at the mouth of the Senegal River, the hassani chiefs in the Gibla had access to a new source of trade revenues and weaponry to reinforce their regional authority. The Trarza and Brakna emiral families

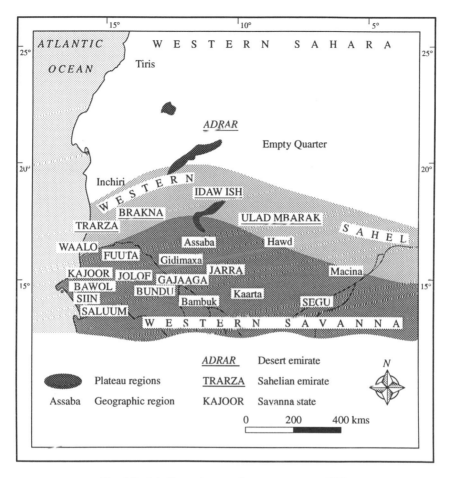

Map 1.3. Sahelian emirates and savanna states, c. 1750.

were able to strengthen their field of authority by successfully representing themselves to the European factors as the legitimate regional authorities through whom the Europeans should negotiate for trading privileges. At times these claims were violently disputed within the emiral lineages and between neighboring emirates. But the emirs were able to secure a measure of security for the Atlantic commerce, if only by guaranteeing their own restraint from violence against the European factors and their agents in exchange for cloth, guns, gunpowder, and a plethora of less significant trading goods.[58]

Another important difference from the earlier patterns of desert tribal confederation was that, from the emirates' establishment in the middle of the eighteenth century (and even earlier in the Gibla), the cultural ideals of the dual hierarchies became established throughout the desert, and the clerical groups, unless impinged on directly, did not militarily challenge the warriors' authority. In part, this was accomplished through the warrior and clerical groups' adoption of different styles of life. Warriors prized mobility. In order to be able to attack and retreat rapidly, they travelled almost exclusively on camels and horses rather than on donkeys or pack oxen. They likewise raised only horses and camels: the production of sheep, cattle, goats, or donkeys would have left them less mobile and more vulnerable to attack. Warriors drew most of their material needs from groups which produced surpluses—from their own slaves, whom they set to work in the south in agricultural villages, from sedentary Black farmers to the south, from other nomadic groups, and from zwaya trade caravans. Warriors lived in smaller groups than the zwaya pastoralists, so as to forage more widely, and this was another dimension of their need to be mobile. In a desert culture with few material luxuries, warriors had fewer possessions, fewer slaves (with the exception of the emiral families), and fewer animals than did the zwaya pastoralists.[59]

Zwaya groups were larger and more numerous than hassani groups, and they tended to have larger camps. Along the desert frontier the needs of their herds circumscribed their movements for much of the year. Most zwaya groups, however, also had diversified economies. Within the desert they allocated the labor of their dependents to farming both within and on the edge of the Black African world, to herding livestock, and to the harvesting of tree crops, particularly gum arabic, that found an expanding market in Europe. And they engaged in local and long-distance trade, across the frontier into the villages and fields and courts of Black Africa.

The most noble hassani and zwaya headed hierarchic systems of social and political relations.[60] The elevated status of these nobles was recognized by other White groups who paid them taxes or labored on their behalf and who acknowledged their own lower social status in a myriad of other ways—seeking their spiritual masters among the more noble zwaya and being willing to fight on behalf of their betters.

The herding groups who were tributary to the hassani were called *znaga*. They either looked after the animals of the hassani or paid their obligation to the warriors with a part of their own herds' production. Znaga status was an ignoble, submissive one. Groups, families, or individuals who had fallen on hard times or who were losers in battle or razzia sometimes accepted this status in return for protection from other warrior groups.

The nomads who accepted the authority of the more noble zwaya groups often had come to their position through similar losses. Those within the sphere of influence of a shaykh from a group other than their own were known as *talamidh*, or *tolba*. Like their counterparts, the znaga, these students contributed labor or material goods to their masters. Sometimes the line between forced and voluntary contributions was ambiguous because students could increase their own social status through their association with a powerful shaykh. Relations between less noble and more noble groups in both hierarchies are difficult to characterize because they had elements of reciprocal obligation and of coercion. In general, less noble groups received protection from the exactions of other predatory groups in return for their contributions, but this protection was not always very effective. Some of the less noble groups were quite independent and capable of defending themselves, and they formalized their submission to a hassani or zwaya group only when required to do so. The larger and more powerful these client groups became, the more their allegiance was sought by the most noble groups for the purpose of securing prestige. Some client groups paid allegiance to more than one master, and under duress a dominant group might be able to activate the allegiance of a less noble group by giving gifts which symbolized the dominant group's largesse. Another mitigating factor in these unequal relations was the fact that, if exactions paid to several groups became too onerous, less noble groups could sometimes switch masters. This was tricky business and sometimes brought on warfare.

The Black African agricultural societies on the other side of the frontier also recognized a fundamental distinction between warriors and clerics. But these distinctions tended to be important only at the highest levels of social and political authority. The social order was not greatly different from that of the desert. Beneath the military and spiritual aristocracy was a large stratum of free people and an even larger stratum of slaves. Free people could be taxed by the authorities and had little recourse before the caprice of their leaders. As in the desert, authority was legitimated through a kinship idiom. Political and religious leaders emerged from powerful descent groups.

The second, profound indication of a shared past among the sahelian societies on both sides of the desert frontier was a common inheritance: the institution of caste.[61] The fact that casted groups of praise-singers and leather, metal, and wood workers were incorporated into the emerging ethnic groups of the desert may reflect an ecological adaptation at the end of the long dry period from c. 1100 to c. 1450 or 1500 to the decline of major towns in the western Sahara such as Awdaghust, where artisanal goods were readily available to the nomadic communities. The incorporation of these casted groups thus may be related to the nomadic communities' disengagement from urban centers and a subsequent shift to a more rudimentary style of life. Although the deepest origins of caste are obscure and probably date to a period of social and ethnic transformation before the period under study, it is an indication both of the geographic limits of the early Sudanic Empire and of the Black African roots of White desert society that the institution is found only in the societies of the western sahel and western savanna, and not farther north in the Arabo-Berber world of the Maghrib.[62]

Another important dimension of shared culture was that of Islamic practice. Islam had been current in areas of the desert and sahel for many centuries, and certain features of Islamic practice had been noted at the courts of Black African potentates in the centuries before our period of study. But over the period 1600–1850, the frontier societies of the western sahel came increasingly to share Muslim cultural practices, including the observance of Muslim dietary rules and the prescriptions for prayer. Some of this Muslim influence was spread peacefully by teaching clerics who were active in Black African agricultural communities. Some Islamic practice was spread coercively through the political violence of religious warfare. When some Black African agricultural communities were incorporated into spheres of White influence, their societies were reorganized along different principles. The sahelian frontier was the crucible in which sedentary societies that had once organized themselves along matrilineal lines came to embrace patrilineal principles of organization.

Political Violence across the Frontier

Across the length of the western sahel, White warriors raided Black communities for slaves and booty. This political violence was possible because the desert warriors, who rode fleet horses or camels, enjoyed the tactical advantages of surprise and rapid flight and were able to launch terror raids. Black resistance was extremely difficult to organize because Black military forces lacked the means to undertake retaliatory expeditions into the desert. And Black reprisals courted the possibility of even more devastating desert raids in the future.

These raids had a political focus. In the contest for scarce resources in a desiccating environment, Whites used terror to gain access to the agricultural production of the Blacks. A common pattern was for hassani to despoil a Black community, raid for slaves, and then bind the survivors and neighboring communities into tributary relationships. Over time, White warriors forced a progressively larger number of Wolof, Tukulor, Soninke, and Bambara communities into vassalage and extorted agricultural goods from them. These arrangements became increasingly important from the first half of the eighteenth century, when, because of the increasingly arid conditions, White warrior communities became unable to depend upon agricultural production of communities within their immediate sphere of influence.[63]

The more noble warriors established their rights to collect agricultural taxes from tributary villagers. *Bakh*, or *ashur* as it was known in the Brakna, was a grain tax taken from Black cultivators who lived in the floodplains along the Senegal River and in the fertile lands of the Assaba region. Bakh was a tax on the individual farmer, not on the land. Warriors collected the tax directly:

they appeared annually in their tributaries' cereal fields and demanded their portion of the harvest. In general, the grain collected went directly to the support of the warrior and his family.

There were differences in the application of this tax between the Trarza and Brakna regions which seem to reflect, at least in part, the relative strength of the emiral lineages. At least from the second half of the eighteenth century, the more powerful Trarza warriors took bakh by force if necessary, because their supremacy was virtually uncontested in the larger region. In the Brakna, from the 1760s, chronic divisions within the emiral lineages rendered the authority of the emir less secure; consequently warriors had to accord more respect to their tributaries—because their tributaries could more easily transfer their allegiance from one warrior group to another or enlist support from Tukulor forces in Fuuta if the Brakna warriors were too heavy-handed in their exactions. Thus, in the Brakna, villagers were said to have given bakh as a "gesture of friendship," rather than having been forced to pay by threat of violence, as was the case in the Trarza.[64]

The agricultural villages in the southwestern Gibla lay between two cultural worlds. They were "Wolof," in that the villagers spoke Wolof among themselves and shared the cultural life of the larger Wolof worlds to the south. But at least by the early eighteenth century, most of the Wolof villagers on the northern bank of the Senegal River also understood Hassaniyya, and their desert overlords considered them as tributaries and collected bakh from them. This general pattern also held true along the southern Brakna and Gorgol regions and in parts of Fuuta, where the villagers were Tukulor and spoke Pulaar rather than Wolof. Likewise in the Gidimaxa region, at least by the nineteenth century, the Soninke had been fully vassalized and paid a grain tax to the warrior nomads from the north.[65]

In the Hawd, the dominant desert groups incorporated large numbers of Bambara and Soninke slaves into desert society and installed some of their captives as tributaries in villages and collected grain from them. Desert groups carried out devastating raids against pagan villages to bring them under their control and justified the political violence in a religious idiom. As the Moroccan merchant Sidi Hamet observed in the early nineteenth century:

> We set out for home from Tombuctoo, in the month of Rhamadan, after the feast, and went back by the same route we had come—that is to say, we went first to the west one moon, along the border of the desart [sic]. We durst not take any thing without paying for it, because we were afraid of the inhabitants, who were a mixture of Arabs and negroes, and all of them Mohammedans, but very bad men: they had also many white men slaves. I saw sixteen or eighteen myself, and a great many blacks. These true believers have very fine horses, and they go south to the country of the rivers, and there they attack and take towns, and bring away all the negroes for slaves, if they will not believe in the prophet of

> God; and carry off all their cattle, rice, and corn, and burn their houses; but
> if they will adopt the true faith, they are then exempt from slavery, and their
> houses are spared, upon their surrendering half of their cattle, and half of their
> rice and corn; because, they say, God has delivered their enemies into their
> hands.[66]

Other raids were more purely destructive in nature and were concerned neither with agricultural taxation nor warfare against nonbelievers. This was particularly true across the southwestern frontier. On their slaving and looting
expeditions, desert raiders went after Blacks—often women and children in
the fields—and took their chattel back into the western Sahara or sold them
into the trans-Saharan trade or to the cross-cultural traders at Saint-Louis for
resale into the Atlantic slave trade or for ransom from the pillaged communities.

In the early period c. 1600 to c. 1675, warfare and pillage on the northern
frontier of Waalo (and perhaps Fuuta as well) generated large numbers of slaves
who were sold north into the horse-for-slave trade. Following the onslaught
of Moroccan raiding in the late seventeenth century, the Trarza and Brakna
swept additional Black African communities under their control. From the
mid-eighteenth century, as the sahelian frontier moved south, many different
hassani fractions and gangs, as well as the emiral forces, began to raid across
the Senegal River. In principle, the dominant warrior groups had to balance
their own political interests in political violence against costs incurred by
disruption in the trade in gum arabic and thus in European revenue payments
or by a break in the flow of grain and other revenues from the Black African
farming communities.

Throughout much of the eighteenth and nineteenth centuries, the heads
of the dominant warrior groups had only very imperfect control over the political violence launched from their spheres of influence.[67] European observers
sometimes referred to the White raiders who operated in Black lands as a separate tribe, but the raiders typically did not belong to an organized political
entity. They were simply hassani who raided on their own account without
undue concern for emiral authority, and these gangs often included individuals from the emiral families who were in dissidence with the ruling emiral
faction. These raids brought terror. As the British lieutenant governor of
Senegal and Gorée observed early in the nineteenth century:

> Mounted on their excellent horses, lightly armed accustomed to abstinence and
> bearing without complaint the extremes of thirst and hunger they astonish and
> overwhelm the unfortunate negroes by the rapidity of their movements and the
> suddenness of their attack. There are among them a tribe (the Assunahs) whose
> sole trade is pillage and who glory in the name of robbers, and who, in larger
> or smaller bodies, are constantly employed in predatory incursions on the
> Neighboring Territories.[68]

Desert Slavery

As a result of White raids into Black lands, a sizable frontier trade in desert-bred and North African horses to the Black cavalry states of the savanna, and a regional exchange of salt and other commodities, a large volume of Black Africans were swept into the desert world. Large numbers of these victims of political violence were forced to march across the Sahara to meet their fates in the Maghrib. But many of these individuals did not make the trans-Saharan journey. From these northbound coffles composed principally of women and children, many Black African captives were put to labor in the White world of the desert edge and the desert itself.[69]

At least by the eighteenth century, sizable slave communities could be found in the plateau regions. There, in the oasis settlements, slaves tended the date palm plantations and cultivated the desert-edge fields. Throughout the pastoral regions surrounding the plateau regions and in the Hawd, White families used female slaves for domestic labor under the tent and male slaves for camp labor and tending the animals. And at least by the late eighteenth century, even in the great camel zone, where both free and slave population densities were low, it was rare to find a family without a slave.[70] Large numbers of slaves, however, were also to be found along the desert frontier itself. As this frontier moved south, new Black communities were forced into servile status. By the nineteenth century, the principal labor of slaves there involved the production of grain to be handed over to their pastoral overlords.

The lives of many first-generation slaves of the Whites who had been uprooted from their home communities were harsh and short. The initial period of adjustment to desert slavery was undoubtedly the worst. Bonds of obligation and affection between masters and slaves had not yet had the time to strengthen, and new entrants experienced high mortality in the struggle to adapt to the rigors of slave life in the sahel. Masters expected abject deference from their disoriented chattel; disobedience elicited beatings and worse.[71]

Food and other material resources in the western sahel and western Sahara were in chronically short supply. Newly acquired slaves who were without kinship ties to the masters could be denied food in times of dearth, and in this sense slaves served as a buffer against White famine in a desiccating environment. Slaves might produce food, but they were not always entitled to consume it. Even in normal times, slaves had a poorer diet, which meant more disease and higher mortality, and they suffered from greater exposure to the elements. The extreme psychological and physiological stresses involved in the adjustment to desert enslavement must also have taken their toll. It is thus perhaps not surprising that, within the larger regional context of slavery in the West African savanna, enslavement in the western sahel and western Sahara had the reputation of being the worst of all possible lots.[72]

Slave communities in the western Sahara, like many slave populations else-where throughout the world, were not self-sustaining.[73] New imports were necessary to maintain or expand the size of the captive populations. In addition to the harsh conditions of desert slavery, which sharply constrained the rate of population growth, cultural rules which governed the social identity of the offspring of White-Black unions had an important role in slave demography. Many young female slaves became the concubines of their own-ers, and the male progeny of these master-slave unions were Bidan if the union was legitimized by freeing the slave woman, as seems to have been the usual case. By contrast, female offspring had slave status.[74]

There were other additional ways to shed slave status. Slaves could acquire freedom from direct servitude as a reward for exceptional service or for advanced religious achievement.[75] This possibility of manumission operated as a powerful social control; slaves understood that they could win improve-ments in their own life conditions or those of their offspring through good behavior. After manumission, the freed slaves, or *haratin*, continued to owe labor service to their former masters.[76] A small number, known as *imragan*, lived in villages along the coast and specialized in ocean fishing. But freed slaves were generally settled in agricultural villages, within the sphere of White surveillance, where they could produce grain for their former masters. These freed-slave villages occupied the lands previously controlled by Black Afri-cans. These haratin communities probably had fertility rates as high as those of other sedentary communities elsewhere along the western sahel.

Viewed over the long term, it appears that, as the southern shore of the desert moved southward and waves of political violence broke onto the savanna, Black Africans were caught in the undertow. Many, probably most, were trans-ferred north to the Maghrib. But many others were dragged into the sahelian world, where, over time, they were transformed into slaves, and then some were freed. Their cultural identities became deeply bound to the White world. The massive slave and freed-slave populations of the Islamic Republic of Mauritania are the legacy of this historical process.

2

The Southwestern Frontier

During the sixteenth and seventeenth centuries, a new nomadic-sedentary frontier in the southwestern corner of the western sahel began to form among Arab, Berber, and Black communities. In the first recoverable stages of this process, Black villagers along this frontier were converted to Islam and drawn into the Muslim world as tributaries. During the course of the seventeenth century, under pressure from drought and inadequate harvests, this frontier began to move south. In the 1670s, an Islamic revolution launched by Berbers from the desert edge engulfed not only the desert steppe but also the Black states of Waalo, Kajoor, Jolof, and Fuuta. The fledgling Islamicized regimes were almost immediately overthrown by the traditional Black aristocracies in league with Arab desert warriors. The jihad had failed, but severe military pressure from the desert continued and came to wreak havoc along the southwestern sahel.

From the 1670s into the mid-eighteenth century the Moroccan Empire in North Africa launched military expeditions in league with the desert hassani against the Black frontier states with devastating effects. Black agricultural lands were lost to the Whites, and large numbers of Black captives were shipped north to western Saharan and Maghribine markets. From the mid-eighteenth century White warrior forces from the desert continued to carry out similar depredations, crossing the Senegal River to raid for slaves, to pillage, and to extort surplus from Black villagers.

Following the French abolition of the Atlantic slave trade in 1816 and their reoccupation of Saint-Louis du Sénégal in 1817, the French began to search aggressively for a replacement for the overseas slave trade. In the process of so doing and by experimenting with agricultural stations and deepening their involvement with the gum arabic trade, the French began to contest the hegemony of the White warriors in Waalo. These conflicts reached a point of resolution only at midcentury. Following the Franco-Trarza war of 1854–58 the French established themselves as intermediaries between the Whites and the Blacks and acted to choke off the chronic violence along the nomadic-sedentary frontier.

The Early Centuries, 1300–1600

In an earlier period of increased humidity, sedentary villages dated from c. 700 to c. 1000 C.E. extended far north into the Gibla.[1] During the dry period which followed, estimated variously from c. 1300s to c. 1450 or from c. 1100 to c. 1500, the nomadic-sedentary frontier moved south. In the 1450s, Cadamosto, the Venetian merchant in the service of the Portuguese, judged the Senegal River to be the northern limit of Jolof and shortly thereafter Duarte Pacheco Pereira made a similar observation.[2] During the more humid period from c. 1450 or 1500 to c. 1600, the lands of the central and northern Gibla came to be settled once again, this time apparently by Bafur villagers. Bafur place-names and desert traditions about the Bafur survive, but little else. The ethnic identity of the Bafur apparently was transformed in the period before the late seventeenth century and absorbed into the ethnic categories of Wolof, Berber, and Peul (pl. Fuulbe), and thus remains somewhat mysterious. Intermixed with the Bafur lands and extending far to the north were the lands of the Berber pastoralists. In the early centuries of the Jolof Empire the Berber pastoralists had apparently posed no threat, perhaps because they were unable to overcome group antagonisms and thus remained too poorly organized to constitute a military threat to the savanna states.

But in the course of the fourteenth and fifteenth centuries, according to desert oral traditions for which dating can be only approximate, several migrations into the Gibla began to change the balance of power at the desert edge. First, a confederation of Berber pastoral groups began to drift south from the central-western Sahara. During this southward movement this confederation of five tribes, known as the Tashumsha, encountered villages of the Bafur. Some of the Bafur agriculturalists began to move south into the Wolof territories, and many of those with herds were absorbed by the Berber confederation. A second migration took place at the end of the fourteenth century. The first of a succession of Arab warrior groups which were drifting south from the Maghrib reached the Gibla. In the midst of the Tashumsha, the most powerful Arab warrior group, the Ulad Rizg, established a sphere of political authority.[3] And over the next two centuries or so, other Arab warrior groups continued to drift south into the Gibla, travelling down the Atlantic littoral, perhaps partly in order to extort payments from the traders active at the Portuguese trading points along the coast.

Authority in these territories in the westernmost sahel was contested. Arab warrior groups struggled among themselves for dominance and brought Berber and Bafur groups under their control. The establishment of these warrior spheres of influence threatened the authority of Jolof. In the aftermath of the mid-sixteenth-century collapse of Jolof, Amari Ngone Sobel (r. 1549–93), the first ruler (*damel*) of Kajoor, struck a blow against this northern pressure. He gathered his savanna forces to repulse the early warrior emirs and drove north into the Sahara, reputedly half the distance to Morocco, farther than any Wolof force had ever penetrated before.[4] Whatever the results of this excursion to beat back the military threat of the Arab warriors, the influence of desert Islamic culture continued to percolate through the western sahel and into the western savanna. According to Wolof tradition, Amari Ngone Sobel chose to submit to a ritual bath prepared by his desert marabouts to mark his enthronement as the founder of Kajoor.[5]

The Immigration of Bubazzul

The White groups of the Gibla which formed in the sixteenth and seventeenth centuries developed traditions built upon the core idea of in-migration from the north of both Arabs and Berbers. The north-to-south direction of these migrations, a trope in the oral traditions, carried a strong cultural value: it was a confirmation of the Whites' North African and Islamic heritage. Yet, although most of the migrations were undoubtedly from the north to the south, it is clear that the unidirectionality of the migrations presented in the traditions glossed a more complex set of historical circumstances. From the east came Berbers from the Malian Sahara, fleeing the increasing aridity that was creating the vast Empty Quarter. Also from the east across the savanna lands came other herding groups, whose descendants trace their origins to the immigration of Bubazzul.

The story of the immigration of Bubazzul (Arabic: possessor of a breast) is remembered today in the village of Tigumatin, a community with Wolof roots which was incorporated into the White world early in our period of desert expansion. According to some accounts, Bubazzul is said to have emigrated from Hausaland in the east, in what is today northern Nigeria.[6] Consider the tradition of Bubazzul's immigration to the lower Trarza:

> During his travels in a westerly direction, Bubazzul stopped at a Black community which was not Muslim and into the heart of which he married. From this marriage was born a son. But the hosts of this Sharif nearly immediately began to be suspicious about the Muslim beliefs of their visitor. Feeling himself threatened, he left his wife's family [and his wife] at night, taking the newborn with him. He began to ask himself if the newborn would be able to survive despite the separation from his mother, while God, in order to lessen his worries and to allow the infant to survive, made a breast to grow on Bubazzul. It was thus that he was able to provide nourishment, through breast-feeding, to the son whose descendants would constitute the five groups. . .[7]

The story is remarkable in several respects. First, it distills neatly into a single episode the arrival of Muslim immigrants in a Black African world. Second, it records the mutual intimacy and distrust that must have characterized the relations between Muslim pastoral peoples and non-Muslim cultivators before the emergence of a shared culture influenced by Islamic values. Third, this tradition may also tell a story about a process from which a new Islamicized culture had to emerge. That is, it may be understood as an allegory about the necessity for groups with matrilineal descent systems to separate themselves from these traditions in order to adhere fully to Islamic and patrilineally based values.[8] Finally, of the five groups which claimed descent from Bubazzul—the Id Agvudya, Ulad Atfagha Haiballa, Id Acheghra, Smassid, and Ahl Gannaar—the first four were Berber and the last was considered to be Wolof. Thus, perhaps most remarkable of all, the tradition of Bubazzul tells a story of group origins before the solidification of White identity, before the widespread insistence on North African and Islamic origins, and refers to an early period of changing ethnic identities at the desert edge, most likely before the seventeenth century.

The Town of Tigumatin and the Black Descendants of Bubazzul

According to other Trarza traditions, the formation of the Ahl Gannaar, the Black descendants of Bubazzul, took place as a result of the southward migration of cattle herders into the Trarza region:

> Among the ancestors of the Ahl Gannaar was Radwan Fall, who was born in A.H. 996 [1587/88 C.E.]. He was a great chief. At the arrival of Al-Mansur Saadi's army, which opened up Songhai to Islam, he was already a great religious chief. At the time his camp was to the north of [the present-day site of] Nouakchott.
>
> One day his son Hamid Fall went to search for a herd of cows, one of which was named Teguemad [Berber: a cow without horns]. After a while he founded the center of the current Tigumatin. So several groups formed around him because of his father's reputation. And the area took the name of Tigumatin.[9]

This tradition is likewise interesting in a number of other respects. First, it confers high religious prestige upon the ancestor of the Ahl Gannaar, by linking Radwan Fall and his descendants with the Moroccan conquest of Songhai in 1591 and thereby establishing the later significance of Islamized pastoral peoples in the region to the north of the Black villagers. Second, it tells the story of the southward immigration of Berber herders with cattle to an area of Black settlement. (In some versions, the region is chosen because the water table is so high that one of Hamid Fall's cattle strikes water with his horn, just below the earth's surface, indicating both that more humid areas lay to the south and that the differential between the north and south was sufficient to induce a migration.) Third, the patronymic Fall is also of strong interest because it provides a window into the earlier culture of the desert frontier. The name Fall (in Wolof: Faal) by the sixteenth century was the name of the royal lineage of Kajoor as well as a typical name in the Trarza.[10] The patronymic is thus additional evidence of early, shared cultural features between the Berbers and Wolof (or proto-Wolof). Fourth, the settlement of Tigumatin (the Berber plural of "*teguemad*") was named by cattle herders after their cattle. This reference to the zebu moor of the Bidan suggests the establishment of the desert-edge breed, introduced from the east into the lower regions of the western sahel, which took place in the context of a rapidly deteriorating environment, when the zebu gobra of the Senegambian Wolof states was driven south by climatic change.

Conversion to Islam and the Establishment of the Frontier

The period of religious conversion was thus probably coincident both with the establishment of a new pattern of land use and with the formation of new ethnic identities. According to other fragments of early Trarza oral tradition, at the time of the founding of Tigumatin there was another settlement in the immediate vicinity which was named Mbul (variant spellings: Mboul, Mboll, Emboul),[11] whose inhabitants were Black. Hamid Fall drew the Blacks to Tigumatin by the force of his religious authority; these Blacks took the name of Ahl Gannaar,[12] and they began to use the surname Fall. The Ahl Gannaar were agriculturalists, but they began to claim descent from the Prophet by virtue of their line of descent both from Hamid Fall and earlier from a son of Bubazzul. This movement brought about the demise of Mbul, and the name Tigumatin came to refer more to a region than to a single settlement. The greater region of Tigumatin included 40 villages and a mosque.[13]

Interestingly, the figure of Hamid (variants: Hammat, Hammar, or Hamet) Fall also occurs in Wolof oral traditions, wherein he is credited with founding the maraboutic village of Pir in Kajoor. Jean Boulègue, working from Wolof traditions, has suggested that the founding of this village took place in the late seventeenth century or that Hamid Fall came to the village under the aegis of the damel Latsukaabe Fall (r. 1695 or 1697 to 1719).[14] (Desert traditions have located Hamid Fall earlier in the seventeenth century.) At all events, the fact that a Muslim center in Pir had been established before the jihad of Nasir al-Din in the 1670s is consistent with the thesis that the religious conversion of the Ahl Gannaar to the north of the Senegal River had repercussions among the Wolof to the south of the Senegal River.

It is possible that this process of the transformation of the Wolof cultivators into the Ahl Gannaar can be dated roughly to the late sixteenth century. This movement signalled the establishment of Muslim control in the lower

Trarza, and it may be that the religious conversion of the Ahl Gannaar was a distant ripple related to the settlement of Saadian military in Timbuktu. Rumors of another coming revolution like that of the Almoravids were rife in the western Sahara about 1600.[15] But in any case, the formation of the Ahl Gannaar secured an agricultural base for the pastoral Bidan as the pastoral frontier moved south, and these events presaged the growing influence of the desert people in the lower Senegal River valley and the importance of Islam as a political idiom in the region well before the more widely noted jihad of Nasir al-Din (discussed below) that convulsed the region in the 1670s.[16]

Other Trarza oral traditions shed additional light on early commercial geography. At its founding, Tigumatin is said to have taken over the commercial functions of the town named Mbul, which is said to have been one of the most ancient inhabited sites in the Trarza, built by the Midlich (a Berber grouping) during the era of the founding of Wadan and Tishit.[17] Thus, there had likely been some commercial connection of long standing between the Trarza region and the Atlantic corridor into the Wolof Empire and the currents of commercial exchange in the trans-Sahara trade.[18] It is likely that Tigumatin was the principal regional market for desert-savanna trade in the central Trarza. It may have also been the major port of entry for Saharan horses into the western Wolof states of the Senegambia.[19]

According to Trarza oral tradition, Tigumatin was the locus for commercial traffic. Although many of the particulars of Tigumatin's importance in the networks of desert-savanna trade are unrecoverable, Trarza oral tradition does hold that Tigumatin had special commercial relations with Wad Nun:

> An eagle was found dead in the Tigumatin region with a large lance in it. Some people in the region recognized the lance as bearing the markings of the people of Wad Nun. And later on when some people at Wad Nun were shown this lance, they told the following story. They said they had been selling meat near Tigumatin when the bird had appeared. And one of the Wad Nun traders, taking up his weapon, threw it. But then both the eagle and the lance disappeared. (This shows us that there were commercial relations between Tigumatin and Wad Nun. The road that ran between them was 10 kilometers wide.)[20]

The Jihad of Nasir al-Din and the War of Bubba, c. 1673–77

In the mid-seventeenth century a saint of the Tashumsha arose in the Gibla, and he began to preach an ascetic doctrine of religious reform. This saint, Nasir al-Din of the Ulad Dayman, wanted the Black riverine and savanna peoples to embrace a stricter, more rigorous adherence to Islamic principles. The ruling elites of the Black states rebuffed the call to reform. The reform movement enjoyed some success among the commoners of Fuuta, Kajoor, and Jolof, who resented the tyranny and pillage carried out by the Black elites,[21] and reform movements sprang into existence which called for the overthrow of the old order. The religious fervor generated by Nasir al-Din likewise gained momentum among some of the zwaya groups in the Gibla, and in 1673, thus mobilized, they launched a military campaign, seeking the forcible conversion of the Black riverine and savanna states to the south.[22] Jolof, Fuuta, Kajoor, and Waalo fell after desultory resistance. To govern the Waalo, Nasir al-Din appointed a man who was linked by matrilineal ties to the Ahl Gannaar.[23]

The second phase of the jihad took place in the lands to the north of the Senegal River. There the ascendant zwaya forces tried to forge a theocratic state, or caliphate, under the command of Nasir al-Din. The militarized zwaya forces began to try to enforce the collection of *zakat*, the tithe paid by Muslims to the caliph. The jihad turned down quite a different path when a tributary of the zwaya Tashidbit refused to pay the zakat. This tributary, a certain Bubba, fled and took refuge with the Bani Hassan. Zwaya forces tried to force the hassani to give up Bubba, but the Bani Hassan refused. Thus the hassani and the zwaya entered into the direct conflict which is known as Shurbubba, or the war of Bubba.[24] This conflict spread through the Trarza, Brakna, and Gorgol regions. Neither all the hassani groups nor all the zwaya groups participated in the fighting, but the warfare did involve many of the major desert groups in these regions. In the first several skirmishes the zwaya forces were victorious, but they were unable to achieve a decisive victory. When the saint Nasir al-Din fell in battle at Tirtillas in the Trarza in 1674, the unity of the zwaya forces began to crumble. A series of successors to the failing caliphate attempted to carry on the war, but the hassani proved triumphant.[25]

At all events, the reform movement in the Black African states failed. The elites were able militarily to reimpose their authority.[26] And in the desert, at the end of Shurbubba, although the circumstances undoubtedly varied from group to group, the victorious hassani institutionalized their ascendancy by imposing three humiliations upon the defeated zwaya. When hassani visited the zwaya camps, they were to be entitled to one-third of the water drawn from the well by the zwaya for the use of their animals. The hassani could require the zwaya to provide animals to transport them from one camp to another. And the hassani could impose on the zwaya to provide them with three days of hospitality (shelter and food) at each zwaya camp.[27]

The two primary documents concerning the jihad of Nasir al-Din and Shurbubba—a contemporaneous account by the French governor of Saint-Louis, Louis Chambonneau, and a historical account written in the first half of the eighteenth century by the zwaya scholar Muhammad al-Yadali—have been subject to diverse historical interpretation.[28] Boubacar Barry in his influential work on the history of Waalo argued that the cause of the "war of the marabouts" lay in a broad shift in patterns of long-distance trade. In his view, although the reform movement launched by Nasir al-Din was couched in religious terms, the underlying reasons for it lay in the economic threat posed to the desert clerics by the French entrepôt at the mouth of the Senegal River. The fledgling Atlantic slave trade represented a danger to the zwaya because it signalled the reorientation of trade toward Saint-Louis, which worked to their disadvantage. In Barry's view the movement of Nasir al-Din was thus defensive and protective of the north-south trade systems.[29]

The evidence concerning climatic change and the social and cultural transformation of the Ahl Gannaar suggests a different interpretation. Nasir al-Din, who is represented in both the Louis Chambonneau and Muhammad al-Yadali texts as something of an other-worldly character, did include an end to pillaging as one element of the plan for reform that his emissaries represented to the Black elites. In the context of an increasingly integrated regional economy, signalled by the incorporation of the Ahl Gannaar into the realm of desert Islam, this call would have had obvious economic importance. The land and labor of the Ahl Gannaar had only recently been lost to the Black African states. The Ahl Gannaar almost certainly would have been among the Black cultivators targeted for raiding. And these attacks would have jeopardized the agricultural base and the expanding sphere of influence of the desert clerics. Thus, Nasir al-Din could expect his call to Black cultivators who were under assault from the Black aristocracies and their minions to fall upon receptive ears. The overthrow of the Wolof and Tukulor elites would have been a necessary step before incorporating other farmers into a new state dominated by desert clerics. In the eyes of the desert clerics the good Black African Muslims were those who would have submitted to their authority. Beyond the ken of the desert marabouts, Black pagan (or insufficiently Islamized) cultivators were considered fair game for raiding. As Barry himself points out, the horse and slave trades, articulated by the desert zwaya, were integral to the political economy of the desert and savanna at this time, and opposition to the broader savanna politic of enslavement would have put Nasir al-Din at odds with the larger ethos of the desert world. The desert forces were not opposed to enslavement in general—far from it; they were opposed only to enslavement that jeopardized their economic interests.

The jihad of Nasir al-Din thus appears to have had an economic rationale embedded in the organization of the regional economy. It is also clear that the Atlantic slave trade could not have represented much of a threat to the long-distance commerce articulated by the zwaya. The Atlantic slave trade offered the Black elite an alternative market for slaves, and it may have promised to bolster the Black states in their confrontation with the expanding desert forces. But the number of slaves sold into the Atlantic slave trade was a very small percentage of those sold into the desert and across the desert to North Africa.[30] And from internal evidence in the Chambonneau account it is clear that, once in control of the Black African states, Nasir al-Din courted the Euro-

pean merchants of the Atlantic slave trade. After the initial successes over-
throwing the Wolof and Tukulor elite, Nasir al-Din sent his brother to the
French to assure them that their interests in the Atlantic slave trade would not
be jeopardized.[31]

The failure of the jihad allowed the Arab warrior groups to establish their
hegemony in the Gibla. The Black African elite resumed its exercise of political authority in Waalo, Kajoor, Fuuta, and Jolof. But the jihad dislodged the
authority of the *brak*, the Wolof ruler of Waalo, over parts of the northern
territories once under Black African control. As the commercial agent Jean
Barbot observed in or about 1682: "This kingdom [Waalo] has very much
declined from what it was in former times, both as to the extent of its dominions and the number of people. The wars it has continually been ingag'd in,
have considerably contracted its limits, for the country of Genehoa [the Gibla],
was once a dependance on it, and therefore in those days indifferently call'd
Genehoa or Senega."[32]

The failed reform movement along the Senegal River also had important
ecological consequences. During the jihad, Berber zwaya from the Gibla had
sought to persuade the common farmers of the riverine and savanna states to
the south (Waalo, Fuuta, Kajoor, and Jolof) to heed the millennial call of the
teachings of the charismatic saint Nasir al-Din. The Wolof of Waalo and Kajoor,
in particular, heeded his millennial call not to plant their grain crops, and when
the grain crops failed to materialize, the Wolof fell to slaughtering their animals to stay alive. The suffering was undoubtedly great. Barbot, who visited
the Senegambia in 1681–82, held that the great famine that racked the region
in 1681 was "in all likelihood" a continuation of the famine occasioned by the
failed jihad.[33] An observer who passed through the region in 1685 was hope-
ful that the Wolof herds would reproduce themselves after a ban upon killing
them was imposed,[34] and an early eighteenth-century writer echoed the hope
that the Wolof would regain their herds,[35] but in the decades following the
war, the pasturelands of northern Senegal must have been underutilized. At
least by the 1720s, the Wolof in Kajoor had reestablished their herds in some
limited measure, but by this time, desert herders had crossed the frontier and
settled in the best pasturelands in the Wolof territories, in Njambuur.[36] By the
1760s, desert herders in Njambuur and in the Trarza were the principal, if not
the only, groups producing cattle for market.[37]

Crossing the Frontier: White Settlement in Northern Senegal
in the Late Seventeenth and Early Eighteenth Centuries

Toward the end of the seventeenth century, the Idaw al-Hajj zwaya group began
to expand from the Gibla, across the Senegal River, into northwestern Senegal.
The Idaw al-Hajj established themselves as teachers of Islam, and through their

students they spread their influence through the villages in Waalo and Kajoor. Their students filled the villages of Barale, Nder, Mbakoul, Waraq, and Sagha in Waalo, where the Idaw al-Hajj were also the religious advisors of the *lingeer*, the powerful female political figure in the region who was usually the mother or sister of the brak. But the largest grouping of Idaw al-Hajj settlements was in the region of Njambuur on the border of Kajoor and Waalo.[38]

By the late seventeenth century, the Europeans at Saint-Louis knew the ensemble of the Idaw al-Hajj in the Trarza, Kajoor, and Waalo by their Wolof name, the Darmankour.[39] The origin of the term is unknown, but it is said to mean "they have incorporated (or encompassed) everybody," expressing the assimilative process which drew Wolof under the aegis of the religious authority of the Idaw al-Hajj. The movement was an analog to that of the Ahl Gannaar a century or so earlier. But where the Ahl Gannaar, who had been Black, had become incorporated into the world of the Whites, the Idaw al-Hajj, who were White, began to assimilate themselves into the Black world. Over time, those White immigrants to Senegal and their progeny adopted Wolof as their primary language, and by continuing intermarriage they became clearly distinguishable from their White cousins in the Trarza. The new families created by these unions were nevertheless set apart. They lived in the midst of Wolof culture but carried the religious prestige of the Idaw al-Hajj.

The Idaw al-Hajj were certainly not the first desert marabouts to establish themselves in Senegal; a certain Mokhtar Mbay had founded the village of Gadde-Nyandoul in Kajoor sometime during the reign of Amari Ngone Sobel (r. 1549–93). And immigrations of families and small groups from other lineages undoubtedly preceded and may have been coincident with the movement of the Idaw al-Hajj.[40] But the Idaw al-Hajj were the largest and most significant movement of desert zwaya to the south of the Senegal River in the post-jihad period. This immigration was in full progress by the turn of the eighteenth century.

The Establishment of White Influence in the Grain Trades

As White groups came to control some of the pasturelands of Waalo and Kajoor, particularly in Njambuur, and to insinuate themselves more deeply into the economic life of these Wolof kingdoms, they intensified the currents of exchange along a north-south axis between the savanna and the desert. And during the course of the eighteenth century, punctuated by droughts and failed harvests, new patterns in the grain trades became established all along the Senegal River valley. Rather than depend upon the grain production of their immediate tributaries and slaves, the Trarza pastoralists came to receive their grain imports from farther to the south—from Waalo, Kajoor, and occasionally from Bawol. This network of exchange was adjacent to a similar one which linked the Brakna with Fuuta, and to a lesser degree, because of its aridity, with Jolof. There was little exchange between these two parallel networks except in times of economic or political disruption. The Trarza rarely traded with Fuuta, or the Brakna with Waalo or Kajoor.

Even before the "war of the marabouts," desert zwaya had been deeply involved with the handling and transport and marketing of local foodstuffs in the Wolof kingdoms. They handled the animal transport for the salt trade from the pits at Ganjool on the border between northwestern Kajoor and southwestern Waalo. The desert traders had hauled salt throughout Kajoor and the wider region and exchanged it for locally grown grain and for cloth garments from the Cap Vert region. Observations from the mid-seventeenth century indicate that a long-distance relay was in place, sending grain back into the desert in exchange for transport services.[41] Yet evidence suggests that in the late seventeenth century the Trarza and Brakna regions were largely self-sufficient in food production, including cereals. Indeed, the earliest account of Europeans provisioning themselves with grain indicates that the French were trading to the north of the Senegal River along the banks of Lake Cayar, where some 500 Black African and Bidan traders were selling cereal surpluses.[42] Proximity to the river, which meant low transport costs, may well have been key.

Much of what we know about these matters comes from the records of the European traders at Saint-Louis and Gorée, because they were dependent upon grain production within the Black African states, and the Whites were adept at exploiting the dependence of Saint-Louis on imported food. This shows up in the high price spikes passed on to the Europeans at Saint-Louis in times of scarcity. In 1698, for example, the price of a barrel of shelled maize weighing 400 pounds, which normally sold for between 4 and 8 francs, fetched up to 20 francs.[43]

By the famine years of 1723–25 in Senegambia, the desert traders had positioned themselves as the principal brokers in the cereal trades with Saint-Louis, and they were able to force the French to trade on terms that they dictated.[44] By the early 1740s, the Bidan had taken over the brokering of virtually all the grain of Kajoor.[45] And by the mid-1740s the desert traders were in such complete control of the grain trade that little was available for sale to the Europeans.[46] The need for food imports was the greatest vulnerability of the European communities, and the desert traders exploited this vulnerability ruthlessly. In 1753, for example, the desert traders bought up grain along the river, sold it sparingly against the imported *guinée* cloth, and thereby drove up the price of grain and strongly depreciated the guinée. The zwaya moved easily in and out of the grain trades, exploiting deftly the opportunity costs of other commerce.[47]

The extent of the grain trade from Waalo and Kajoor for desert society is difficult to estimate because annual demand varied as a function of weather, warfare, and production. But it is clear that after the great drought of the mid-eighteenth century (1747–58) the desert peoples were deeply dependent upon the importation of grain.[48] In comparative terms, it seems certain that the demand from the sahel was at least several times greater than the combined demand from Saint-Louis and Gorée. The populations of these enclaves grew in the late eighteenth century and did so rapidly in the first half of the nineteenth century; but even then their demand for grain was far inferior to that of a single desert region like the Trarza.[49] During the era of the Atlantic slave trade, the grain demand from the Atlantic communities was probably also inferior to the grain necessary to maintain the Wolof cavalries, a trade-off between "guns and butter" if there ever was one.[50]

Table 2.1. Regional population estimates, 1755–1848

Year	Saint-Louis	Gorée	Trarza	Brakna
1755[a]	2,500	—	—	—
1767[a]	—	1,094	—	—
1776[a]	4,622*	1,569	—	—
1779[a,b]	3,018	—	—	—
1785[a]	6,000	1,636–1,646	—	—
1786	5,460[a]	—	—	—
	5,000[b]			
1801[b]	10,000	—	—	—
1810[a]	5,200	3,268	—	—
1818[c,d,e]	6,000	—	30,000†	—
1832[a]	9,030	5,261	—	—
1837[c]	13,000	—	—	—
1838[a]	13,717	—	—	—
1840[e]	13,000	—	—	—
1848	—	—	50,000[a]	60,000[a]
			55,000[d]	63,000[d]

Sources:
   [a] Curtin, *Economic Change*, vol. 2, appendix 7.
   [b] Pierre Labarthe, *Voyage au Sénégal pendant les années 1784 et 1785, d'après les memoires de Lajaille* (Paris, 1802), 177.
   [c] E. Bouët-Willaumez, *Commerce et traite des noirs aux côtes occidentales d'Afrique* (Paris, 1848), 12–13, 33–34.
   [d] ANFSOM, DFC Sénégal, carton 83, no. 115, Rapport sur les établissements . . . , par M. Schmaltz.
   [e] Anne Raffenel, *Nouveau voyage dans les pays des nègres* (Paris, 1856), vol. 1, 125.
   * Adults only.
   † Men only.

The external demand for grain exports from Kajoor, a region styled by one observer as "the granary of this part of Africa,"[51] exacerbated conditions of food shortage there during bad years. Even in good years overall production was dampened sharply by the practice of pillage and the disruption caused by warfare. Wolof villagers produced far below capacity by design. Indeed, successful harvests were an invitation to pillage. With the establishment of colonial rule and the cessation of pillage, Wolof farmers began to produce large agricultural surpluses for export, without the need for food imports.[52]

Hassani Dominance across the Desert Frontier

In the second half of the eighteenth century, hassani forces in the Gibla established their intermittent dominance of Waalo, Kajoor, Fuuta, and Jolof. In part this was accomplished through the exercise of political terror—raiding, enslavement, destruction of villages, and acts of random violence—that brought individual villages and families into relations of vassalage with their sahelian overlords, who offered some degree of protection from the depredations of other hassani groups. And in part, the White warriors established their hegemony through military pacts with the Black elites or through military invasion.

The earlier period, from the jihad of Nasir al-Din until c. 1760, was also marked by political violence launched by Whites into Black Africa. In the war of the marabouts desert clerics toppled the Black African elites of the Wolof states and Fuuta, but these victories were short-lived, and members of the Black aristocracies regained their ascendancy with the assistance of the desert-edge warriors. In this sense the war of the marabouts heralded the rising influence of the hassani in the Black African states.

The war of the marabouts also unfolded at the beginning of a period of the expansion of Moroccan influence in the southwestern Sahara. Beginning in the 1670s expeditionary forces sent by the sultan of Morocco had begun to wage warfare against the Black riverine states. These marauding forces wreaked havoc along the desert edge. In the lower Senegal River valley, it was likely this military pressure that forced the brak by about 1697 to move his capital Ngurbel from the north to the south bank of the river.[53] Waves of political violence pushed other Blacks as well to the south side of the river, and many thousands of Black villagers who were not so fortunate were captured as slaves. This violence was determinative in the sense that never again would the Wolof of Waalo attempt to control the northern bank of the river. Fuuta's control over the Assaba and Tagant was also definitively broken.

These military interventions also shook up the balance of power in the Gibla. In 1720 when the Brakna emiral grouping moved against the Trarza emiral grouping (aided by the Ulad Dalim from along the Atlantic coast), Ali Shandhora, the Trarza emir (r. 1703–27), sought and received military assistance from the sultan of Morocco.[54] The conflict was not contained in the Gibla, but spilled over into Kajoor, where the Trarza chief chased after the Brakna with a force of 1,000 cavalrymen and 2,000 foot soldiers.[55] Ali Shandhora was eventually able to defeat the Brakna forces, thereby freeing the Trarza region from the yoke of tribute. In the course of this military campaign, Ali Shandhora seized 4,000 slaves in the Brakna and conscripted them as slave soldiers.[56] These soldiers made up the Trarza infantry, useful for expeditions into the Black states.[57] To put this in a regional perspective, this single seizure of 4,000 slaves equalled the number of slaves exported into the Atlantic slave trade from the entire lower and middle reaches of the Senegal River valley over a period of 10 years or more.[58]

This violence took place in the midst of a period of widespread military intervention along the entire length of the Senegal River valley.[59] In Fuuta, beginning in the early 1720s, marauding armies which were apparently composed of Moroccans, Whites, and Blacks from the Hawd were able to raid almost at will and to depose *saatigis* [rulers]. Although at least one of these originally Moroccan armies was called in by the ruling Deeniyadkoobe lineage to stave off an internal challenge, the desert military forces soon began to operate on their own accounts.[60] The violence also brought about realignments within the political order of the Black African states. In 1722, some of the forces of Fuuta joined with the Moroccans and Arabs to attack Waalo, presumably at least in part because in 1715 the brak of Waalo stopped making the customary payment to Fuuta. They struck Waalo hard, taking women and children, including two of the brak's wives, and destroying most of the livestock that they came across.[61] Violence, enslavement, and the imposition of tribute devastated Fuuta, and kept it prostrate from the 1720s into the 1770s. Oumar Kane, the historian who has studied this desert military pressure on Fuuta in depth, has argued that it was by far the singular and determinant factor in the collapse of the Deeniyadkoobe regime.[62]

The threat of Moroccan raids also hung over Waalo and Kajoor, and by 1720 Ali Shandhora already had grand designs to depose the brak and establish Trarza hegemony on the south bank of the Senegal River.[63] During the course of the 1720s Trarza influence tangibly expanded in both Waalo and Kajoor. Neighboring Waalo was the more powerful of the two Wolof states, and the Trarza chief solidified his political alliance with the Wolof elite by marrying the sister of the brak.[64] But this arrangement afforded the population of Waalo no special protection from the violence. The military incursions from the desert continued to be nearly annual affairs, and they took their toll. By 1726, agricultural production in both Waalo and Kajoor was disorganized, and the populations were suffering.[65] The violence continued into the 1730s and 1740s.

It was not, however, until after the great famine of 1747–58 that the regional balance of power began to shift decisively in favor of the desert hassani. This shift took place in the midst of an internal struggle for succession to the office of damel of Kajoor. At the death of the damel in 1747, the legitimate heir, Meïsa BiGe, was not yet of age to exercise authority. Those who exercised the powers of damel in his stead hatched a plot against him, and Meïsa BiGe took refuge in the Trarza (or Waalo). At maturity, the damel gathered his supporters and marched upon Kajoor in an effort to establish his authority. After three battles, in the last of which the usurper lost his life, Meïsa BiGe in 1758–59 took over the reins of Kajoor. The *buur ba* (ruler of) Jolof took advantage of the civil warfare in Kajoor and attacked the new damel. He succeeded, installing himself as ruler from 1759 to 1760. About 1760 Meïsa BiGe sought the military assistance of the Trarza hassani, and the damel's forces in league with a Trarza military expedition led by Sidi al-Mokhtar Wuld Sharqi Wuld Haddi fought a pitched battle against the buur ba Jolof and his forces. In this battle the buur ba Jolof was killed, and Meïsa BiGe again regained control of Kajoor, again if only briefly.[66] According to Trarza oral tradition, upon the defeat of the buur ba Jolof, the damel of Kajoor's mother is said to have declared, "In all the world there are only three good women: the mother of Allah, the mother of the captain of the Trarza army that defeated the Jolof [Sidi al-Mokhtar Wuld Sharqi Wuld Haddi], and myself, the mother of the damel!"[67] And according to Trarza oral tradition, the Trarza intervention came at a price. The damel had to agree to pay an annual tribute to the Trarza emiral family of one camel load of cloth and one *mud* (about two liters) of gold and beads each year. And for one month of each year the Ulad Ahmad Bin Daman warriors could circulate freely within the domains of the damel. During this month the warriors were free to pillage at will, carrying off as many slaves and as much grain and other goods as they could. Sometimes the damel designated a particular village for the Trarza forces to destroy completely, burning it to the ground and carrying off its inhabitants.[68] Kajoor had been forced to cede part of its sovereignty.

The civil war in Kajoor and the subsequent intervention by the Trarza hassani took place during and immediately following the period of low rainfall and general famine (1747–58) which struck the entire Senegambia.[69] Of the riverine states, Fuuta proved more resilient than Waalo in the face of the drought. Because the Tukulor of Fuuta practiced a dual economy of agriculture and livestock herding, during seasons of drought Fuuta could disperse some of its population into the pastoral nomadic sector, and these groups were then free to travel where necessary to secure adequate pasture.[70] Waalo was not so fortunate. Waalo was dependent upon cereal production and thus was deeply disturbed by years of low rainfall and low streamflow. The Wolof of

Waalo could flee to neighboring African states during times of famine, but where shortages prevailed these refugees were unwelcome arrivals. When drought disrupted the usual social and economic patterns in Waalo, the part of the population suddenly rendered surplus by the natural disaster became easy prey for raiders from the north. Trarza hassani generally stole children and women rather than adult men from the fields, because they could be more easily integrated into the desert world or sold across the desert into North Africa. And violence begat violence. When desert warriors fell into the hands of Wolof villagers, they had their throats cut.[71]

In the years after the drought, the political lives of the Wolof states in the lower Senegal River valley were severely disturbed, and the Trarza presence grew ever more aggressive. The civil warfare in Kajoor and its new tributary relationship to the Trarza warriors left Kajoor in a weakened position in relation to Waalo to the north. In 1762 a new brak tried to expand his authority by blocking tax payments from the Europeans to the damel. This effort succeeded in the short term, but in 1764 forces from Waalo and Jolof joined together to attack Kajoor.[72] The attack failed and the brak was forced to retire to Waalo after six weeks. By August of 1765 the damel's forces had counterattacked and practically conquered Waalo. By 1766, civil war had broken out in Waalo.

The Waalo political system could still elect a candidate to the office of brak, but when opponents to the brak sought support from the desert warriors to the north, the Wolof elite could not provide a reasonable degree of protection for its political allies. Trarza forces exploited the divisions between the Waalo political factions, and they stepped up their raids into Waalo. The Trarza hassani began to exact bakh payments from the Wolof villagers under the nominal authority of the brak. Ali al-Kori, the Trarza chief at this time (r. 1757–85), backed one contender, Mambodje Kumba, against a succession of braks advanced from the core Waalo political lineages, and one after another of these braks died by assassination or in warfare.[73]

In 1771–72 a severe drought struck the Trarza region, and this only exacerbated the Trarza pressure on Waalo. This drought apparently did not affect the riverine or savanna peoples directly, but it was so severe that, according to a Trarza historical poem, it caused warfare to break out within the Trarza emiral grouping.[74] The effect of this warfare on Waalo was that the desert warrior pressure was less focussed than ever, and groups from the Atlantic coast, which usually had been reined in by the Ulad Ahmad Bin Daman, also began an assault on Waalo.[75]

In 1775, the Trarza attacked Waalo in force and to devastating effect. It is possible that the Trarza chiefs acted in collusion with the British governor of Senegal, although the charge raised that Governor O'Hara bore principal responsibility for the attacks would seem to rest on the implausible assumption that O'Hara was able to manipulate the Trarza warriors to European advantage.[76] At all events, the results of the Trarza assault in 1775 on Waalo are clear enough: the attacks permanently changed the balance of power at the desert edge. The destruction of Waalo fields and villages was severe. The desert raiders and the Wolof elite sold many of the Waalo villagers into the Atlantic slave trade. In 1774 and 1775 alone, the British shipped 5,135 slaves from Senegal.[77] The raids continued into 1776, and although no export figures have been found for that year, the number of slaves entering the Atlantic slave trade likely continued quite high.

The Trarza warriors also took unknown numbers of captives from Waalo into the desert. Many of these slaves travelled north to Saharan and North African markets, but others were retained along the desert edge. This presented something of a problem because the new slaves were in close proximity to their former Wolof society and because the influx was so rapid that it was difficult for the Whites to establish rights in ownership. Seven years later desert society still had not perfectly absorbed the new slaves. In 1783 an observer noted that the Blacks to the south of the river were making forays into the desert, attempting to steal back captives from the Whites, and that the desert people were stealing slaves from one another.[78]

The pattern of hassani dominance which held sway in Fuuta, along the middle valley, over the course of the century 1675–1775 was similar in many respects to that along the lower valley.[79] Continual raiding and warfare left the desert hassani able to pillage at will. And the additional exactions of the Deeniyadkoobe ruling class fuelled resentment among the commoners. Over the long decades from 1720 to 1770 this violence took its toll. Perhaps the principal impact was demographic. Slave raiding considerably thinned the Fuutanke population,[80] and the slaves were channelled almost exclusively to the north, into sahelian, Saharan, and North African markets.

Along the middle valley, however, Fuuta's response to tyranny from both within and without was remarkably different from that of Waalo and Kajoor in the lower valley. In the 1760s, pious Muslims in small communities in Fuuta banded together to build an Islamic reform movement to resist the exactions of the Deeniyadkoobe and the Brakna. Fortuitously for the Fuutanke, in the same decade the Brakna emirate was weakened by the death of the emir Ahmad Bin Hayba Bin Nagmash; the emir's son seized power in 1766 but was unable to reestablish the full authority exercised by his father. And downriver the destruction of Waalo by desert forces in the mid-1770s must have given additional urgency to the Muslim initiative. By 1776 the Fuulbe reformers had purged the ruling Deeniyadkoobe and called into existence a theocratic Muslim state. This revolution had significance that reverberated beyond Fuuta itself. The White warriors had held that slave raiding was permitted against non-Muslims. One thrust of Fuuta's revolution was to deny the hassani this rationalization of warfare against nonbelievers. It called specifically for immunity for Muslims in the face of the threat of slave raiding, and the revolution succeeded in blunting the White attacks.[81]

Thus the decades of the 1760s and 1770s marked a watershed in the evolution of White influence in Black lands. From this point onward, in the Wolof states of Waalo and Kajoor, White warriors could undertake slave raiding and pillage with impunity. The balance of power had tipped sharply. Even a few warriors found that they could terrorize a Black village. The threat of even more brutal retaliation sharply circumscribed the villagers' resistance to marauding raiders.

The hassani policy of raiding was at great variance with that of the commercial zwaya, particularly those deeply involved in Senegambian trade and transport. The commercial zwaya had a vested interest in the maintenance of substantial peace. In the years following the Trarza devastation of Waalo, the Idaw al-Hajj themselves came under attack from the Trarza warriors. They moved the site of their gum market and invented kinship ties to the Brakna emiral lineage to legitimate the change of allegiance.[82] In 1790, the marabouts in Njambuur revolted against the authority of the damel of Kajoor and appointed a *qadi* [Islamic judge]—a Tukulor from Fuuta—to rule themselves. He reigned for seven years. During this period, the people of Njambuur successfully resisted the Trarza incursions. But with the reestablishment of rule by the damel, desert incursions began again.[83] By the 1810s, the Trarza were ascendant in the larger region, collecting tribute from Waalo, Kajoor, and Jolof.[84]

The Franco-Trarza Struggle for Dominance, 1817–58

By time of the French reoccupation of Senegal in 1817, Waalo had become partly repopulated through natural increase and through emigration from Kajoor and Fuuta. The Idaw al-Hajj had reestablished their position in the Trarza region. The French were anxious to find a new, secure footing for trade after the abolition of the Atlantic slave trade and negotiated with the brak to lease lands in the Waalo for plantations. The Idaw al-Hajj agreed to provide labor.[85] But the plantations failed miserably, in part because the lands themselves were unsuitable and because conflict over succession in the Trarza emiral grouping broke out and spilled into Waalo.[86]

Waalo was once again the site of Trarza raids and counterraids, but this time, the central conflicts were between factions of the Trarza emiral group and between these factions and the French, if the French got in the way. When the chain of hassani authority was in hot dispute, the French and métis traders along the river sometimes fell victim to violence. When Muhammad al-Habib gained firm control of the Trarza emirship in 1827,[87] the hassani groups divided up the Waalo villages. The French decided to contest the Trarza control of Waalo in the early 1830s, and the Trarza emir responded by formalizing his authority in Waalo by marrying the sister of the brak. Warfare broke out between the French and Trarza from 1833 to 1835.

In this conflict a new pattern developed that indicated the complexity of the interests at play along the river. The French had no direct, effective means through which to put pressure on the White warriors. The French policy was to blockade the river to prevent the zwaya grain caravans from crossing over to the north bank. The river blockade squeezed the zwaya directly, but it was indirectly effective in influencing the White warriors because the zwaya in turn put pressure on the warriors to make peace. The warriors likewise attempted to exert pressure on the French indirectly, by way of the zwaya. The Trarza emir's strategy was to threaten to ban the sale of gum to the French during these conflicts. This proved a somewhat effective strategy as long as Portendick on the Atlantic desert coast, where the British gum ships traded irregularly, appeared a credible threat to French commerce. The Saint-Louis traders agitated strongly for making peace with the Trarza in order to establish normal commercial relations at the river markets.[88]

The Trarza emir Muhammad al-Habib invoked this strategy again during the 1854–58 Franco-Trarza war, but this time, influential zwaya stood up to the emir. According to a Trarza oral tradition:

> When the emir gave the order to stop trade with the French no one was able to buy clothes or any other European goods. A group from one camp went to see Muhandh Baba, the grandfather of Mokhtar Wuld Hamidun, to ask him to support their request to the emir for permission to send a caravan to the European *escale* [river market]. The marabout Muhandh Baba refused at first but finally agreed to lead the caravan himself. The emir had frontier guards to ensure that his orders were carried out. A group of these guards saw the tracks of this caravan and went to see the emir. The emir sent out a warrior with an army to stop the marabout. When the captain saw that Muhandh Baba was at the head of the caravan, he went to the emir to say that this marabout was a respected scholar. The emir then cancelled his plan to stop the caravan.[89]

This Franco-Trarza war ended in defeat for the Trarza. They lost 500 men in battle; the French captured another 500 of their men along with 30,000 cattle, 12,000 sheep, 200 horses, 1,000 asses, 500 camels, 2,500 slaves, and considerable booty. They had more influential warrior nobles killed than had been lost in many years of intergroup warfare in the desert.[90] In 1858, Muhammad al-Habib and Governor Faidherbe finally reached an accord that ended the war and forbade further Trarza warrior transgressions to the south of the river. The French agreed to act as an intermediary between the Trarza emir on one hand and Kajoor, Njambuur, Dimar, and Jolof on the other. The French agreed to collect the tribute owed to the Trarza emir from the Black states. In exchange the Trarza emir agreed not to send an army into these territories without the prior consent of the French governor and to try to prevent other Trarza warriors from crossing the river to collect their due.[91]

This peace treaty defined a sphere of Bidan influence to the north of the river and a sphere of French influence to the south of the river, a division that would define the boundaries between Mauritania and Senegal in the French colonial system, and later as independent states. From a political and military point of view, this treaty marked a formal beginning of French imperialism in Black Africa. The desert zwaya, however, had quite a different perspective. Relieved that the hassani had been reined in at last, the zwaya coined "the year of justice" for the year the treaty with Faidherbe was signed.[92] The end of an era was at hand.

Thus after a period of some 250 years, the military and political expansion of the desert frontier was effectively ended by the imposition of French colonial authority along the lower Senegal River valley. White warriors would no longer have free rein in their Black dependencies to the south of the Senegal River; thereafter, White raids into Black lands would court French punitive retaliation. Following the death of Muhammad al-Habib in 1860, Trarza emiral factions fought each other to determine the succession of emiral authority, but all recognized the limitations of their positions relative to the French. A new configuration of regional power under French direction had formed and was in the process of consolidation.[93]

As the Trarza emiral forces were forced to accept a sharply circumscribed role in the larger region, their desert dependents such as the Ahl Gannaar accepted diminished prestige within desert society. The fortunes of the Idaw al-Hajj, the desert merchants closely allied with the Trarza emirate who had exercised special influence and authority in the regional trades, including the horse and slave trade and the export trade in gum arabic, had begun to decline even earlier during the 1830s and 1840s, when the Trarza emir acted to enforce his dominance of the booming gum arabic trade along the lower Senegal River.[94]

But for most zwaya groups involved with the grain trades and livestock herding along the southwestern frontier, the second half of the nineteenth century would open up new possibilities for the reorganization of production and for regional commerce. In the Gibla, Shaykh Sidiya al-Kabir of the Ulad Ibiri, who was based in Butilimit, organized an impressively large system of grain production by slaves and freed slaves along the middle Senegal River valley.[95] And to the south of the river, the explosive growth of the peanut trade attracted sahelian herders to the peanut basin of Senegambia to provide animal transport services. These new patterns of organization and trade evolved in an environment of greatly decreased political violence, which had the effects of broadening the economic franchise and boosting production.

3

The Southeastern Frontier

During the more humid sixteenth century the influence of the Songhai Empire (1492–1591), centered in Timbuktu, extended north to Taghaza in the west-central Sahara. To the west-northwest beyond the control of Songhai lay the greater Adrar-Tagant plateau region, which was known in Azayr, the Soninke-Berber dialect, as Shinqit, which meant "springs of the horses." Along the major western Saharan trade route which linked the Maghrib to Black Africa, Soninke populations mixed with Berber populations in the principal caravan towns of Wadan, Tishit, and Walata. To the east lay another trans-Saharan route in the west-central Sahara. It ran from Tuat in Algeria south to Timbuktu on the Niger River.

From the mid-sixteenth century, Moroccan initiatives to control the trans-Saharan trade routes had a profound influence on the development of the desert world. In 1543–44 the Saadian Empire of Morocco sent a first expedition into the western Saharan trade corridor. The expedition marched south with 1,800 horses and a large number of camels and reached Wadan. When it received word that the forces of Songhai, reputedly numbering 300,000, had been sent against it, the Moroccan expedition retreated north to Tarudant. In 1584, a second expedition was sent toward Wadan, with the goal of pushing on to Timbuktu. This second expedition perished of thirst. Other Moroccan initiatives were directed toward the trans-Saharan route in the west-central Sahara. The Saadian Empire conquered Tuat and Gurara in 1583, seized control of the Taghaza salt mine from Songhai in 1585 and established royal tax collection there, and finally conquered Timbuktu in 1591.[1]

These Saadian military initiatives had important consequences for the western Sahara. One was to decrease the amount of commercial traffic on the western trans-Saharan route, which ran through Walata, Tishit, and Wadan. According to Michel Abitbol, the desert trade returned in full volume to this western route only in the 1620s, when Moroccan control over the Tuat-Taghaza-Timbuktu route fell apart.[2] Although the dating can be only approximate, it appears that during this hiatus serious disturbances broke out within the dominant Idaw al-Hajj trading community in Wadan, and a part of the Idaw al-Hajj left Wadan to settle in the Trarza.[3] In addition, the most powerful confederation in the Tiris-Adrar region, the Tadjakanet, broke apart, dispersed, and reorganized.[4] The Kunta groupings, which were to play an important role in both the western and west-central areas of the Sahara, emerged from the Tadjakanet confederation, centered in the larger Tiris-Adrar region, sometime between the mid-sixteenth and early seventeenth centuries. Following the migration of the Idaw al-Hajj to the Trarza, a group of Kunta (Kunta al-Mitghambrin: the masked ones) came to establish itself at Wadan.[5]

In this same period Timbuktu entered its definitive decline.[6] The military conquest by the Moroccan army may have disorganized the commercial center for a short time. But the military conquest is inadequate to explain the fact that Timbuktu never regained its position. The failure to do so may be explained, at least in part, by the onset of desertification. The increased aridity also likely explains, in part, the seventeenth-century out-migration of populations from Wadan, in the easternmost Adrar, at the edge of the Empty Quarter. From the town of Shinqiti, also in the eastern Adrar, migrants left to settle the new towns of Atar (1675) and Ujaft (foundation date unknown) in the western Adrar.[7] It is interesting to note that under conditions of increasing aridity, when conflicts caused town groupings to split apart in the eastern Adrar, the groups which left founded new towns rather than taking up a life of herding. The western high plateau regions apparently continued to capture most of the reduced rainfall while the eastern Adrar became too dry for either dense human settlement or much caravan traffic.[8]

Alawite Initiatives (1668–) and Arab Military Pressures

After a lengthy interval following the conquest of Songhai, the new Moroccan Alawite dynasty (established in 1668) again began to extend its influence into the western Sahara. In A.H. 1089 (1678/79 C.E.), for example, the Moroccan sultan Mawlay Ishmaïl sent an expedition to "Aqqa, Tata, Tassint, and Shinqit, up to the borders of the Sudan." It brought back to Morocco some 2,000 haratin with their children. The adults were armed and incorporated into the army.[9] This was only the first of many groups of Black Africans who were transported from the edge of the western Sahara apparently to serve in the sultan's army.[10] The benefits of displaying allegiance to the Moroccan sultan seem to have outweighed the costs. Deputations from various Saharan tribes arrived in Morocco shortly after the expedition to bring evidence of their submission.[11]

New military pressures were also exerted farther to the southeast in the Soninke lands of the Jarra kingdom in the Hawd. There, civil war had broken out between rival Daabo and Sagone Soninke lineages in the second half of the seventeenth century.[12] The rival lineages formed alliances which extended the conflict to the north and across the savanna. Desert hassani forces (perhaps with Moroccan assistance) entered the conflict on the side of the Daabo lineage, but in short order this military assistance turned into an extension of desert power through these territories. The progressive domination of desert forces in the Hawd can probably be dated from about 1672 onward. One observation of the military confrontation along the southeastern frontier comes from the account of Cornelius Hodges, who travelled on behalf of the Royal African Company into the region of Bambuhu (Bambuk) along the upper Senegal River valley in the winter of 1689–90. He sent an advance party of men to the north of the river to the town of Tarra (probably Jarra, the capital of the kingdom of Jarra), said to be the principal market for slaves in the region. While his men were there, a large desert military force of horse and camel cavalry laid siege to the town and then attacked it, but were ultimately rebuffed.[13]

Moroccan army invasions continued from the late seventeenth century to the mid-eighteenth century and became annual, if seasonal, affairs in the 1720s and 1730s.[14] When these attacks were directed against Black Africans, the Moroccans, like the Whites of the desert edge, were obliged to withdraw from the savanna lands when the rains began in order to preserve their animals. With the return of the dry season, the Moroccans would launch new raids upon the sedentary communities. According to a report from 1726, one pattern was for the Moroccans to take hundreds of captives in a raid and then sort out the children over the age of five or six, who would presumably be sold into North Africa. The others would be kept for sale to the French or, if that was not possible, be chased away.[15] The few accounts that exist of the raids attest to their severity. As a Frenchman in Galam noted in the aftermath of a Moroccan raid: "It has been four days since the Ormans [Moroccans] fell upon the country of Galam and took a number of Blacks as slaves, stole all the grain and their livestock, and burned the villages. This is going to cause a severe shortage of food."[16] These raids severely disrupted the organization of Black African communities. Some communities were destroyed by slaving; other communities simply abandoned their settlements and fled south; yet others succumbed to the demands of desert settlers who could offer them protection.

Warfare in the Savanna: The Bambara Conquest of Jarra

In the middle of the eighteenth century, warfare between the Bambara states spread west into Jarra. This intensified the conflict between the warring Daabo and Sagone lineages of the Soninke, and finally the political violence overwhelmed Jarra itself. The warfare generated large numbers of vanquished and disoriented people, who would be swept up in the slave trades. In 1753, the

Bambara chief Sie Banmana Kulubali crossed into Kaarta, offered his army's military services to the Sagone, and in exchange demanded the division of the country's spoils. In a bloody conflict at Kingi, the Daabo were slaughtered. The Bambara thus established themselves in Kaarta and from this base launched wars of expansion in all directions. The Soninke kingdom of Jarra was reduced to the single province of Kingi.[17]

By the end of the eighteenth century, the town of Jarra, the former capital of the Soninke kingdom of Jarra, had been incorporated into the desert world. As Mungo Park noted on his travels in this region in 1796:

> The town of Jarra is of considerable extent; the houses are built of clay and stone intermixed, the clay answering the purpose of mortar. It is situated in the Moorish kingdom of Ludamar [Ulad Amar, a fraction of the Ulad Mbarak]; but the major part of the inhabitants are Negroes, from the borders of the southern states, who prefer a precarious protection under the Moors, which they purchase by tribute, rather than continue exposed to their predatory hostilities. The tribute they pay is considerable; and they manifest toward their Moorish superiors the most unlimited obedience and submission, and are treated by them with the utmost indignity and contempt.[18]

The Whites Move South: From the Adrar to the Tagant

Beginning in the second half of the seventeenth century, coincident with the devastating lineage warfare which broke out among the Soninke of Jarra and with the Moroccan incursions along the desert edge, White migrants from the Adrar began to move southeast into new areas of the Tagant plateau regions. In these newly opened up regions the nomads held the upper hand and were able to impose their own wills on the Black cultivators who found themselves at the edge of the desert frontier. Here, as along the southwestern frontier, the White settlements involved taxation of the agricultural production of Black African cultivators and the emergence of new communities professing a fervent Islam. These new settlements in the plateau regions signalled the emergence of a new system of regional exchange that linked the Tagant and the Adrar with the western savanna and the upper Senegal River valley.

In some respects, this southward movement was a continuation of the new settlement building that was taking place in the western Adrar. When the Smassid left the town of Shinqiti to found Atar and Ujaft, the Idaw Ali, another of the major groups then at Shinqiti, split into two, and the emigrating group went south to found the important caravan town of Tidjikja in the northern Tagant in 1660.[19] Similarly, at the same time that the Kunta were making inroads into the Idaw al-Hajj town of Wadan, a splinter group of Kunta from the Azawad, to the north of Timbuktu in the central Sahara, moved west and established two towns in the Tagant plateau region: at Talmust in the first half of the sixteenth century and at Ksar al-Barka about 1690. Later, from the Tiris-Adrar region, a group of Kunta nomads went south to establish themselves at Rashid, also in the Tagant, either in 1722/23 or 1765.[70]

Oral traditions about the founding of Ksar al-Barka and Rashid make explicit the fact that the Tagant settlements continued to push the desert frontier south. At Ksar al-Barka, for example, the founder of the Bidan community, a man named Muhammad Talib Wuld Bajid, is said to have encountered Black cultivators there. He built a mosque and began to tax the cultivators who served as a "bank for the Muslims." The proceeds collected were used to pay for the religious education of the Black students, for strangers fulfilling religious obligations, and to support the warrior groups in the region.[21] At Rashid the

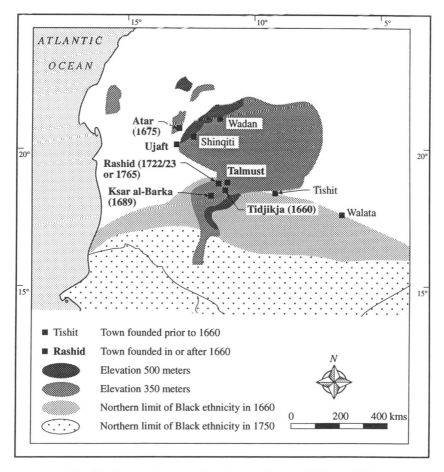

Map 3.1. New settlements in the plateau regions, c. 1660 to c. 1765.

earlier occupants, two Pulaar-speaking communities known as Tass and Tertellas, had moved south to escape continual pillaging on the desert frontier by the time the Kunta grouping tried to settle there. Even so, according to oral tradition, it was a Tukulor who showed the Kunta where to build along the wadi.[22]

The Kunta and the Idaw Ali were not the only major groupings to establish themselves in the Tagant. In the late eighteenth century, warfare broke out between the remaining Idaw al-Hajj factions at Wadan. Some left and headed south for the Tagant, following a shaykh named Sidi Mahmud of the Idewbje. In the new pastoral spaces created by the evacuation of Black African communities, there was still room for the formation of major desert groupings. Once in the Tagant, these Idaw al-Hajj immigrants attracted many other groups to them and formed the Ahl Sidi Mahmud, one of the largest, perhaps *the* largest, of the maraboutic-warrior groups in the Tagant.[23]

Regional Trade

By the eighteenth century, desert groups in the Adrar, whether engaged in livestock herding, rainfall agriculture, oasis cultivation, or a mix of these practices, did not consistently produce enough calories to meet their own needs, and thus one of the deepest imperatives of desert life was trade with the savanna. The degree of dependence of desert people on imported foods varied by region and by year. Desert people traded some livestock to the savanna, but the net flow of calories was from the savanna to the desert. In part, this was accomplished through "invisible exports," that is, through the transport services provided to savanna farmers by desert caravans. But a principal exchange was desert salt for savanna grain: minerals for calories.

Many camel nomads were nearly self-sufficient, living on camels' milk for much of the year, but these pure camel nomads were at one extreme of a continuum of desert diet, and they made up only a small percentage of the total population. To the south of the Adrar, some desert-edge communities, particularly those in the Tagant, were able to produce enough food in good years to sustain themselves, but during years of low rainfall or abject drought, these same communities fell back by necessity upon the agricultural production of Black Africans to the south.[24] By the eighteenth century the trade in cereals was at the heart of the caravan trade, and by extension of desert society as a whole. Most of the caravan trade in the western Sahara involved the importation of grain from the Black African savanna, and virtually all zwaya groups took part in the trade systems through which cereals travelled north from the savanna into the desert. Even with this trade, nomads in the desert lived a meager material existence. But one result of this trade with the Sudan was that it allowed greater desert population densities, particularly in the plateau regions, than otherwise would have been possible.[25]

Desert Imports: Grain and Other Savanna Goods

The single most important good imported into the western Sahara from the savanna was grain—and by the late eighteenth century that grain was sorghum. Desert people combined sorghum with milk in a preparation known as *aysh*, which was the basic staple in the White diet. Except during the months just before the cereal harvests in the Sudan, when sorghum stocks in the desert ran low, the majority of the desert population ate aysh in the evening, as the sole meal of the day, for much of the year.[26] The preparation of milk and sorghum together yielded a higher percentage of usable protein than did milk and sorghum consumed separately (in much the same way that a preparation of grain and beans increases the yield of protein for the peasantry of Latin America today),[27] and the consumption of aysh was a pervasive and fundamental benefit which the Whites drew from their trade with the lands below the Sahara. Within the desert, the market for sorghum was deep and wide. And although sorghum had the lowest value-to-bulk ratio of any good carried by the desert caravans, it was the most important.

As the progressive desiccation of the Sahara brought about the southward retreat of Black African cultivators and simultaneously decreased the opportunities for desert herders to cultivate desert fields using rainfall, the trade relations between herders and agriculturalists intensified. Over time, the newly settled Bidan communities in the plateau regions had increasing need for food imports. They paid for these imports, in large part, through the export of salt.

European observations regarding the salt-for-grain trade are suggestive about the southward movement of this grain-trading zone. When Cornelius Hodges travelled in Bambuk in 1689–90, he was sufficiently far to the south of the grain-exporting northern savanna regions to note that desert salt was traded only for gold, cloth, and slaves along the upper Senegal River valley.[28] Only 10 years later, at the beginning of the eighteenth century, salt was commonly exchanged for grain in the region of Gajaaga. Commercial records concerning the French trading post along the upper Senegal indicate that salt was traded against grain by volume in a range of 1:3 to 1:15 over the period 1700–1736, for which data have been found.[29] One common pattern was for grain or cloth to be sold for salt in the northern savanna, and then for savanna merchants to resell the salt in the central and southern savanna.[30]

These exchange relations did not guarantee a sure supply of food to desert and desert-edge communities. The savanna, like the sahel and the desert itself, was subject to the vagaries of erratic rainfall. Grain was often available in the savanna, but it often was not abundant. And during years of duress, competition for grain was intense.[31] Cultivators at the desert edge and in the desert tried to insulate themselves from shortfalls. The main strategy was to raise cereal substitutes which grew successfully on less rainfall. Along the Senegal River and up into the desert, cultivators grew a bean plant and a melon whose seeds could be cooked with cereals in order to stretch the stocks of cereals when they were in short supply. Along the river where milk was less abundant, the villagers mixed the bean of the *nyebe* plant (*Vigna sinensos*) and the seeds of the desert melon (*Coloxynthis citrullus*), which were known as *vundi* or *sherkash*, with grain; and this mixture, like aysh, yielded more protein than did the grain and cereal substitutes consumed separately. Desert people also grew nyebe and vundi both in open fields under rainfall and in irrigated plots under the date palms, and in the desert these seeds and beans were sometimes prepared together with grain and milk. Vundi played a particularly important role at Walata, where farmers devoted the fields surrounding the town nearly exclusively to the melon; they fried a bread made with the seeds which was called *mun* and was unique to Walata. Desert people did not prize either the beans or seeds as foodstuffs. During years when grain provisions were sufficient, nyebe and vundi were reserved for slaves and haratin. But stocks of vundi could be conserved up to 10 years or more, and it proved a good hedge against the years of bad harvests which struck the cereal-producing areas.[32]

The deep trade ties that linked desert people with the savanna farmers extended far beyond their need for food. Zwaya groups imported goods from the western savanna which were at the heart of desert culture. Until the expansion of the gum arabic trade during the first half of the nineteenth century which pumped the blue trade cloth from India known as guinée into the Adrar and along the southeastern frontier, desert people along this axis imported all their cloth from the savanna.[33] Desert people used their animals' hair and hides for their artisanal industries, but these materials alone did not provide a base for desert material culture. The materials used in the construction of the *khayma*,[34] the Bidan tent used by nomadic pastoralists and camel nomads throughout the western Sahara, illustrate this interrelation. Bidan traditionally fabricated the tent top of the khayma from a wool woven from the hair of camels or goats or sheep. This thick woven covering provided protection from the direct radiation of the sun and some insulation from the chill of the desert night. Each khayma required two tent poles about 8–10 feet in length to hold up the tent top, and these poles needed to be straight, light in weight, and durable. Trees in the desert and at the desert edge were too small, gnarled, and crooked to support the desert tent, and the wood of the date palm, while straight and durable, was simply too heavy to be transported easily. Consequently, Bidan imported their tent poles from the woodland savanna.[35] For the side panels of the tents, the desert people used cotton cloth called *giv* from the Sudan. This cotton cloth was thinner and less dense than the desert wool made from animal hair, and in moderate daytime weather the cotton side panels could easily be rolled up, allowing light to enter and allowing for the free circulation of air. During very hot weather and dust and sand storms, the cotton side panels still allowed sufficient circulation of air while providing a modicum of protection from the heat, sand, and wind. At night they served as mosquito netting.[36] Under the tent, the savanna influence was likewise apparent. The basic cooking and serving utensils in use under the Bidan tent—particularly calabashes and ebony bowls—were imports from the south.

Desert Exports: Salt, Livestock, and Dates

In earlier centuries, the export of salt from the Sahara to the western savanna had been an important sector of trade for the western savanna empires and for the states of the Maghrib.[37] The early Arabic accounts contain numerous references to a trade in salt for gold, and indeed perhaps as late as the 1640s, the volume of sporadic gold exports from the western savanna to the Maghrib appears to have been considerable.[38] Whatever the exact nature of the early salt-for-gold trade (some accounts refer to a trade of salt for gold in equal measure), it seems certain that the quantities of salt exported in the period before 1600 were inferior to the vast salt trades of the eighteenth and nineteenth centuries. The large-scale exploitation of both broken crystal and rock salt deposits in the western Sahara apparently came into full importance only with the southern extension of the desert frontier.

Over the period 1600–1850, the principal good exported by caravan from the western Sahara to the western savanna was salt. This desert trade to the savanna was part of a larger system of salt trading into the interior of West Africa.[39] The savanna agricultural communities' demand for imported salt was particularly strong, for three principal reasons. First, savanna people, like people who live in other hot lands, require greater quantities of salt than do people who live in cooler climates, because human beings lose body salts through perspiration. Second, agricultural communities in general have greater needs for salt than do livestock herders because the level of their consumption of livestock products is lower, and the vegetable material which makes up the bulk of their diet has a lower salt content than do animal products. And finally, the savanna as a whole lacked naturally occurring salt deposits. Savanna people knew how to manufacture a low-grade salt from vegetable ash, and thus were not strictly dependent upon the importation of salt. Savanna people, however, preferred the desert salts, and this preference allowed for the growth of the desert salt trade.[40] So central was the salt trade to the Bambara of the western savanna that they referred to the Sahara simply as Kokhodugu, or the country of salt.[41]

Pastoral communities in the desert also needed salt for their own survival. They had less need to supplement their own diet than the savanna communities did, because their diet contained a higher proportion of meat and milk. In addition, the concentration of salts in desert well water was generally high in comparison to water from savanna wells and rivers. To meet their own needs and the needs of their animals, desert people exploited the loose crystal salt and rock salt deposits in the western Sahara.

Loose crystal deposits were found throughout the desert, but many of those exploited lay near the plateau regions, between the Tagant and the Adrar, and others lay farther to the east near Tishit and Walata. Much of this loose salt, or *amersal*, was mixed with sand and other impurities, and the desert herders considered it suitable only for their animals. The trade in rock salt was by far the more important. From the western Sahara, most salt exports were rock salt cut from the underground deposits at Ijil, a site in the northwestern corner of the larger Adrar region. The Ijil salt could be cut into bars and transported easily, and savanna people preferred it to amersal, and in this sense desert and savanna peoples shared a hierarchy of preference in salt use.

From the late eighteenth century, as far south as the Tagant, the Assaba, and even the Hawd, zwaya caravans travelled to Ijil to provision themselves with salt. Most salt caravans originated in the Adrar, however, because transportation costs to Ijil were lower from the Adrar than from more distant points, measured in terms of the wear upon the pack camels and the time spent in making the journey. The Adrar was the jumping off point for the salt trade, and virtually all zwaya groups in the Adrar participated in the salt caravans. By the late eighteenth century, the increasing environmental desiccation meant that the Adrar was no longer in the transitional zone of the sahel but was in the full desert. The salt caravans were recognized to be so vital to general survival in the plateau regions that the warrior chiefs in these plateau regions and in the Hawd did not levy taxes on the caravans as they made their way to the western savanna.

About 1766/67 the salt mine at Ijil came under some sort of Kunta control, and it was during this period—the late eighteenth and early nineteenth centuries—that the Kunta grouping associated with the mystic Sidi al-Mokhtar al-Kunti (d. 1811) reached its point of greatest influence.[42] The Kunta were propagators of the Qadiri order of Islam, and the efflorescence of Kunta influence at the Ijil salt mine was one evidence of their considerable success in spreading the Qadiriya from the Azawad into the western Sahara. Some of their principal competition came from the Idaw Ali at Shinqiti and Tidjikja, who embraced the Tidjani order between 1780 and 1830 and became its propagators.[43] Additional competition came from the Ahl Sidi Mahmud grouping. It is not yet possible to evaluate fully the significance of the Kunta success either in regional or comparative terms because comparable studies of the economic activities of the Idaw Ali and the Ahl Sidi Mahmud have not been undertaken. Even the available evidence is somewhat difficult to assess. By the late eighteenth century, a Kunta grouping was dominant at Wadan, but this town, ruined by warfare and at the edge of the desiccated Empty Quarter of the western Sahara, was in full decline.[44] The commercial center of the Adrar had shifted from Wadan to Shinqiti, and to Atar and Ujaft in the western Adrar. Not one of these towns was controlled by a Kunta grouping, and indeed, a Kunta grouping did not have a significant presence in any of them. In addition, the Kunta did not control a single caravan town along the main trade route in the southeastern desert quadrant, which ran from the Adrar towns through Tidjikja, Tishit, and Walata.

On the other hand, the western Kunta themselves did have a system of taxation at the sebkha itself. The caravanners seeking salt brought water, grain, and firewood to the Kunta laborers at Ijil, and the grouping of these goods was

Illustration 3.1. The ruins of Wadan.

known as *ujih*. Although these goods and their transport were not free, because grain was valuable and the transport somewhat wearied the caravanners' camels, the goods did travel upon the backs of camels which otherwise would have arrived totally unburthened at the salt mine. The quantities of these goods paid to the laborers were small, and in fact the caravans going to Ijil, like those going to the Maghrib, were called *azalai*, which means "camels without loads."[45] At Ijil the laborers loaded salt onto the camels, and in return the caravanners deposited every seventh bar of salt at the house of a commercial agent of the Kunta in one of the Adrar towns. All caravanners paid these taxes except for those whose animals carried the Kunta brand. It is uncertain when this taxation was in force (the oral data on this point are varied and conflicting, which suggests that this power to tax did not last for long in the same form) but while the tax was in force, it indisputably gave those Kunta a special trade advantage.[46] They received free transportation of their salt from the Ijil mine to the Adrar. Once in the Adrar they were free to sell the salt to other groups who did not want to undertake the journey north to the sebkha, or they could load it onto their own animals and carry it south.

Pack camels were the best transport animals for desert conditions, but they were not indefatigable. Travelling for six to eight hours per day, pack animals were capable of hauling freight for up to two months at a time, but after a period of extended exertion the pack camels required long rests. Zwaya groups chose not to push their camels unnecessarily hard, and thus most of the zwaya who hauled salt from Ijil to the western savanna did so in two stages. The first journey was to the sebkha itself and then back to the caravanners' settlement, or camp, or nearby town. The length of the segments of this journey along the *triq al-milh*, or salt route, varied considerably by region and by town. Ijil lay only one week's travel from Wadan, but more than two weeks from Rashid, and even longer from the Assaba. After stopping to take on salt at the sebkha, a task which might be accomplished expeditiously or might entail weeks of waiting, the caravans would usually return to their initial point of departure. The camels would be exhausted from this journey, and if the caravanners intended to use the same camels for the trip to the western savanna, they would give them three months' interim rest.

The second stage was the journey to the savanna along the *triq al-zra*, or sorghum route, and it required up to about one month if the loaded caravans started off from the Adrar. Once in the savanna, the purchase of goods could easily take another month or two, depending upon the markets there, and during this time the pack camels again gained a needed respite from hauling, after which they would return fully loaded with sorghum and other goods. For the Adrar caravans which undertook both the salt and the grain routes, this travelling could take up a good part of the year.[47]

Prices of goods in the desert-savanna trade, in general, reflected the costs of transportation from the point of origin. For example, Tidjikja was several days farther removed from Ijil than Shinqiti was, and salt bars were more expensive at Tidjikja than at Shinqiti; and salt became increasingly expensive as the caravans moved southeast toward the agricultural lands. Grain also increased in price as the caravans moved away from the savanna, back into the desert. Annual variations in the supplies of salt and grain, due to warfare or drought either in the desert or in the savanna, meant that prices could fluctuate considerably even in the course of a single year. For example, during the famine that hit Fuuta, Walata, and Arawan in A.H. 1249 (1833/34 C.E.), the price of a bar of salt dropped to the value of the same measure of grain, from its usual price of 20–25 measures of grain.[48]

One strategy to lessen the vulnerability to swings in the availability of salt and grain was to stockpile these goods in the desert. To do so, it was essential to protect the goods from theft and spoilage by rain. There were three basic storage techniques. Along the northern desert coast, camel nomads stored their grain underground, but this was somewhat atypical for the rest of the western Sahara.[49] It was more usual for pastoral nomads to store their grain in animal-skin bags in their camps. In oasis and caravan towns, desert people kept their grain in the storage rooms which were a standard feature of houses in these settlements.

Salt, on the other hand, was too bulky to store indoors, and the desert solution was to rebury the salt in the earth. Salt could be stored for years this way, and the amount of labor necessary to uncover the salt, even if its exact location was known, helped to prevent marauding nomads or rival groups from seizing stockpiles of it. Caravanners often buried their salt in and around their towns, to be dispensed later for the caravan trade or for purchasing goods in town, but some caravanners buried their salt between the plateau regions and the savanna when the price of salt fell to an unacceptably low level, or when the threat of robbery was too great, or when transport was lacking.[50]

In principle it was possible to store grain for years. But grain stocks were an inducement to plunder. Zwaya groups never found a completely successful response to the threat of grain theft. If warned of an attack in time, zwaya could pour their grain into the sand. The labor required to separate sand from the grain was generally great enough to extinguish the raiders' interest. Another response was to fortify the storage houses. This was the case at Walata. Its distinctive architecture of heavily reinforced doors and narrow windows which served as gun portals was effective, but for some reason it was never tried elsewhere in the desert.

In a broad sense the zwaya groups' participation in the salt and sorghum trade was partly a function of their geographic location in relation to Ijil and to the western savanna. Most caravanners from the Adrar and some from the Tagant carried salt from Ijil all the way to the savanna and then carried grain back to their desert towns and camps. These northern caravans often deposited part of their salt supplies at the large towns of the Adrar and at Tidjikja, Tishit, and Walata. These entrepôts were the major points of brokerage between caravans coming south from Ijil and north from the savanna. At these entrepôts, pastoral nomads from the surrounding hinterlands could purchase salt, link up with other caravanners, and haul their salt to the savanna for sale.

The caravan towns and oasis settlements in the plateau regions and in the Hawd were the central places in the local networks of trade, and the flow of goods northward from the rainfed agricultural lands allowed groups in the surrounding areas to participate in the larger system of desert-savanna trade according to their needs. Owing to differences in desert ecology, the food requirements of groups in the different desert regions varied, and, even within a single desert region, groups could engage in specialized production, exploiting the local microenvironments. The participation of desert groups in the larger system depended fundamentally upon the nature of their investments and seasonal conditions. Groups took into account the condition of their herds, their stocks of salt and grain, the pasturage conditions along the salt route and the sorghum route, the prices of salt at the local caravan entrepôts, and the political conditions in their region and in the desert at large, to mention some of the most important considerations. Conditions changed every year, and desert people tailored their responses accordingly. Zwaya by and large were free to buy from and sell to whomever they chose. Only overt warfare between zwaya groups would prevent parties from trading.

In general, the closer the sahelian groups' territories were to the savanna, the less strict was their dependence upon the trade in salt. There is little detailed information available for earlier periods, but the oral data referring to the late nineteenth and early twentieth centuries give some indication of the complexity of the currents of exchange. In the Hawd, for example, the trade in livestock was easily as important as the trade in salt. Many herders took their animals south on transhumance and traded animals for grain in the savanna villages. In the caravan towns, currents of long-distance trade and local production mixed freely. Traders made their living by stockpiling goods and by provisioning the caravanners who did not want to travel the entire distance to the Sudan, or who wanted a mix of desert and savanna goods. At Walata, many townsmen made their living by trading savanna goods, particularly grain, cloth, and slaves, to herdsmen from the surrounding region of the Hawd and to caravanners from the plateau regions, and they integrated their own local production into this trade. The Walata townsmen traded their vundi to the caravanners from the plateau regions in exchange for salt, exchanged this salt in turn for grain in the savanna, and then traded sorghum to the local herdsmen in exchange for livestock.[51]

At Tishit the pattern of organization was somewhat different. Tishit was originally a desert-edge port where the trading diasporas of Soninke and Bidan met to exchange goods. Even after other Soninke groups had retreated from the desert during the collapse of the Songhai Empire, Tishit remained a multi-ethnic town, with one section for the Masna, who were the descendants of the Soninke, and one each for the Shorfa and the Ulad Billa, who were Bidan. At Tishit the ethnic differences between the three groups were not sharply drawn, and the Masna in most respects were not culturally different from the Bidan, particularly in the desert-side sector of their diaspora. But the Masna maintained a transethnic identity. They operated a specialized trade in loose crystal salt from their own sebkha at Tishit (where they collected a tax in grain on the exploitation of this salt), and they were active in towns throughout the western part of Mali, which had special quarters for the Masna traders.[52]

Before the French occupation of the western savanna in the late nineteenth century, salt caravans from the plateau regions were large. Pastoral nomads from the wider region, after picking up their salt at Ijil, would gather at the closest caravan town and proceed south. Often these caravans numbered hundreds of camels and in some cases over a thousand.[53] Caravans from the Adrar in general were not organized along tribal lines. The towns themselves were multitribal settlements, and zwaya from the Tagant often joined the Adrar caravans after picking up their salt at the sebkha. Then the caravans would travel south, taking the name of the town of residence of the caravan leaders, for example, "the caravan of Shinqiti." Outside the Adrar, tribal ties were more important in the composition of the caravans. Caravans from the Tagant or Assaba, which carried previously stored stocks of salt or salt bought along the sorghum route, were generally smaller, and they travelled highly armed. These caravanners derived their security from their military might and the threat of retaliation rather than from the religious prestige (and the implied threat of devastating supernatural intervention) which protected some of the Adrar caravans.[54]

A part of the desert trade in livestock also fed into the desert-savanna exchange of salt and sorghum. At least by the nineteenth century, two principal variations took place near either terminus of the larger system. Camel herders, occasionally from as far away as the Atlantic coast, travelled to the Adrar to buy grain with their camels. Some of these camels then entered a livestock trade north to the Maghrib. Several caravans of 200–400 camels left the Adrar each year to go to market in southern Morocco and Algeria. There, the caravanners sold them for slaughter, to supply the northern desert towns with meat. In exchange, Bidan herders and traders carried back to the Adrar assorted manufactured goods from the Maghrib and Europe: cotton and wool garments, firearms, rugs and blankets, and, from the early nineteenth century, black tea from China.[55] At the other end of the trade system, along the southeastern frontier, some pastoralists from the Hawd traded livestock against grain at Walata rather than taking their livestock south to the Sudan.

From a desertwide perspective the trade in dates ran a distant second to the trade in salt, and from within the western Sahara, date exports to sub-Saharan Africa were never as important as the date trade from the oasis settlements of the northern fringe of the desert to the Maghrib. The oasis communities in the Adrar and the nomads from the wider region consumed most of the dates grown in the Adrar; the date growers did not trade bulk volumes of these dates to the savanna. Nevertheless in some areas the export date trade played a bigger role, and in the Tagant—particularly at Tidjikja—the date trade was a pillar of the town's commerce.

The general level of wealth in the savanna was lower than that in the Maghrib, and for most Bambara and Soninke cultivators who traded a part of their cereal harvest for salt, dates were a luxury. Except in years when the rates of the salt-sorghum exchange strongly favored the cultivators, it seems likely that the market for dates in the savanna was rather circumscribed. In years when the rhythm of the salt and sorghum exchange was seriously disrupted for one reason or another, the savanna demand for dates dropped off precipitously. Recurrent drought plagued the savanna, and the markets there probably were not as stable as those in the Maghrib. In addition, dates could be stored successfully only for about a year before they began to go bad, and thus they were not a good hedge against these market fluctuations. But a market for dates did exist, even if it was unstable, and the Tagant palm groves, which were farther south than the Adrar groves and which produced more dates, supplied most of the dates that did enter the savanna market.

Currencies and Commerce

Desert merchants and caravanners conducted this regional trade using staple commodities, or commodity moneys, or gold, whichever was the most convenient and most profitable. Although a single commodity money might be used in the majority of exchanges in a given region, in practice this meant that there were multiple currency zones.[56] In the Adrar, for example, the Whites often used salt as the unit of account, standard of deferred payment, store of value, and medium of exchange, although many exchanges also took place in guinée cloth, which desert traders carried north from the Senegal River trade and south from the Maghrib; or in sorghum and millet, which they carried north from Bambara and Soninke lands; or in gold, which came primarily from the Bambara but which haratin also mined in small quantities in the desert at Walata.

In the trade across the desert frontier, multiple currencies were also in use. Savanna people used cloth currencies, both the *pièce de guinée* and the long narrow strip cloth from the western savanna, as well as a black cloth from Hausaland, although for some transactions they required the desert traders to use cowrie shells. This drew a kind of distinction between the money zones of the desert and of the savanna. Cowries had value for the desert people only in their trade with the savanna; they were not used as a currency in the desert. Traders from Walata carried back to their town the small stocks of cowries left after trading in the Sudan. They stored the cowries until their next trip south into the savanna.[57]

Much exchange in the desert took place on terms of deferred payment, using an institution called *mudaaf*. Mudaaf circumvented the Islamic proscription of usury, which was interpreted to mean the loaning of goods or currencies at positive rates of interest. The desert institution of mudaaf allowed for positive rates of interest to be paid to the lender on loans of goods and/or gold (usually in the form of dust), because the transacting parties could specify that the return payment be made in goods or currencies other than those lent. For example, a caravanner could loan a standard guinée cloth on terms of deferred payment in livestock at two or three times the rate which the cloth would have brought in livestock had immediate exchange of these goods taken place.

Mudaaf was common practice throughout the desert, and the permutations of exchange it allowed were nearly infinite. A great number of exchanges took place between herdsmen and caravanners. Herdsmen often paid for trade goods with heads of livestock, and there was a certain rhythm to this. Herdsmen repaid debts in camels at the end of October, when their animals were most valuable. Then, the camels had survived the rainy season, fattened on new pasture, and were ready for use as transport animals. Herdsmen repaid cattle debts in September, when the animals were in their best condition owing to new pasture.[58]

Slave Imports

The number of slaves crossing the southeastern frontier in any given year was highly variable, a function of numerous political, climatic, and military factors.[59] Many of these slaves were purchased with horses rather than salt or livestock, and the savanna demand for horses was at least in part conditioned by warfare. In exceptional years, slaves flooded across the frontier. At the time of the jihad of Umar Tall, for example, Black Africans poured into the desert, and the mortality rate for slaves was so high that one contemporary European traveller in the western Sahara called it "the grave of slaves" and spoke of its immense consumption.[60]

Many of these slaves came from the Niger bend region. There, according to Richard Roberts, the Segu Bambara and the Segu Tukulor states practiced an economy of slave raiding, producing slaves for export both for the northern markets of the Sahara and the Maghrib and for the Atlantic slave trade.[61] Many of these slaves, perhaps most, reached the market as a result of the slave raiding of the military elites which terrorized the savanna lands in an effort to consolidate their power, to eliminate their rivals, and to build states. The military capability of these savanna elites in the Niger floodplain as well as the great distance of the Niger floodplain from the hassani territories apparently discouraged desert raiders from attempting to seize large numbers of slaves there through concerted political violence. Desert traders, however, were active in the Niger bend region and were among the principal purchasers of slaves.

At the desert edge, along the upper Senegal River and along the southern regions of the Hawd, desert warriors did exercise concerted political violence against Black communities, intervening in civil wars and launching raids of pillage, enslavement, and general destruction across the frontier. The Ulad Mbarak were particularly implicated in the political violence which tore the Soninke communities asunder.[62] Farther to the east along the Hawd, many Bambara villages were destroyed when desert raiders sought slaves and pillage. Many enslaved Bambara were taken to labor villages at the desert edge, overseen by their Bidan masters. Others made the journey north to the plateau regions or beyond to North Africa. The southward movement of the southeastern frontier created an undertow that dragged Black Africans north.[63]

The demand for slaves in the desert itself was probably highly price elastic. For many pastoral nomads, personal slaves were useful but not essential, and in "good years" when many slaves reached the desert markets and their price was low, the number of nomads who could afford to buy slaves increased. Sidi Hamet, a caravanner with considerable experience in the early nineteenth-century trade, reported that "a good stout man" could be had in the Timbuktu market for the price of a woolen garment worth two dollars in Morocco.[64] He also reported that the ruler of Timbuktu had amassed some 1,000 slaves to send north with the yearly caravans, and eventually headed north with a very large caravan which included 2,000 slaves.[65] Large numbers of slaves entered the western Sahara during exceptional years, such as during the Umarian jihad of the late 1850s and early 1860s, when jihad forces sold inexpensively to the desert traders the homeless, impoverished individuals left in the wake of the destruction of their crops and villages. White traders recall today that slaves were at times so inexpensive on the savanna markets that they could be purchased for a piece of salt the size of the slave's foot.[66] But oral data insist that there was also a regular flow of slaves in normal years; slaves were usually available for purchase in the major caravan towns, particularly Walata and Tishit.[67]

Slave Exports to Saharan, Maghribine, and Atlantic Markets

The zone of political violence along the southeastern frontier of the desert was broader and deeper than that along the southwestern frontier, and the volume of slaves generated through political violence in the southeast was far greater. Desert traders bought slaves on the savanna markets for resale in the Maghrib, in the Sahara, and to European factors along the upper Senegal River for export into the Atlantic world; Black African traders bought slaves on savanna markets for resale to European factors along the upper Senegal River and to other Black Africans elsewhere in the savanna. Rough estimations of the numbers of slaves shipped to the Maghribine and Atlantic markets have been developed from a wide variety of historical data.

At least from the late seventeenth century, the Alawite state in the Maghrib was a massive importer of slaves from the Sudan. Ralph A. Austen has recently brought together scattered data in order to estimate the numbers of slaves which were imported into Morocco and Algeria in the period 1700–1890.[68] The number of slaves shipped from Senegambia into the Atlantic market has been estimated by Philip D. Curtin, Paul E. Lovejoy, and, more recently, by David Richardson.

Table 3.1. Estimates of Moroccan and Algerian imports of Black African slaves, 1700–1890

	Per annum	Subtotal
Morocco		
1700–1810	2,000	220,000
1811–40	3,000	90,000
1841–75	2,000	70,000
1876–95	5,000	100,000
Algeria		
1700–1839	500	70,000
1840–79	700	21,000
1800–1900	500	10,000

Source: Ralph A. Austen, "The Mediterranean Islamic Slave Trade Out of Africa: A Tentative Census," in Elizabeth Savage (ed.), *The Human Commodity. Perspectives on the Trans-Saharan Slave Trade* (London, 1992), 227.

Table 3.2. Estimates of annual slave exports from Senegambia into the Atlantic world

	Curtin[a]	Lovejoy[b]	Richardson[c]	
1700–1710	—	1,840	1700–1709	2,223
1711–20	3,090	3,090	1710–19	3,626
1721–30	2,250	2,250	1720–29	5,253
1731–40	2,620	2,620	1730–39	5,721
1741–50	2,500	2,500	1740–49	3,500
1751–60	2,250	2,250	1750–59	3,010
1761–70	1,410	1,440	1760–69	2,759
1771–80	1,210	1,240	1770–79	2,440
1781–90	2,030	2,210	1780–89	1,524
1791–1800	620	700	1790–99	1,832
1801–10	200	—	1800–1809	1,800
Totals	181,800	201,300		336,880

Sources:
  [a] Curtin, *Economic Change*, vol. 1, 168 (Table 4.3). Estimates are of French and British slave exports.
  [b] Paul E. Lovejoy, "The Volume of the Atlantic Slave Trade: A Synthesis," *JAH* 23 (1982), 485 (Table 5). Estimates are of French and British slave exports.
  [c] David Richardson, "Slave Exports from West and West-Central Africa, 1700–1810: New Estimates of Volume and Distribution," *JAH* 30 (1989), 17 (Table 7). Estimates include French, British, and North American exports.

If one takes the higher estimates for slave exports from all of Senegambia advanced by Richardson and accepts the estimate that two-thirds of these slaves came from along and from below the southeastern frontier in a vast shed that stretched east to the Niger bend, south to the upper Gambia River, and west to the Ferlo of central Senegambia, this would yield a total of 245,810 (336,880 x 0.67) slaves for the period 1700–1809, or 2,458 slaves exported per annum (with considerable interannual and interdecadal variation). For the trans-Saharan trade, one might estimate that two-thirds of the slave imports into Morocco and Algeria similarly originated from the same vast shed. This would yield a total of 184,250 (275,000 x 0.67) slaves for the same period, or 1,824 slaves exported per annum. Thus the trans-Saharan slave trade would have absorbed more individuals than the Atlantic slave trade over the period 1700–1709 and from 1770 onward. The trans-Saharan and Atlantic trades would have been near parity during the decade 1760–69. The Atlantic slave trade would have absorbed more slaves during the period 1710–59.[69]

Estimation of the numbers of slaves absorbed into the Sahara is even more problematic and more speculative. It is clear, however, that the numbers of desert imports were large. If one were to speculate that the total human population of the southern and central reaches of the western Sahara at the end of the eighteenth century numbered 250,000, or roughly 25 percent of the White, slave, and freed slave populations of the Islamic Republic of Mauritania in the late twentieth century, two-thirds of this total, or roughly 167,000, would have lived along the axis which extended from the Adrar and Tagant to the south and southeast. Of this population, roughly one-quarter to one-third, or 41,750–55,667, would have been slave.[70] If the average net demographic decline in the slave population had been on the order of 2–5 percent per year, maintenance of this slave population would have necessitated imports along the southeastern frontier within a range of 825–1,113 (with a decline of 2 percent) or 2,087–2,783 (with a decline of 5 percent). And these estimates would not take into account the fact that over the course of the late seventeenth and eighteenth centuries, larger slave imports were necessary to build the initial slave population to these levels. Slave exports from the savanna into the Sahara along the southeastern frontier might thus be very roughly estimated to lie within a range of 50–135 percent of savanna exports to Maghribine markets.[71] Put differently, over the course of the period 1700–1809, the number of slaves shipped north (to the Maghrib and into the desert) appears to have been larger than the number of slaves shipped west into the Atlantic markets.

The regional patterns of trade and enslavement along the southeastern frontier were probably influenced significantly by the ending of the Atlantic slave trade. It is likely that the price of slaves dropped and that the market position of sahelian traders was strengthened, as was the case along the southwestern frontier. It seems certain that a major change in these patterns did take place during the decade of the 1850s, when the jihad of the Tukulor Islamic reformer Umar Tall spread warfare east from the middle Senegal River valley, engulfing the savanna region over to the Niger inland delta. The destruction occasioned by this jihad was probably on a larger scale than the region had known for at least a century, that is, since the Moroccan raids of the first half of the eighteenth century. The numbers of Black African slaves reaching the Maghrib were greater; slaves flooded the desert markets; and desert traders sold yet other slaves to the Soninke, who settled them in agricultural villages.[72]

4

The Horse and Slave Trade

At least from the fourteenth through the sixteenth century, the trades in war horses from North Africa and from the southern frontier of the western Sahara played critical roles in the political economies of the Malian and Jolof empires, and from the sixteenth to the mid-nineteenth century, in the political economies of smaller, cavalry-based states across the western savanna. Following the onset of the increasingly arid period beginning in the first half of the seventeenth century, the zone of desert horse breeding was pushed south, and through crossbreeding with the small disease-resistant indigenous horses of the savanna, new breeds were created. Although the savanna remained an epidemiologically hostile environment for the larger and more desirable horses bred in North Africa and along the desert fringe, Black African states continued to import horses into the late nineteenth century.

The fundamental problem with the importation of North African (or Saharan) horses was that they lacked immunity to the disease environment of the savanna and suffered extremely high mortality.[1] The principal killer, although certainly not the only one, was trypanosomiasis.[2] One solution was to interbreed: over time, the Barbary horse was thereby able to pass on, in some measure, the virtues of size and speed; the West African pony contributed a measure of increased resistance to trypanosomiasis.[3] The resultant mixes were not particularly attractive aesthetically, but were serviceable and often praised for their hardiness and spirit.[4] Another solution was to continue to import, even in the face of devastating mortality. The logic here lay in the superior equine qualities of the Saharan and North African breeds. Their greater height at withers translated directly into greater speed. Their increased weight meant that they were capable of carrying greater burdens over longer distances. Their larger overall size projected more fearsome power. All were important for the smaller cavalry-based states of the seventeenth, eighteenth, and nineteenth centuries. For the slave raiding of entire villages, mounted warriors typically surrounded a settlement, then burned it, and during the attack ran down on horseback those who sought to escape. Captives were then tied together in coffles and attached to the tails of the warriors' horses. For small-scale raiding into agricultural fields, warriors needed to strike quickly, to stuff smaller children into sacks and tie them on the horses' backs, and, if exigencies permitted, to abduct the larger children and the adults as well, and then to flee quickly in order to escape the wrath of the raided community. And although horses did not figure as a direct assault force in large-scale conflict between states, the cavalry, held in reserve, did carry out raids and pillage when an enemy force dispersed in flight.

The imported horses were generally exchanged for slaves, and the link between imported horses and exported slaves was direct. Horses were used in state warfare, which produced large numbers of prisoners of war, who were then sold into the Atlantic, Saharan, and North African markets; they were used as well for predatory pillaging, which likewise produced slaves for export. In the Atlantic, Saharan, and North African trades there was an internal dynamic element. Horses did not live long in the savanna, and slave mortality within the desert and on the trans-Saharan crossing was high. In the Atlantic sector, particularly during the eighteenth and early nineteenth centuries, slaves were sold, in part, for guns and gunpowder, which facilitated more warfare and raiding. Thus, the horse and slave trades fed upon one another and reinforced the cycle of political violence.

Many historians have assumed that the horse and slave trade into Senegambia was a principal feature only of the early historical centuries of desert-savanna trade. Robin Law, in his pioneering study *The Horse in West African History*, suggested that the era of the dominance of the horse and slave trade from the Sahara ended in the sixteenth century.[5] Philip Curtin, in his landmark *Economic Change in Precolonial Africa*, documented an apparent collapse in horse prices and inferred that from the late seventeenth century the horse trade from North Africa or from the Sahara no longer played a major role in the political economy of Senegambia.[6] Other historians of Senegambia have maintained that the Atlantic slave trade was the dominant influence on the political economy of the coastal Wolof states, at least from the second half of the seventeenth century, and have paid scant attention to the horse and slave trade.[7]

This chapter presents evidence from a broad range of historical sources to demonstrate the continued importance of the horse and slave trade between the western Sahara and Senegambia throughout the eighteenth century and into the second half of the nineteenth century. It will argue that the horse and slave trade was fundamental to the success of the smaller cavalry states of the savanna and that the number of slaves exported into the western Sahara from the coastal Wolof states of Waalo and Kajoor (and likely from the other Black African states of northern Senegambia) was quite possibly larger than the number of slaves exported into the Atlantic slave trade.

The Cavalry Revolution in Senegambia

The indigenous Senegambian pony was small, between 0.95 and 1 meter in height to the withers. It was, in fact, too small for many purposes to which the full-sized mounts could be put, including carrying warriors on its back. By contrast, the Arabian and Barbary horses introduced from the Sahara and from the Maghrib—and by the Portuguese in the early centuries of European contact—were much larger, the Arabian horses ranging in size from 1 meter 40 centimeters to 1 meter 45 centimeters and the Barbary horses ranging from 1 meter 42 centimeters to 1 meter 48 centimeters.[8] Interestingly, although the indigenous pony was established long before the introduction of the Arabian and Barbary horses, the Wolof words for horse are derived from Arabic, indicating that in the Senegambian corridor the imported horses were indeed a breed apart. By contrast, in the Malian savanna, the terms for horse have local language roots,[9] perhaps suggesting a longer-standing pattern of horse imports, perhaps before the establishment of Arabo-Berber influence in the Adrar. As further evidence of a distinct equine history in northern Senegambia, one might cite the Senegambian adoption of the Arab saddle rather than the Bambara, Macina, or Mossi saddles of the western Sudan, suggesting that formative influences came from the north rather than from the east and that these influences arrived after the establishment of Arabo-Berber hegemony in the horse trade. This linguistic and cultural evidence would also argue for a Sahara-to-Mali trade in horses, perhaps bred in the Adrar, that predated the cavalry revolution in Senegambia.

At least since the fourteenth century, Barbary horses had been associated with Sudanic imperial authority. These imperial horses appear to have been imported both from North Africa and from breeding grounds at the desert edge.[10] We know little about the supply of horses from North Africa in this early period, apart from two brief comments: one by the Portuguese Valentim Fernandes, writing in 1506–7, to the effect that Sanhaja traders sold horses from Safi (in Morocco) to Jolof in exchange for slaves,[11] and another by the geographer Leo Africanus, writing in the mid-sixteenth century, concerning a community in the Moroccan Sahara that was involved in purchasing horses from the kingdom of Fez and selling them into Black Africa.[12] Information about the supply of Saharan-bred horses is not much better. In the wetter period, 1500–1630, the southern edge of the western Sahara was far to the north of its present location, probably approximately at the latitude of the Adrar plateau. Although the origins of the horses imported into the savanna cannot be established with certainty, linguistic evidence suggests that the Adrar was an important breeding ground. The name Shinqit means "springs of the horses" in Azayr,[13] and this would argue for horse breeding there, before the consolidation of Bidan ethnicity and before the establishment of Bidan hegemony. Similarly, Wolof linguistic evidence points to the importance of the Adrar, and specifically to the caravan town of Wadan, in the horse trades: the Wolof term for mare is *"fas wadan,"* meaning "horse from Wadan."[14] In addition, Tukulor tradition indicates that during the fifteenth century there were large numbers of horses in the Hawd, and this is supported by Fernandes' account.[15]

To the west of Mali, the trade in horses had also been important to the political cohesion of the Jolof Empire, perhaps since its inception. The evidence for the patterns of horse supply in this early period is not extensive, but it does indicate that the trade in horses for slaves was not centralized. Networks of desert traders operated not only at the heart of the empire, but also fanned out to the courts of petty Black princes. In the mid-fifteenth century, for example, Cadamosto noticed Berber zwaya of the Tashumsha who had insinuated themselves at the courts of the Wolof aristocracies in the western provinces of Jolof, where they enjoyed prestige handling the horse and slave trade.[16] Some of these horses imported to the provinces of Jolof were in turn drawn toward the center of the empire through the collection of tribute. The African provincial elites seem to have supported themselves by slave raiding in villages within their spheres of influence and by warfare against neighboring groups and to have expressed their allegiance to the buur ba Jolof by sending horses and slaves and other goods to the imperial court. Indeed, the fact that rulers required their subject populations to pay tribute in horses underlines the fact that there were multiple routes of supply from the desert into the savanna.[17]

In the second half of the fifteenth century, Jolof began to import large numbers of horses. Fortunately it is possible to date this change with some precision. In the mid-fifteenth century, Cadamosto noted that there were very few horses in Jolof;[18] of those, only a few were bred locally in Jolof, the rest were imported.[19] But by the early sixteenth century, according to Fernandes and Duarte Pacheco Pereira, the buur ba Jolof had a cavalry of either 8,000 or 10,000 horses, although these figures may refer to the larger Wolof region, including Waalo, territories lost to desert forces in the Gibla of the southwestern Sahara, Kajoor, Bawol, and Jolof.[20]

The massive buildup of Jolof cavalry by the early sixteenth century was momentous. It transformed the political geography of the western savanna; other polities struggling against the dominance of the center were obliged to follow suit. This revolution of the horse cavalry states apparently brought common cultural elements to the broader region. The Black Africans of northern Senegambia and western Mali, as well as the Whites of the western Sahara, adopted the Arab stirrup.[21] It allowed the warrior to manipulate weaponry such as pikes and spears with greater force, using leg and upper torso strength more efficiently than a bareback rider could. With the adoption of the stirrup the horse came to be more fully exploited as an animal of war and predation. It allowed for the elite of sedentary states to exercise the same kind of dominance over agricultural communities in the savanna and at the forest edge that horse- or camel-riding nomads could at the desert edge.

It is at least possible that a substantial number of the horses in late fifteenth- and early sixteenth-century Jolof were bred locally. But judging from later observations of cavalry forces in Waalo in the seventeenth century, when increasingly arid conditions more favorable to horsebreeding obtained and most horses were still imported, it is highly likely that the majority of the horses in Jolof were likewise imported. These animals had no immunity to savanna diseases and must have suffered the staggering mortality of later similar imports. Because of the large number of horses that would have had to be imported, it seems clear that the Portuguese contribution to the buildup of the Jolof cavalry state could not have been decisive and may in fact have been of minor significance. The majority of the imported horses must have been either led overland from the distant Maghrib by desert traders or sold off the desert frontier.[22]

About the last decade of the fifteenth century, a Fuulbe group from western Mali interposed itself between Jolof and its source of desert remounts. Led by Koli Tengella, the Fuulbe were successful in warfare to the north of the Senegal River in the region of the Hawd. According to the Tukulor chronicler Siré Abbas Soh, the Fuulbe were able to seize more than 40,000 horses of the best quality and to control a massive cavalry.[23] Whatever the number of horses involved, the control over cavalry seems to have been critical. By about 1510 the Fuulbe succeeded in dominating the middle Senegal River valley. Shortly thereafter, probably between 1530 and 1550, Jolof's control over her provinces dissolved completely. In the resulting power vacuum, Fuuta, the Fuulbe state on the middle Senegal, was able to expand its own sphere of influence. It dominated the agricultural groups to the north of the river, and Fuuta began to collect tribute from Waalo downriver and from Kajoor to the southwest. When Jolof lost control in the middle valley, the coastal provinces broke away conclusively.[24] The new horse cavalry states emerged from the political disintegration of the empire. Those near the desert edge, in particular, needed to control large cavalries to deter aggression from hostile neighbors. Toward this end, they imported large numbers of Barbary horses and began to develop the new crossbreeds.

Crossbreeding, Horse Mortality, and Sahelian Cavalry

Over centuries, the pony breeds of Kajoor and Bawol, known as the Mpar and the Mbayar, respectively, were improved through crossbreeding principally with the Barbary horse of the Sahara and the Maghrib. This crossbreeding produced the smaller, less aesthetically pleasing, but still serviceable horses of Senegambia. But this was a long process indeed. By the mid-twentieth century the Mpar, for example, had been successfully bred up to a height of 1 meter 25 centimeters to 1 meter 35 centimeters. But although this Kajoor horse was praised for its exceptional endurance and hardiness, by French judgment the Mpar was still too small for any effective military use. And there was no way to improve the breeds further by using local stock. A French government mission at the end of the nineteenth century sent to improve the Mbayar breed of Bawol, for example, found that it was impossible to do so with local stallions. Stud horses had to be brought in, as they had been during the long centuries of the horse and slave trade, from North Africa.[25]

By the late nineteenth century, to the north along the Senegal was another spinoff of the desert horse trade known as the *cheval du fleuve*, or river horse. Colonial specialists considered it to be a degenerated subspecies of the desert breeds. So did the desert herders, who referred to the horses as haratin (freed slaves).[26] The river horse was larger than the Mpar or the Mbayar and enjoyed prestige in the river regions. But like its desert progenitors, it too was susceptible to trypanosomiasis, and this confined the expansion of the river horse to the river region, where presumably it was pastured in the Ferlo and in the desert steppe during the unhealthy rainy season. Colonial efforts to cross the river horse with the Mbayar came to nought.[27]

In the first half of the twentieth century, the pattern of horse breeding that was found in the savanna lands along the southeastern desert frontier was markedly different from that along the coastal corridor of the Wolof states of Senegambia. Along the southeastern frontier the importation and breeding of the Saharan or Maghribine Barbary horses were much more successful. Even so, the horse stocks there tended to deteriorate in the more epidemiologically harsh savanna environment. Colonial veterinarians charted the progressive degeneration of the pure Barbary horse of the Hawd through the horse herds of the savanna. By contrast, in western Senegambia crossbreeding produced more stable new breeds that were able to reproduce themselves. The difference probably lay in the genetic differences of the small, distinct pony herds of the Senegambian Wolof states, apparently the only such horse stock to the west of Timbuktu.[28]

The supply patterns of the desert horse trades have left few traces. Late seventeenth-century sources leave the impression that horses were raised to the north of Waalo (perhaps in the northern Trarza or Inchiri), although desert oral traditions give no indication that horses were ever bred in the Trarza or Inchiri. By the eighteenth century or so, most western Saharan horses exported to Black African markets probably were raised in the Tagant and Hawd regions by White groups, who themselves exercised a formidable military capacity, and this pattern held into the nineteenth century and beyond. By the mid-nineteenth century at least some of the horses of the Trarza emirate were imported from the Tagant.[29] The largest concentrations of desert horses, however, seem to have been in the Hawd. There, the largest breeders, particularly the Mashduf, are said to have raised six breeds and had herds of hundreds each.[30] By the twentieth century, French sources indicated that the Hawd (*cercle du Sahel*) was a center of horse breeding and that there were additional sources of supply in the western Adrar, the Tagant, and the Awker.[31]

Even though conditions in the savanna became considerably more arid beginning in the early seventeenth century, the mortality of the imported pure Barbary horses does not seem to have improved. Evidence from the period of early French colonial rule is persuasive. From the conquest of the French Soudan until the very end of the nineteenth century, the French colonial cavalry rode only on Arab horses imported from Algeria. This presented a great problem to the French, because the horses died out rapidly. The figures for horse mortality in the 1880s in the French Soudan are indicative of the severity of the problem (see Table 4.1).

Table 4.1. Annual horse mortality of the colonial cavalry in the French Soudan

	Percent
1882–83	92
1883–84	87
1884–85	95
1885–86	86
1886–87	73
1887–88	75

Source: C. Pierre, *L'élevage dans l'Afrique occidentale française* (Paris, 1906), 83. The high mortality of Arab horses was generally attributed to an unhealthy climate.

Compounding the problem was the fact that the disease environment for animals was changing, in part as a result of the importation of new breeds. Epizootics of "horse-sickness," referred to in the veterinary literature as a bilious typhoid infection and apparently quite distinct from the familiar trypanosomiasis (often referred to as a typho-malaria), were first noticed by the French in the 1880s. This sickness affected local horses as well the imported Barbary and French breeds.[32]

In 1898–1900 the colonial service decided to purchase horses from the desert traders. They bought 12–15 horses per year, brought down from the

Adrar or from Morocco. But this initiative failed as well. A solution to the problem in the French Soudan was to purchase local horses there. They were large enough for the purposes of the military cavalry, but they apparently were still quite vulnerable to disease. The French estimated that they had to replace a third of their horses annually.[33]

The high mortality of the desert horses clearly posed enormous problems for the horse cavalry states of the western savanna. The early eighteenth-century traveller Francis Moore made an interesting observation about the internal dynamics of the Saharan horse trade in the Gambia that bears on this issue. He stated that the sale of desert horses below the Wolof kingdoms was brokered by the Wolof themselves, and that he had seen no mares in his travels in the region: "The Generality of Horses in this River, are brought from the borders of *Barbary*; but as the Grand *Jolloiffs* are nearest them, they buy them up, and reap an Advantage, by selling them to the *Mundingoes* and *Mahometans*. They never sell Mares, so that in all the Time I was in *Gambia* I saw no more than one Mare, and she was brought . . . from *Cape de Verde* Islands."[34]

Several historians have taken Moore's comments to mean that the horse traders were able to keep horse prices artificially high by refusing to sell mares. The importation of stallions, in this view, would have been critical in maintaining dependence upon the areas of horse supply.[35] The model, though not explicitly stated, seems to be that this monopoly was eventually broken by the importation of mares. The Wolof linguistic evidence is equivocal. As mentioned above, the Wolof term for mare translates as "horse from Wadan," while the Wolof for white Arab horse is rendered "Arab male horse."[36]

The fact that interbreeding was both possible and apparently widely practiced casts a rather different light on the presence of stallions in early Senegambia. A stallion put to stud could produce more crossbreeds than a mare, and for just this reason stallions were able to command high prices. The importation of stallions into zones of endemic trypanosomiasis would have made economic sense. Most imports would not survive for a full year, and thus the possibilities of breeding pure Barbary horses were practically nonexistent. The viability of the crossbred fetuses *in utero* was greatly enhanced when they were carried in non-Barbary mares. In addition, stallions were larger and more powerful than mares, and thus more desireable for military purposes.[37]

Seventeenth-century observers drew sharp distinctions between locally bred horses and imports from the desert edge and from the Maghrib. The different horse breeds were understood to have discrete capabilities, and consequently they brought vastly different prices. According to Louis Chambonneau, in the mid-1670s in Waalo there were both imported and locally bred horses available for sale whose prices ranged from a low of 1 slave up to 10 or 15 slaves, indicating the gap between savanna breeds and the best of the imported horses. Other late seventeenth-century observations confirm the high prices that desert mounts would bring. Jean Barbot noted that horses were commonly bought from desert traders, and that some of them cost 10–12 slaves apiece. La Courbe, writing of his journey up the Senegal River in 1685, stated matter of factly that a good horse would bring 25 slaves; and J.-B. Labat, drawing from the work of André Brüe and others, noted that desert people "have horses of great beauty, [and] they are valued at fifteen slaves apiece." These were not exceptional horses collected by avid horse fanciers. These were the war horses sought by the Black African princes and heads of state. It was these horses which enabled the brak of Waalo "to make frequent excursions into the dominions of his neighbours, to get cattle, slaves, or provisions."[38]

And at least by the 1670s, the military use of horses along the desert frontier of the western Sahara was well-established. A fragment of Trarza oral data relates that at the time of the jihad of Nasir al-Din "every man had a horse."[39] Similarly, evidence from the southeastern frontier of the western Sahara makes plain the fact that there were large desert-side cavalries raiding the Black African settlements at the end of the seventeenth century. The advance party sent by the traveller Cornelius Hodges to Tarra in the upper Senegal River valley in 1689 credited the Moors with mounting a cavalry of 40,000 horses and camels to attack the town.[40] And as La Courbe makes clear, the horse and slave trade was not on its last legs in the late seventeenth century: "These desert people wear their hair long and dressed in the back, clothe themselves like the Blacks, always go bare-headed and are armed with long pikes and with spears; they are great horse traders and raise a lot of horses which they barter with the Blacks for slaves who they then will sell later on far away."[41]

The same seventeenth-century sources provide information concerning the limited extent to which crossbreeding had crowded out the market for desert imports. By the late seventeenth century, the brak of Waalo was credited with having the largest cavalry in the Senegambian region, at least 10 times as large as that of the damel of Kajoor. The brak's cavalry stood at between 3,000 and 6,000 horses and, according to Chambonneau, most were imports.[42] Similarly in 1697, when André Brüe saw a display of the saatigi of Fuuta's cavalry, both imported and locally bred horses were in evidence. The large stable of the saatigi, however, was stocked with pure Barbary horses.[43]

To the south of the Senegal River states, horse mortality in the late seventeenth century may have been sufficiently high to prevent crossbreeding. Prices rose as traders ventured farther south into the zones of intense tse-tse fly infestation. Barbary horses were much less expensive in Waalo than in Jolof, for example, and the Jolof consequently had few, if any, to serve for war.[44]

Table 4.2. European observations of cavalry strength in the sahelian emirates and savanna states, c. 1450 to c. 1850

	Strength	Polity	Comments
c. 1450[a]	very few	Jolof	
Early			
sixteenth	8,000	Jolof	
century	10,000	Jolof	
c. 1681[c]	3,000	Waalo	"The great Brak maintains about three
	few or none	Jolof	thousand horse; because he can pur-
			chase horses of the Moors, at a much
			cheaper rate than the Jolofs, who are
			at a great distance from them, and
			therefore have few or none to serve in
			the war; but their foot are very good,
			and some ride on camels, whereof
			there is plenty in their country."
	5,000–6,000	Waalo	"The *Brak* has more horse in his army,
			than any of the other black kings,
			because he can have as many horses
			as he pleases from the *Azuaghe Moors*
			his neighbours, of the country of
			Genehoa, in exchange for slaves.
			Besides, he is so great a lover of
			horses, that it is sometimes observ'd,
			when provisions were very scarce in
			the country, that he would be so spar-
			ingly of millet to feed them, as to live
			himself upon little besides tobacco and
			brandy. . . I have been told, that this
			king maintains five or six thousand
			horse after this manner, which enables
			him to make frequent excursions into
			the dominions of his neighbours, to get
			cattle, slaves, or provisions."
	300	Kajoor	"When king *Damel* has resolved on
			any martial expedition, he orders
			Conde, his generalissimo, to assem-
			ble the chief men, and all the *Blacks*
			of the country, from among whom a
			draught is made, to form a body of
			horse and foot, seldom exceeding
			1500 men, most infantry, because the
			king has scarce 300 horse at command
			throughout his dominions."
1695[d]	2,000	Kajoor	In the campaign against Jolof, the
			damel set out with 2,000 horses and
			2,000 infantrymen, of which only 200
			were armed with rifles.

(table continued on following page)

Table 4.2. European observations of cavalry strength in the sahelian emirates and savanna states, c.1450 to c.1850 (*continued*)

	Strength	Polity	Comments
1697[e]	700	Fuuta	"This prince [the Siratick of Fuuta] is powerful, the Brak and all the nobles of Waalo are his vassals and every four years make a tribute payment to him of forty-three slaves and a number of cattle. He has cavalry, and the means to have as many horses as he wishes from the Moors who are his neighbors."
1723[f]	1,000	Trarza	Ali Shandhora with 1,000 horses and 2,000 foot soldiers in Kajoor on a campaign against the Brakna forces
1734[g]	200–300	Waalo	"The brak is the closest neighbor of the fort at St.-Louis du Sénégal, his forces consist of two or three hundred cavalrymen and of three thousand foot soldiers of which half carry firearms."
	—	Kajoor	"[The damel] . . . has numerous cavalry, and . . . can turn out twelve thousand foot soldiers."
1762[h]	≈ 2,000	Waalo	"Brak is the most powerful."
	≈ 2,000	Brakna	the same force that the brak had
		Fuuta	The king of Fuuta could put 7,000–8,000 men in the field when he joined forces with the several Moorish tribes. In this number was a lot of cavalry.
	1,000–1,500	Galam	Galam could field 2,000–3,000 men, half in cavalry, half of whom carried firearms and half of whom used arrows.
	3,500–4,000	Bundu	Bundu could field 7,000–8,000 men; half were cavalry.
		Bambuk	Bambuk was in the process of putting together an army of 5,000–6,000 men, all foot soldiers, three-quarters of whom would fight with poisoned arrows. Beyond, near the mines was an army of 35,000.
	7,500	Moors	The Moors (in the Hawd) had 15,000 men, half in cavalry.
1769[i]	at most 1,000	Kajoor	300 to 400 cavalrymen were used to pillage a province (canton). "Their largest armies are of ten thousand men and include three to four hundred cavalry charged with pillaging within their own realm, and at the most twenty thousand including one thousand horse when there is war to make against outside the kingdom."

Table 4.2. European observations of cavalry strength in the sahelian emirates and savanna states, c.1450 to c.1850 (*continued*)

	Strength	Polity	Comments
1785[j]	2,000	Kajoor	The damel's forces have been exaggerated; nevertheless he was known to have assembled 2,000 cavalrymen and 300–400 foot soldiers.
1787[k]	3,000	Kajoor	
1795–97[l]	2,000	Ulad Amar	"The military strength of Ludamar [Ulad Amar] consists in cavalry . . . This body is not very numerous; for when Ali [the chief] made war on the Bambarra, I was informed that his whole force did not exceed two thousand cavalry. They constitute, however, by what I could learn, but a very small proportion of his Moorish subjects."
1798[m]	10,000	Kajoor	The damel raised 10,000 horses from all the village chiefs, who paid him obedience to crush the revolt against his authority on Cap Vert.
1811[n]	—	Kajoor	The damel in this year was not as powerful as his predecessors, but he could still field 5,000 or 6,000 men in an emergency.
1848[o]	1,500	Kajoor	The damel refused Saint-Louis the right to set up grass huts at Ganjool to trade for peanuts, and the damel sent a force of 1,500 cavalrymen to enforce his will.

Sources:

[a] Crone, *The Voyages of Cadamosto*, 17, 49, cited by Law, *Horse*, 52. Evidence for the scarcity of horses in the desert itself in the fourteenth century can be found in Ibn Khaldun's *Histoire des Berbères* (Paris, 1968–69), 331–332. In discussing the Berbers of the western Sahara, Ibn Khaldun remarks, "Only a few horses are to be seen amongst them." A passage from this work by Ibn Khaldun appears in H. T. Norris, *Arab Conquest*, 28–29.

[b] Pereira, *Esmeraldo de Situ Orbis*, 47, cited by Law, *Horse*, 52.

[c] Barbot, *A Description of the Coasts of North and South Guinea*, 39, 57–58.

[d] Labat, *Nouvelle relation*, vol. 4, 145, cited by Lucie Ann Gallistel Colvin, "Kajor and Its Diplomatic Relations with Saint-Louis du Sénégal, 1763–1861" (unpublished Ph.D. dissertation, Columbia University, 1972), 98, but incorrectly. She misreads the cavalry figure as 200 rather than 2,000.

[e] Labat, *Nouvelle relation*, vol. 2, 195: "Ce Prince est puissant, le Roy Brac & tous les Grands du Royaume d'Oüal sont ses vassaux, & luy payent tous les quatre ans un tribut de quarante-trois captifs & d'un nombre de boeufs. Il a de la Cavalerie, & le moyen d'avoir des chevaux tant qu'il veut par les Maures qui sont ses voisins." See also Labat, *Nouvelle relation*, vol. 3, 234–235.

[f] Bibliothèque Nationale (Paris), Fonds français, MS 24222, Journal de André Brüe, folio 335.

(*table continued on following page*)

Table 4.2. European observations of cavalry strength in the sahelian emirates and savanna states, c.1450 to c.1850 (*continued*)

---

[g]ANF C[6] 11, Mémoire sur la Concession du Sénégal, 8 octobre 1734. In regard to Waalo: "Le Roy Brack est le plus voisin du fort St Louis du Sénégal, ses forces consistent en deux ou trois cent Cavaliers et en trois milles fantassins dont la moitié portent des armes à feu." In regard to Kajoor: "[Le Damel] . . . qui a une Cavalerie nombreuse, et qui peut mettre sur pied Douze mille fantassins."

[h] "'Brak' est des plus puissants du pays, il peut avoir 4 à 5000 hommes capables de porter les armes dont près de la moitié en cavalerie" (Bibliothèque Nationale [Paris], Fonds français, MS 9557, 30 novembre 1762, Mémoire sur les mines de Bambouc). The data on the brak of Waalo alone are cited by Barry, *Waalo*, 202.

[i] Doumet, "Mémoire," 39.

[j] Pierre Labarthe, *Voyage en Sénégal pendant les années 1784 et 1785, d'après les mémoires de Lajaille* (Paris, 1802), 110.

[k] Pierre Cultru, *Les origines de l'Afrique occidentale française: Histoire du Sénégal du XVe siècle à 1870* (Paris, 1910), 233, cited in Colvin, "Kajor and Its Diplomatic Relations," 98.

[l] Park, *Travels*, 119–120.

[m] Mollien, *L'Afrique occidentale en 1818*, 66.

[n] PRO, CO 267/29, 1 January 1811, Answers to the Questions proposed to Lt. Colonel Maxwell, Lieutenant Governor of Senegal and Goree by his Majesty's Commissioner for Investigating the Forts and Settlements in Africa. One of the damel's predecessors was said to have brought 5,000 cavalrymen to bear upon a rebellion in Kajoor, presumably in the eighteenth century, although no date was mentioned.

[o]ANS, 2 B 27, Gouverneur Baudin au Ministre, 12 février 1848.

European observations of the cavalries of the various Black African states are informative and bear upon the question of relative parity in military force between these states. The figures suggested by European observers may not be precise, but they are accurate enough to detect a significant change in the regional distribution of military power. In the eighteenth century, Kajoor came to rival and then to supersede the cavalry state of Waalo as the dominant horse power in the Wolof and Sereer states. Waalo's cavalry force declined from 3,000–6,000 in the 1680s to 2,000 in the 1760s. By contrast, the cavalry of the damel of Kajoor increased from approximately 300 in the 1680s to 2,000–3,000 by the 1780s.[45]

The principal demand for North African and Saharan horses came from the rulers of the Black African states and their courts. The case of Kajoor is the best documented. The damel of Kajoor, for example, had his own stable of exclusively Barbary horses. It is likely that slave soldiers of the damel used these horses to carry out raids against villages within Kajoor and on the borders of neighboring states. Nobles and village chiefs apparently also owned desert horses, which conveyed prestige and affiliation with the political economy of rapine. Thus, by 1681, for example, the damel of Kajoor did not have a great number of suitable horses under his immediate control, but he was able to raise 300 horses throughout his realm.

By the middle of the eighteenth century, many more horses were available to the damel for large-scale military conflict. The midcentury observer

Doumet (1769) thought that the damel might be able to raise 1,000 horses for state warfare. By the end of the century, observers credited the damel with being able to raise 2,000, 3,000, or even 10,000 horses. Under increasingly arid conditions, Kajoor, the Wolof state to the south of Waalo, was able to mount a cavalry force to rival that of Waalo in the previous century. There can be little doubt that the nature of interstate warfare in the region was changing as a result.

Although there are few data concerning the size of the cavalry forces of the states to the east of Waalo and Fuuta, the scant information that exists does suggest that there was a similar pattern of cavalry use in those states and that the cavalries were of a size comparable to those farther west. In the 1760s, one observer noted that approximately half of the military forces of the states of Galam (Gajaaga) and Bundu were in horse cavalry, and that these cavalries numbered roughly 1,000–1,500 in the case of Galam and 3,500–4,000 in the case of Bundu. To the southwest of Bundu in a moister ecozone was Bambuk. Its army consisted of some 5,000–6,000 men, but all were foot soldiers. In the Hawd the desert forces were said to be able to muster 15,000 fighting men, half of whom were mounted cavalry.[46]

By the late eighteenth century, when Mungo Park travelled into the region of the southeastern desert frontier, the military strength of the desert forces was entirely in horse cavalry. In 1796, when Park was held captive by Ali, chief of the Ulad Amar of the Ulad Mbarak, he commented upon the military capabilities of the desert forces:

> Of the number of Ali's Moorish subjects I had no means of forming a correct estimate. The military strength of the Ludamar [Ulad Amar] consists in cavalry. They are very well mounted and appear to be very expert in skirmishing and attacking by surprise. Every soldier furnishes his own horse, and finds his accoutrements, consisting of a large sabre, a double-barrelled gun, a small red leather bag for holding his balls, and a powder horn slung over the shoulder. He has no pay, nor any remuneration but what arises from plunder. This body is not very numerous; for when Ali made war upon Bambarra, I was informed that his whole force did not exceed two thousand cavalry. They constitute, however, by what I could learn, but a very small proportion of his Moorish subjects. The horses are very beautiful, and so highly esteemed that the Negro princes will sometimes give from twelve to fourteen slaves for one horse.[47]

Park was generally impressed with the desert horses and credited their superior fleetness for the desert warriors' ability "to make so many predatory excursions into the Negro countries."[48]

Along the southeastern frontier, under the pressure of increasing desertification, the raising of crossbred horses likewise became established at least by the late eighteenth century. The Fuulbe raised equine crossbreeds along with their cattle.[49] Apparently some attempts at horse breeding there had gone awry, perhaps disrupted by the high level of political violence. Park noticed wild horses, presumably an inferior breed with little economic value, at the frontier of Kaarta and the desert-edge territories under the dominance of the Ulad Amar. There, the Blacks hunted them for food and held their meat in high esteem.[50]

Comparison of the Atlantic and Trans-Saharan Slave Trades

Simple calculations are useful in giving some rough idea of the magnitude of the slave raiding that must have supported the northern Senegambian cavalries. For the late seventeenth century, if one takes the lower figure of 3,000 horses in the Waalo cavalry, and estimates that only half came from desert traders, and assumes that the vast majority of horses imported from the desert were new crossbreeds from the desert edge with at least some resistance to trypanosomiasis (and thus would have had to be replaced at a minimum of one-third per annum, which is the replacement figure for locally bred horses in late nineteenth-century French Soudan), Waalo would have had to export into the desert 500 slaves per annum. An unknown number of these mounts would have been pure Barbary horses and would have sold at roughly 15 slaves apiece. The number of annual exports was thus likely considerably in excess of 500 slaves per year, which should be taken as a minimum figure; the actual number was more likely a low multiple of this figure. By way of comparison with the Atlantic slave trade, approximately 60 slaves per year were sold from Saint-Louis du Sénégal during the 1680s.[51]

These estimates of slave exports suggest that in the early years of the French presence at Saint-Louis, the number of slaves exported from Senegambia across the Atlantic was a small percentage of the slaves which passed from Senegambia into the desert. Even at the minimum price of one slave per horse reported by Chambonneau in the 1670s, the exports from Waalo alone to the Sahara and North Africa may have equalled or surpassed the export of slaves from the entire Senegambia, including the Senegal and Gambia river basins, into the Atlantic sector.

Along the Senegambian coastal corridor below Waalo, the Wolof states likewise seem to have been dependent upon the importation of horses acquired from desert traders. In 1686, for example, when the *teeñ* [ruler] of Bawol defeated the damel of Kajoor's army, he took many prisoners. He needed to equip a military force. Guns and gunpowder were available through the Atlantic trade, and horses from the Sahara. The teeñ sold only 80 of the prisoners of war into the Atlantic trade. He sent the rest north to be exchanged for horses, to mount his cavalry.[52]

Across the western sahel, during the eighteenth century, the importation of war horses from the Sahara and the Maghrib continued to be directly implicated in the political violence of enslavement. But in some respects the dynam-

Table 4.3. Prices of horses in the western sahel and western savanna states, c. 1450 to c. 1900

	Price*	Comments
c. 1450[a]	9–14 slaves	horses sold by the Portuguese
	10–15 slaves	horses sold by desert traders
1460[b]	6–8 slaves	
Early six-teenth century[c]	< 6 slaves	The price for horses imported by the Portuguese had fallen from 10 slaves to 12 as a result of "bad organization." Horses were "of little value."
1675[d]	from 1 up to 10–15 slaves	"Horses are rare and more expensive than slaves . . . most are Barbary horses that the Moors sell . . ."
c. 1681[e]	up to 10–12 slaves	"They commonly buy horses of the *Moors* of *Genehoa* their neighbours, which tho' small, are extraordinarily mettlesome, like those of Barbary. Some of them cost ten to twelve slaves a-piece, or about one hundred pounds sterling. One *Catherine* of *Rufisco* . . . had a horse when I was there, which she valu'd at fourteen slaves, and afterwards presented him to the king of *Kayor.*"
1680s[f]	2/3 slave	
1685[g]	25 slaves	"a good horse"
1685[h]	15 slaves	Moors "have horses of great beauty, they are valued at fifteen slaves apiece."
1697[i]	15 slaves	"The Master of the Horse of the King [of Fuuta] rode several of the Prince's horses. . . These are very nice, true Barbary horses; they cost fifteen slaves apiece."
Mid-eighteenth century[j]	100 slaves 100 cattle and 20 camels	"The Arab horses of these countries are the most beautiful that I have seen. . . I have seen one of these horses sold to a Negro king; he paid one hundred slaves, one hundred cattle, and twenty camels for it."
Mid-eighteenth century[k]	100 young virgins	Virgins were gathered in 10 *ceddo* [slave soldiers] raids on villages around Ganjool. (Here, a mid-nineteenth-century account provides detail on a raid said to have taken place in the previous century: it may be apocryphal.)
1749–53[l]	15–30 slaves	". . . their Barbary horses which are considered with good reason to have the finest lines, to be the speediest at racing, and to be the best built in the universe, if one excepts the angular hindquarters, and of

(table continued on following page)

Table 4.3. Prices of horses in the western sahel and western savanna states, c. 1450 to c. 1900 (*continued*)

	Price*	Comments
		which the ordinary price is 15 to 30 slaves each of 100£, thus between 1500£ and 3000£. . ."
1769[m]	up to 30 slaves	Moors sold their horses to the damel of Kajoor.
1785/86[n]	up to 10–12 slaves	". . . in Africa one hears it said that horses are sold for up to ten to twelve slaves. It is true that black kings, to whom this sort of money [the slave] costs nothing . . . have paid up to twelve slaves for a nice horse; but one must not think that this is the going price for a nice Moorish horse, and besides these slaves only represent in merchandise the value of some four hundred pounds per head; the price of a horse selling for twelve slaves would only be forty-eight hundred pounds. . .
	50 pièces de guinée (3 slaves)	"But after having questioned many Moors, . . . I was reassured that one could obtain twenty [16 mares and 4 stallions], which would cost fifty guinée each, and which would total one thousand pièces de guinée. . . ". . . for twenty-five thousand francs, one could have . . . twenty horses, whether stallions or mares. . ."
1789[o]	12–20 eunuchs	"For every horse brought the King of Timbuctoo gave from twelve to twenty eunuchs, and some 400 slaves were annually imported, though many of them were passed on to Algeria."
1796[p]	<1/2 slave	Mungo Park purchased (for travelling) "a small, but very hardy and spirited beast, which cost . . . the value of £7, 10s."
	up to 12–14 slaves	"The horses are very beautiful, and so highly esteemed that the Negro princes will sometimes give from twelve to fourteen slaves for one horse."
An IX[q]	up to 10–12 slaves	"The blacks value highly the horses of the Moors. I have seen black Princes give up to 10 or 12 slaves for a horse, and make a raid expressly for the purpose of paying for the horse."
1811[r]	up to 26 slaves	"The Moorish breed of horses is highly esteemed; and at the period when the Slave Trade was carried on, twenty-six slaves have been given for one by a negro

Table 4.3. Prices of horses in the western sahel and western savanna states, c. 1450 to c. 1900
(*continued*)

	Price*	Comments
		prince, such was the comparative value of the two animals."
1818[s]	up to 15 slaves	". . . horses of the true Arab breed . . . their prices vary according to their beauty . . ."
	1/2 slave	"a good horse" (for travelling)
1821[t]	3 or 4 slaves	"the people of El Giblah [Gibla] sometimes go far to the southward . . . whence the Arabs obtain black slaves . . . for each horse"
1854[u]	20–30 slaves	"a fine horse"
1855[v]	400–500 francs (≈ 2 slaves) 1,200 francs (6 slaves)	Three different "races" of horses were raised. The first was divided into three families—Déeïnia, Mérass, and Séguemm—and could only live in the desert. Sold in country, a male was worth 400–500 francs and a female 1,200 francs. The second race was known as Tellïïa, could acclimate itself to Senegal, and was worth
	150–250 francs (≈ 1 slave) 200–300 francs (≈ 1 slave)	between 150 and 250 francs. The third race was called Cheurguya (the river horse). Its price varied between 200 and 300 francs. It was possible to purchase up to 200 or 300 horses of the Cheurguya breed per year if one ordered one year in advance.
	2 pièces de guinée	inferior horses
	100 cattle	Arabian horses
1856[w]	120,000 cowries (≈ 3–5 slaves)	price of a horse in Segu; price of a male or female slave given as 25,000–40,000 cowries
1881[x]	20 slaves	price paid by a Bidan caravanner for his horse
1890[y]	4 slaves 5 slaves	prices of stallions in Fuuta from an oral tradition, recorded in 1969. The source does not indicate the provenance of these stallions and may not indicate average price.
Late nineteenth century[z]	15–20 slaves or 100 cattle	Frequently (during the French conquest) one saw chiefs exchanging 15–20 slaves or 100 cattle, garnered in a razzia, for a horse that was pleasing to them.
c. 1900[aa]	800–1,000 francs (3–6 "ordinary" slaves)	horses, raised by the "maures du Sahel" (Hawd), known as Krékibas, Djdejats, and Djraibs and sold locally
	1,500–2,000 francs (5–12 "ordinary" slaves)	The same horses sold in Senegal would have brought approximately 1,500–2,000 francs if their pedigree were established.

(*table continued on following page*)

Table 4.3.   Prices of horses in the western sahel and western savanna states, c. 1450 to c. 1900 (*continued*)

	Price*	Comments
1906[bb]	100–200 francs	Colts were sold by the Moors to Wolof merchants in the cercle du Sahel. After two years of care, these merchants resold them at Medina, where other merchants
	1,200–1,500 francs	paid up to 1,200 or 1,500 francs. According to an expression then current in the
	4 slaves	French Soudan, a mare was worth four slaves: "Each hoof is worth a slave."

Sources:

[a] Crone, *The Voyages of Cadamosto*, 17, 49, cited by Law, *Horse*, 52.

[b] D. Gomes in J. M. Garcia (ed.), *As Viagens dos Descubrimentos* (Lisbon, 1983), 45–46, cited by Elbl, "Horse," 99.

[c] Pereira, *Esmeraldo de Situ Orbis*, 47, cited by Law, *Horse*, 52.

[d] Chambonneau, in Ritchie, "Deux textes," 332.

[e] Barbot, *A Description of the Coasts of North and South Guinea*, 38.

[f] PRO, T 70/456, Gambia Journals, 1683–1688, cited by Curtin in *Economic Change*, vol. 1, 222.

[g] La Courbe, *Premier voiage*, 126 ("un bon cheval").

[h] Labat, *Nouvelle relation*, vol. 3, 68: ". . . ils avoient des Chevaux d'une grande beauté, ils les estimoient quinz Captifs piece. Voilà une assez plaisante monnoye, mais chaque pays a ses modes. Il est bon pourtant de dire aux curieux qu'en ce quartier-là, on estime un Captif dix piastres ou trente livres tournois, & que par consequent le prix d'un cheval barbe étoit de quatre cent cinquante livres." Attribution of year 1685 is from Cultru's analysis of the work published by Labat (see Cultru, *Les origines de l'Afrique occidentale*, 95).

[i] Labat, *Nouvelle relation*, vol. 3, 235. Attribution of year 1697 is from Cultru's analysis of the work published by Labat (see Cultru, *Les origines de l'Afrique occidentale*, 129).

[j] Pruneau de Pommegorge, *Description de la Nigritie*, 16–17. The purchaser was probably the damel of Kajoor.

[k] Faidherbe, "Notice historique sur le Cayor," 527–529.

[l] Michel Adanson, "Mémoires d'Adanson sur le Sénégal et l'île de Gorée," presented and commented upon by C. Becker and V. Martin, *Bull. IFAN*, série B, 42 (1980), 759. Adanson's memoir was written in 1763 and referred back to his years in Senegal from 1749 to 1753.

[m] Doumet, "Mémoire," 43: "Ils vendent des cheveaux au roy qui en achette jusqu'à trente captifs, qu'ils conduisent en leurs terres du côté opposé de la rivière et les y emploient à la culture de leurs terres et à la garde de leurs bestiaux."

[n] Golberry, *Fragments d'un voyage*, vol. 1, 322–324: "On s'est plu à exagérer le prix de ces cheveaux maures, et en Afrique on entend dire qu'ils se vendent jusqu'à dix et douze captifs. Il est vrai que des rois-nègres, à qui cette sorte de monnaie ne coûtait rien à prendre ne à donner, ont payé pour un beau cheval jusqu'à douze esclaves; mais il ne faut par croire que ce soit là le prix nécessaire d'un beau cheval de race maure, et d'ailleurs ces captifs ne représenteraient qu'une valeur réelle de quatre cents livres par tête, en marchandise; le prix d'un cheval de douze captifs, serait donc représenté par la somme de quatre mille huit cents livres.

"Mais après avoir questionné beaucoup de Maures, et Sydy-Moktar particulièrement, sur le prix auquel on pourrait acquérir de ces chevaux de la plus belle race, dans le cas où l'on voudrait en acheter un certain nombre à la fois, pour les répandre dans nos haras, j'ai eu lieu de m'assurer, qu'on obtiendrait vingt chevaux choisis, qui coûteraient chacun cinquante pièces de Guinée, ce

Table 4.3. Prices of horses in the western sahel and western savanna states, c. 1450 to c. 1900 (*continued*)

---

qui ferait mille pièces de Guinée soldées à la fois, et formerait une somme très considerable pour les Maures du Désert.

"On peut donc assurer, que pour vingt cinq mille francs, on pourra chaque année, extraire des oasis du Zaarha, vingt pièces, soit étalons, soit jumens, choisis entre tout ce que ces races maures peuvent offrir de plus parfait."

The slave price was calculated by converting Golberry's horse price of 50 pièces de guinée at 25 francs each, or 1,250 francs in total, to 43 pounds sterling using the conversions table in Curtin, *Economic Change*, vol. 2, 56, and to approximately three slaves using the price of a slave on the lower Senegal in 1783 from Curtin, *Economic Change*, vol. 2, 49.

[o] Budgett Meakin, *The Moors. A Comprehensive Description* (London, 1902), 178 footnote, citing a document in the PRO, Morocco, vol. 17 (1789).

[p] The first price is cited by Curtin, *Economic Change*, vol. 1, 222. Park, *Travels*, 21 and 119–120.

[q] Pelletan, *Mémoire sur la colonie française du Sénégal et ses dépendances*, 55, footnote 11.

[r] PRO, CO 267/29, Answers to the Questions proposed to Lieutenant Colonel Maxwell, Lieutenant Governor of Senegal and Goree, by His Majesty's Commissioners for investigating the Forts and Settlements in Africa.

[s] Mollien, *L'Afrique occidentale en 1818*, 40–41 ("un bon cheval").

[t] Major Rennell, "An Account of the Captivity of Alexander Scott among the Wandering Arabs of the Great African Desert," *Edinburgh Philosophical Journal* 4, no. 8 (Apr. 1821), 229.

[u] Louis Faidherbe, "Les Berbères et les Arabes des bords du Sénégal," *BSG*, 4e série (fév. 1854), 109 ("un beau cheval"). This corrects typographical errors which appeared in the *JAH* version of this table.

[v] Carrère and Holle, *De la Sénégambie française*, 74, 216–217.

[w] ANFSOM, Sénégal II, dossier 4, Notes sur l'Afrique Occidentale Comprenant le pays de Ségou, les sources du Dhioliba & un Essai de vocabulaire contenant quelques mots de la langue parlée par les ingiènes de Grand Bassam 1856, M. Vignon.

[x] Alex. Will. Mitchinson, *The Expiring Continent: A Narrative of Travel in Senegambia* (London, 1881), 249.

[y] Kane and Robinson, *Islamic Regime*, the account of Aali Gay Caam, "Sammba Jaadanaa," 162–165.

[z] Meniaud, *Le Haut-Sénégal-Niger*, vol. 2, 139.

[aa] Horse prices from Meniaud, *Le Haut-Sénégal-Niger*, 134 and 138. Price of ordinary slave (given in pièces de guinée valued in French francs) from Dr. Lasnet et al., *Une mission au Sénégal. Ethnographie-botanique-zoologie-géologie* (Paris, 1900), 30. This work also includes a price for more expensive "captifs de case" that appears to pertain principally to the southwestern corner of the western Sahara.

[bb] Pierre, *L'élevage dans A.O.F.*, 36 and 43.

* Prices in slaves that are shown parenthetically indicate the equivalent of their immediately preceding entry.

ics of the horse and slave trade did change fundamentally over the eighteenth century, as horse breeding became a more successful concern in some regions of Senegambia. This was due, in part, to the increasing aridity, which over time eliminated the habitat of the tse-tse fly in the northern zones and pushed the zone of trypanosomiasis infection to the south. This, in combination with the breeding of new savanna horses that enjoyed greater immunity to trypanosomiasis than did the North African and the desert steppe horse, made horses common in northern Senegambia. But it is also clear that the breeding of horses in the savanna did not eliminate the demand for desert mounts. In 1736, for example, David Langlois de la Bord noted a continuing demand for desert horses in Waalo: "Few slaves were taken along the river this year, Brak made five or six raids which produced *nothing* [for the French], the larger part passed into the hands of the Moors in exchange for their horses . . ."[53] And in Kajoor the royal cavalry horses available for pillaging, which necessarily would have been faster than those available to hapless villagers, also continued to be imported from the desert traders. There is little evidence of the numbers of horses involved in these raids, other than the observations of Doumet, who estimated in 1769 that there were 300 to 400 cavalry horses used for pillaging within the realm of the damel. Most of the mounts would have been the more ordinary sort available from the desert traders at a price of roughly three slaves per horse or perhaps the largest of the new crossbred horses with a considerable resistance to trypanosomiasis.[54]

In Kajoor, the damel was the single largest purchaser of the best Barbary horses, many of which were probably brought down along a coastal route from Marrakech.[55] These Barbary horses in the mid-eighteenth century sold at the "ordinary price" of 15–30 slaves and generally must have died within the year of purchase. Some of the slaves used for this purpose probably came from the annual tribute that the damel drew from his kingdom, which Doumet estimated at 400 slaves and an unspecified (though considerable) number of cattle.[56] Of these slaves, perhaps 100–200 were sold into the Atlantic sector.[57] Many of the rest were likely destined for sale into the desert; the sale of 200–300 slaves would probably have yielded only between 10 and 20 horses fit for the damel. Other slaves for export were gathered in pillaging expeditions carried out on the initiative of either the damel or other nobles.[58] The nobles also needed to own high-prestige desert horses, and on occasion they undertook pillage for the explicit purpose of gathering slaves to sell into the Saharan trade.[59]

Any estimate of the annual number of slaves which moved north to Saharan and Maghribine markets must remain somewhat speculative. Much detail about the sale of horses, which were central to the prestige of the cavalry-based states, escaped the notice of (or was shielded from) European observers. But it is possible that at the time of Doumet's observations (1769) the number of slaves drawn solely from tribute revenues who were then sold for horses and exported to the desert sector from Kajoor equalled or exceeded the number of slaves sold into the Atlantic slave trade. And it is important to emphasize that slaves drawn from tribute revenues made up only part of the total number of slaves exported north to the Sahara and North Africa. Other slaves were gathered either through pillage by the damel and his nobles or through raids by desert forces. And it is certain that the volumes of these additional two streams of slave exports were sizable.

Europeans commented frequently upon the pillages committed by the damel and his soldiers. Desert raids into Kajoor occasioned less commentary, but it is nonetheless clear that these raids could produce significant numbers of slaves, particularly from 1760, when desert warriors helped secure the authority of the damel and in exchange received the right to pillage within Kajoor for one month per year.[60] And following successful large-scale slave raids into Waalo in 1775, desert warriors began to raid with greater impunity in the Wolof states. Unfortunately it is not possible to determine the number of slaves taken in desert raids that were destined for North African markets as opposed to the Atlantic slave trade. Some eighteenth-century writers described the sale of Black slaves by Bidan to brokers in the Atlantic slave trade and made little or no comment about the northward flow of slaves.[61] On the other hand, Silv. Meinrad Xavier Golberry, writing from his experiences in Senegal during the mid 1780s, indicated that the Whites had a major market for their captives in North Africa: "They [the desert people] are merchants; they travel great distances in the Sahara in all directions; they pillage for slaves on the banks of the Senegal and the Niger, and they sell them [the slaves] on the shores of the Mediterranean. , ,"[62]

The existence of a significant western Saharan and Maghribine demand for Senegambian slaves casts new light on the Atlantic slave trade from Senegambia in the eighteenth century. The number of slaves from the Wolof states exported into the Atlantic sector decreased during the second half of the eighteenth century, from approximately 300–400 per year in the period 1700–1750 to 200–300 per year in 1760–90, when prices were rising over the course of the century. This suggests that the critical inputs in the political economy of slave raiding during the era of the Atlantic slave trade came not from the Europeans and that the Black African rulers and princes satisfied their demand for European guns and gunpowder and for cloth and other imported goods with a smaller expenditure of slaves in the second half of the eighteenth century than in the first. Indirect confirmation of this price elasticity of demand comes from the report of a Wolof river captain who related details of his interview in 1775 with the damel: "The Damel was speaking to me one day [at his compound] in Kajoor. I was saying to him, "you don't gather as many slaves for sale as you did previously." He said to me "I am going to explain why. It is because at the present time I receive for one slave what I used to get for five.". .he made me see that we were fools to pay 120 bars for slaves, which is the going price."[63] In fact, the revenues from tribute, pillage, and warfare seem to have left Black rulers at times with a surplus of expendable slaves. This would go some distance toward explaining the fabulously high price of 100 slaves, 100 cattle, and 20 camels that one "Black prince" (probably the damel of Kajoor) was willing to pay for a single, if spectacular, desert horse.[64]

From the second half of the seventeenth century through the eighteenth century, to the east of the coastal Wolof states, the number of slaves generated by political violence was probably much greater than along the Senegambian littoral. Along the southeastern frontier of the western Sahara, the horse and slave trade was intertwined with the large-scale political violence launched from the desert edge and from Morocco, which rolled back Black African settlements from the Tagant and saw the rise to military dominance of desert forces in the Hawd. And farther to the south, from Galam and Bambuk, slave exports to the Maghrib apparently continued at high volume throughout the eighteenth century. From Fuuta, however, the massive exodus of northbound slaves was greatly reduced by the successful Toroodbe revolution in the mid-1770s.

Illustration 4.1. A chief of the Assounas.

Illustration 4.2. A Negro horse soldier.

Illustration 4.3. View of the village of Ben in Cayor.

Illustration 4.4. A chain of slaves travelling from the interior.

Illustration 4.5. Moors surprising a Negro village.

In the Aftermath of the Abolition of the Atlantic Slave Trade

The horse and slave trade did not stop with the abolition of the Atlantic slave trade. But with the closing of the Atlantic slave market, the slave-raiding states of the western savanna were left without a direct means to purchase imported European goods. For the Black African rulers and princes, it was still possible to obtain guns, cloth, and other imported goods through the sale of slaves, but it was now necessary to sell their slaves to desert traders in order to do so. The collapse of the Atlantic market thus strengthened the position of the desert traders who purchased slaves. And it brought immediate repercussions for the slave-raiding states because the desert traders were able to exploit their newly bolstered, dominant market position.[65] Comparing the slave trade of the northern Senegambian states before abolition with the slave trade after abolition, Lieutenant Colonel Maxwell testified in 1811:

> As there still exists a considerable demand for slaves amongst the Moors who receive them in exchange for Horses, Cloths, and other Merchandize and convey them into the interior of their Country for Sale, there is no difficulty hitherto in getting rid of them and the numbers in all probability are not lessened.[66]

And in 1818 Gaspard Théodore Mollien visited the towns of Ganjool and Kelkom, which had been recently devastated by the damel. He commented explicitly on the increase in warfare and pillage that was necessary to support the damel's court:

> The abolition of the slave trade was a grand gesture, generous, worthy of an enlightened century, but illusory, until we force the Moors to subscribe to it. Let me explain: the Blacks sell to the Moors the slaves which are forbidden to the Europeans to buy; and the king, who had sufficient revenue to maintain his court by selling two hundred prisoners to the French at 600 francs apiece, at present makes more frequent incursions against his neighbors, and against his own subjects, to double the number of his slaves and to have the same revenue, because the Moors pay only half as much for slaves as the Europeans did.[67]

The depredations of the damel of Kajoor continued well after the ending of the Atlantic slave trade, sometimes with the explicit purpose of gathering slaves to purchase horses.[68] And even as late as 1854, the Kajoor elite was pillaging Wolof villages with impunity and selling the victims into desert slavery.[69]

Many of these slaves must have moved north along the trans-Saharan route which ran along the Atlantic littoral up to Wad Nun in the Moroccan Sahara, the point at which the slaves moved into the control of Moroccan traders.[70] In the late 1840s, a trade spur opened up that linked Kajoor with Wad Nun via the Adrar and apparently supplemented the coastal route. General Faidherbe provided some details on a single caravan from Wad Nun that travelled this spur and arrived at the Trarza escale. The caravan was originally composed of 200 camels and 150 mares, of which half had already been sold along the way.[71] The 75 remaining mares apparently were destined for the markets of Kajoor, and although the quality of the horses is not commented upon explicitly, the reigning price of 15 slaves per pure Arab steed translates to 1,125 slaves for export to the Saharan and North African markets. And indeed, this calculation does not take into account the sale of truly fine horses. Faidherbe, as late as the mid 1850s, for example, noted that "a fine horse" could bring 20–30 slaves in the desert market.[72] At the other end of the range, if all these horses had been desert bred, in which case they would have been bought for three or four slaves each, the value of the horses in this single caravan would have been between 225 and 300 slaves.

The Ending of the Horse and Slave Trade

On the heels of a crisis in the gum arabic trade, the French conquered the lower Senegal River valley (1854–58).[73] The French presence in the lower Senegal blocked easy access by the desert horse and slave traders to the Wolof states. For the lower Senegal the era of the horse and slave trade was drawing to a close. As Faidherbe noted presciently in 1859: "Marabouts from the Tiris, the Adrar, and the Trarza come to buy slaves in Kajoor in exchange for their horses and [then] take them to Morocco. This migration, which is leading to the depopulation of our colony, will soon cease, thanks to our [new] situation in Senegal." [74] The French were also successful in preventing large-scale desert-raiding expeditions into the Wolof states or Fuuta, [75] and in this regard, too, they helped staunch the northward flow of slaves. By the 1860s the states of the Atlantic littoral were far from demilitarized, but from this point onward the Wolof cavalry forces apparently rode almost exclusively upon the local crossbreeds.

Along the middle and upper portions of the Senegal River valley and as far east as the Niger River, horse cavalry continued to be central to the wide-scale religious and political violence of the jihads of the second half of the nineteenth century. In the upper valley and farther east along the western savanna, where the jihad of Umar Tall wrought awesome destruction, most of the war horses used in the religious and political violence seem to have been the adapted crossbreeds. Umar Tall purchased his cavalry remounts in Segu; Ahmadu Shaykhu oversaw royal stud farms in Banamba. [76] Along the middle Senegal basin, combatants in the internal conflicts of Fuuta Tooro in the 1870s needed a steady supply of horses, and at least some were probably obtained from the desert. [77] And by the late nineteenth century, under the conditions of increasing aridity that forced the desert frontier south, Soninke-bred horses became an important element in the trade; these horses were sold to remount the cavalry of Samori Ture. [78]

By the turn of the twentieth century, desert caravans from the Adrar and southern Morocco were still making their way toward Saint-Louis du Sénégal to sell horses, principally mares, to local merchants. These horses were often ill-treated and arrived in poor condition; they brought 250–400 francs; the merchants fed and cared for them for two years and sold their colts as "river horses." From 1898 through 1900, the French bought 12–15 of the desert horses per year. But with the French occupation of the Trarza beginning in 1901, desert caravans stopped coming. [79] Horses from the Hawd, however, continued to be sold into Senegambia—sometimes as race horses—and into the French Soudan well into the twentieth century.

The horse and slave trade was a major sector of the desert-edge economy during the period 1600–1850. Under conditions of increasing aridity, the zone of desert-horse breeding was pushed south, and new crossbreeds were created. Over time, the new ecological conditions allowed for the use of horse cavalry in the Black African states farther to the south. These cavalries were bolstered by the continued importation of the larger and more desirable horses bred in North Africa, the high desert, and the desert fringe. The volume of slaves exported north into the Sahara and across the Sahara to the Maghrib declined considerably from a high in the late seventeenth and early eighteenth centuries, but slave exports appear to have continued relatively strongly until the imposition of French colonial rule. Along the southwestern frontier this denouement came in the 1850s. Along the southeastern frontier, the French would not consolidate their conquest until the 1890s.

5

The Trade in Gum Arabic

Gum arabic was a natural exudate of several varieties of acacia tree (principally, *Acacia verek* and *Acacia senegal*) which grew wild in the sandy soil of the desert edge. Over the period 1600–1850, under conditions of increasing aridity, the acacia groves were forced far to the south. Some tentative evidence may be adduced from early European maps. In the late seventeenth century, for example, the gum "forests" of the western Sahara were represented in the interior as far north as the St. John River, approximately 200 kilometers to the north of Portendick. By the late eighteenth and early nineteenth centuries, cartographers depicted the gum groves 200–300 kilometers farther to the south.[1] But it is also possible to chart this southward movement, if only indirectly, by following the displacement of the gum trading stations down the Atlantic littoral. In the seventeenth and eighteenth centuries a substantial trade in gum arabic took place from the ports of Arguin, Portendick, and occasionally Jiwa (Petit Portendick) along the western Saharan coast. By the late eighteenth century this trade had virtually ceased at Arguin, the northernmost of the desert ports, and by the mid-nineteenth century the trade had become too dangerous at Portendick and Jiwa as well.[2] The lack of potable water and the increasing barrenness and aridity of the coastal regions had raised the risks of carrying the gum to the coast beyond acceptable levels. Although some gum had been brokered at gum stations along the Senegal River as early as the seventeenth century, over time an increasing percentage came to be transported south. At least from the turn of the nineteenth century, most of the export gum trade was conducted along the Senegal River.[3] This southward displacement of the gum groves is itself powerful evidence of ecological change. Gum trees stabilize dunes by means of their lengthy lateral roots, enrich the soil by fixing atmospheric nitrogen, and, owing to their cover and underground biomass, slow down wind erosion and decrease runoff.[4]

Over the course of the period 1600–1850, the export trade in gum arabic had a considerable impact on the regional economy of the desert frontier. The importation of large quantities of cotton cloth, particularly the indigo-dyed guinée from India, in exchange for gum resulted in the gradual replacement of the traditional cotton cloth manufactured by Black Africans.[5] Tax payments made by the Europeans to the regional desert authorities helped to legitimate the extension of desert authority; the payments amounted to a stock of wealth from which the desert emirs could distribute largesse to their clients. In the early years of the gum trade, the imported goods may have also constituted a source of prestige: in the view of one eminent desert historian, the emir of the Trarza, Ali Shandhora (r. 1703–27), may well have adopted the name of a superb Dutch trade cloth.[6] Over time, the prestige associated with imported goods would have been severely diluted both by the growth in the gum trade and by the powerful movements in the terms of trade in favor of the White merchants which pumped large volumes of imported cloth and other goods into the desert sector. And by the mid-eighteenth century the new wealth also cushioned the impact of the ecological deterioration of the desert edge, allowing desert people yet another means through which to import grain.

The labor hours dedicated to gum harvesting were a small percentage of the total labor hours dedicated to productive pursuits by the slave populations of the Gibla. Not only were the labor requirements for gum harvesting relatively slight, but they also fell during the nonagricultural season. A slave worker set to this task could on average harvest four kilograms per day, and thus in principle the harvesting of a given ton of gum arabic could be accomplished by two harvesters during a period of roughly three months. But zwaya could harvest gum only in territories to which they had specific rights, and thus the gum harvesting season was generally shorter than three months and less productive than half a ton for an individual slave. In addition, gum harvesting fitted easily into the daily routines of those who were charged principally with the management of livestock herds, so it could be undertaken as a supplemental activity. Thus, during the eighteenth century, the gum harvest, if carried out by slaves set exclusively to this task, would have engaged the seasonal energies of some 2,000 individuals, a small fraction of the slave population of the Gibla. Many more individuals were undoubtedly involved in this process; yet it is clear as well that the harvesting of gum arabic could not have been constrained by a shortage of labor. Even during the boom in the gum arabic trade during the first half of the nineteenth century, the desert-side slave populations would have been able to accommodate easily the increased demand for seasonal gum labor. Along the desert edge, Whites imported Black slaves principally to perform agricultural labor, as well as to work in the livestock sector, to carry out domestic labor under the tent, and to harvest gum arabic. Thus, the importation of Black African slaves into the societies of the desert edge was driven by a complex set of factors.[7]

The Demand for Gum Arabic

Peoples of the western sahel had traditionally used gum arabic as a food stuff, thickener for drinks, medicinal treatment (particularly for diarrhea), cosmetic hair treatment, and for making ink, glue, painting on wood, and glazing mud walls.[8] Not surprisingly it also entered into the regional trade networks, and it figures in some of the early Arabic accounts of exports from Awdaghust to Morocco.[9] We know little, however, about the organization of gum harvesting or marketing in the period before 1600. The quantities marketed seem to have been modest, and gum arabic was a humble product compared with the slaves and gold, which most impressed the early chroniclers.

Europeans in the preindustrial age likewise employed gum arabic to similarly diverse ends—as a stiffener in making hats, paint, paper, gild, glue, and ink, in preparing foodstuffs and cosmetics, and in sizing cloth. From the time of the Portuguese maritime expansion in the mid-fifteenth century, quantities of gum arabic were purchased by the Portuguese, and by the seventeenth century it was purchased by the French, Dutch, and Brandenburgers at the coastal trading fort of Arguin and at Portendick farther south along the western Saharan littoral Before the European maritime revolution, Europe's gum had come from Arabia and the Nilotic Sudan. But, by the sixteenth century, gum from the Gibla had begun to reach European markets, and by the eighteenth century the southwestern corner of the Sahara had become virtually the sole supplier of gum arabic to Europe.[10]

From the second half of the seventeenth century, industrial uses for gum arabic in the new cotton calico textile printing factories began to stimulate a steady and diffuse demand. From the early centers in London, Amsterdam, and Marseilles, calico printing found its way to Germany and Switzerland in the late seventeenth century. Over the course of the eighteenth century, the scale of calico printing in England and in France expanded enormously, and the techniques spread to other European states. According to S. D. Chapman and S. Chassagne, calico cottons enjoyed a veritable consumer craze. For the first time in European history consumer taste was nearly uniform; calico prints were an inexpensive substitute for tapestries, exotic silks, and expensive imported chintzes. The exact uses to which gum arabic was put are difficult to identify; each printer had his own proprietary formulas and guarded them as such. But printers in London who testified before the House of Commons in 1752 stressed the indispensability of gum arabic in the production of silk, silk handkerchiefs, (cotton) stuffs, linen, and calico cotton goods, particularly in the processes of penciling and applying colors.[11] Additional industrial uses for gum arabic were developed shortly after the middle of the eighteenth century. Gum arabic was found to be the best mordant for use on the new, large, engraved copper plates, which allowed for great strides to be made both in the fineness in printing and in the size of pattern to be repeated.[12]

As the use of gum arabic in textile production became increasingly important, gum exports from the western Sahara increased from 500 or 600 tons per year in the early eighteenth century to nearly double that amount by the 1780s. During some periods in the first half of the eighteenth century, the French gum trading companies were very concerned with garnering control of the gum supply. They purchased all the gum on the market and then dumped a great deal of it into the ocean in order to keep prices high. Thus, gum exports from the western sahel (Senegal and the "gum coast") may not correlate with gum imports into Europe.

The overall estimates of European consumption of gum arabic are valuable because they complement the single, relatively complete series for gum imports to England during the period 1699–1808.[13]

Table 5.1. Estimates of European gum consumption (in tons*)

	France	England	All Europe
1734[a]			300
1752[b]		120	
1757[c]			600
1766[d]		1/5 of gum senegal	
1783[e]	1/6 of gum sold in Senegal		
1785–86[f]			1,000
1795[g]	200–250		
1803[h]			1,000

Sources:

[a] ANF C[6] 11, Mémoire sur la Concession du Sénégal, 8 octobre 1734.

[b] Great Britain, House of Commons, "Report from the Select Committee respecting the importation of gum senega." The estimate of gum arabic consumption of the printing industries only.

[c] ANF C[6] 14, Extraits relatifs au commerce de la Gomme tirér d'un mémoire sur la concession générale du Sénégal (1757?) (unsigned).

[d] PRO, CO 267/1, Chas. O'Hara to Lords Commissioners for Trade and Plantations, 28 May 1766, at Fort Lewis.

[e] ANF C[6] 18, Mémoire sur la commerce du Sénégal, février 1783.

[f] Richard Phillips (ed.), *A Collection of Modern and Contemporary Voyages and Travels*, vol. 4 (London, 1806), the account of Jean Baptiste Léonard Durand, "A Voyage to Senegal," 142.

[g] ANF C[6] 20, Sénégal, 26 Brumaire de l'An 3.

[h] ANFSOM, DFC Sénégal, carton 83, no. 105, Des peuples qui habitent les cotes du Sénégal et les bords de ce fleuve, Des royaumes sur la cote de Gorée, Cayor, Baol, Sin, et Salum, 1803 (unsigned); P. Herbin de Halle (ed.), *Statistique générale et particulière de la France et de ses colonies*, vol. 7 (Paris, An XII), 98.

* The type of tonnage is not specified in the sources. French sources are assumed to refer to metric tons; English sources are assumed to refer to long tons.

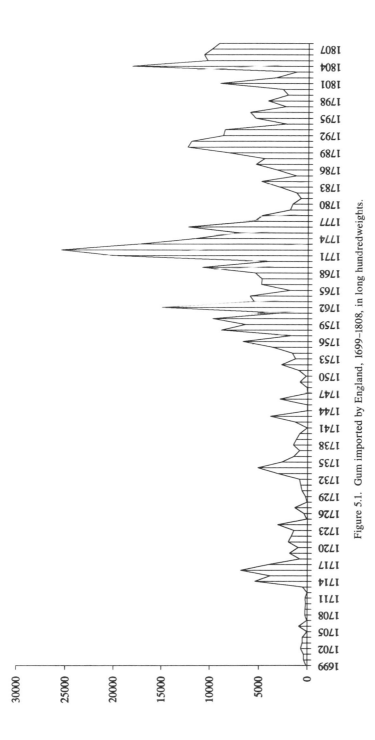

Figure 5.1. Gum imported by England, 1699–1808, in long hundredweights.

101

Table 5.2. Gum imported by England, 1699–1808, in long hundredweights

	Directly from Africa					Via the New World					Grand total
	Arabic	Senegal	Arabic and/or senegal	Sandrake	Total	Arabic	Senegal	Arabic and/or senegal	Sandrake	Total	
1699	64	0	0	56	119	0	0	0	0	0	119
1700	45	0	0	324	369	0	0	0	0	0	369
1701	200	0	0	178	378	0	0	0	0	0	378
1702	585	0	0	89	674	0	0	0	0	0	674
1703	285	0	0	217	503	0	0	0	0	0	503
1704	501	0	0	0	501	0	0	0	0	0	501
1705	Book missing										
1706	304	0	0	581	886	0	0	0	0	0	886
1707	41	0	0	0	41	0	0	0	0	0	41
1708	74	0	0	180	255	0	0	0	2	2	257
1709	0	0	0	235	235	0	0	0	0	0	235
1710	32	0	0	129	161	0	0	0	0	0	161
1711	2	0	0	174	175	0	0	0	60	60	235
1712	Book missing										
1713	10	0	0	489	500	0	0	0	0	0	500
1714	3,693	1,600	0	99	5,392	0	0	0	0	0	5,392
1715	2,649	1,075	0	131	3,855	0	1	0	0	1	3,856
1716	3,764	2,009	0	54	5,827	0	1,000	0	0	1,000	6,827
1717	2,241	1,730	0	33	4,005	0	0	0	0	0	4,005
1718	321	0	0	180	501	294	0	0	0	294	795
1719	0	1,605	0	51	1,656	79	61	0	72	212	1,867
1720	840	31	0	85	956	0	0	0	0	0	956
1721	0	1,849	0	38	1,887	0	105	0	9	114	2,001
1722	0	1,661	0	14	1,674	0	0	0	0	0	1,674

Year											
1723	0	1,117	0	17	1,134	250	0	0	40	290	1,424
1725	19	0	0	40	59	0	0	0	0	0	59
1726	0	0	0	108	108	255	0	0	0	255	363
1727	1,216	0	0	114	1,330	0	0	0	0	0	1,330
1728	11	0	0	20	31	2	0	0	0	0	31
1729	154	0	0	50	203	0	0	0	0	2	206
1730	533	0	0	42	576	100	0	0	0	0	576
1731	488	0	0	120	507	0	0	0	0	100	707
1732	805	4	0	20	330	0	0	0	0	0	830
1733	583	2,504	0	11	3,098	0	0	0	0	0	3,098
1734	679	4,390	0	81	5,150	0	0	0	0	0	5,150
1735	533	2,105	0	32	2,670	0	2	0	27	29	2,698
1736	7	1,341	0	88	1,436	0	0	0	0	0	1,436
1737	743	0	0	97	840	0	0	0	0	0	840
1738	1,221	0	0	263	1,484	0	8	0	0	8	1,492
1739	149	0	0	265	413	0	768	0	0	768	1,181
1740	154	520	0	128	802	0	0	0	0	0	802
1741	2	0	0	26	28	0	0	0	0	0	28
1742	73	1,232	0	12	1,317	0	0	0	0	0	1,317
1743	0	0	3,887	16	3,903	0	0	0	0	0	3,903
1744	30	0	0	11	11	0	0	0	0	0	11
1745	2,913	0	0	0	30	0	0	0	0	0	30
1746	0	0	0	16	2,929	0	0	0	0	0	2,929
1747	0	0	0	0	0	0	0	0	0	0	0
1748	0	0	60	6	66	0	0	0	0	0	66
1749	758	0	0	41	800	0	0	0	0	0	800
1750	0	0	98	84	182	0	0	0	0	0	182
1751	0	0	720	206	926	0	0	0	0	0	926
1752	0	0	2,467	29	2,496	0	239	0	0	239	2,735
1753	0	0	1,263	10	1,272	0	0	0	0	0	1,272
1754	1,420	0	0	55	1,475	0	111	0	0	111	1,586

(table continued on following pages)

Table 5.2. Gum imported by England, 1699–1808, in long hundredweights (continued)

	Directly from Africa					Via the New World					Grand total
	Arabic	Senegal	Arabic and/or senegal	Sandrake	Total	Arabic	Senegal	Arabic and/or senegal	Sandrake	Total	
1755	0	0	3,589	105	3,694	0	0	0	0	0	3,694
1756	0	0	5,907	8	5,915	0	771	0	0	771	6,686
1757	0	1,734	0	22	1,756	0	0	0	0	0	1,756
1758	8,511	140	0	176	8,826	0	26	0	0	26	8,852
1759	0	0	5,727	50	5,777	0	688	0	0	688	6,465
1760	0	3	9,731	0	9,733	0	0	0	0	0	9,733
1761	0	0	2,775	44	2,819	1	0	0	0	1	2,819
1762	0	0	12,152	4	12,156	30	2,285	500	33	2,848	15,004
1763	0	1,605	3,141	0	4,746	423	375	0	20	818	5,564
1764	0	7	5,600	0	5,607	168	0	204	16	388	5,995
1765	29	769	0	389	1,187	610	0	0	55	665	1,852
1766	11	4,653	0	0	4,664	130	0	0	50	180	4,844
1767	69	4,700	0	12	4,782	0	0	0	0	0	4,782
1768	595	4,201	0	668	5,464	0	0	0	0	0	5,464
1769	222	10,583	0	0	10,805	0	0	0	0	0	10,805
1770	114	3,944	0	2	4,060	0	0	0	0	0	4,060
1771	121	19,898	0	79	20,099	0	0	0	0	0	20,099
1772	927	24,521	0	34	25,482	0	0	0	0	0	25,482
1773	273	16,889	0	94	17,257	0	39	0	0	39	17,295
1774	131	11,321	0	54	11,507	0	0	0	0	0	11,507
1775	276	6,833	0	31	7,140	0	2	0	0	2	7,142
1776	221	12,013	0	58	12,292	0	0	0	0	0	12,292
1777	18	5,607	0	4	5,629	0	0	0	0	0	5,629
1778	210	4,499	0	21	4,729	0	0	0	0	0	4,729
1779	68	1,771	0	20	1,859	0	0	0	0	0	1,859

Year											
1780	1,098	472	0	30	1,600	0	0	0	0	0	1,600
1781	0	670	0	0	670	0	0	93	0	93	763
1782	648	556	0	0	1,204	0	0	0	0	0	1,204
1783	805	2,136	0	0	2,941	89	0	0	0	89	3,030
1784	4,805	63	0	0	4,867	0	0	0	0	0	4,867
1785	1,226	6	0	0	1,232	0	0	0	0	0	1,232
1786	2,007	1,289	0	0	3,297	0	0	0	0	0	3,297
1787	3,006	2,440	0	0	5,446	0	0	0	0	0	5,446
1788	3,192	1,353	0	0	4,545	0	0	0	0	0	4,545
1789	4,130	4,080	0	0	8,209	1	0	0	0	1	8,210
1790	4,134	8,220	0	0	12,354	2	0	0	0	2	12,357
1791	6,030	5,941	0	0	11,971	0	0	0	0	0	11,971
1792	5,597	3,148	0	0	8,745	0	0	0	0	0	8,745
1793	3,926	4,677	0	0	8,602	0	0	0	0	0	8,602
1794	2,284	0	0	0	2,284	0	0	0	0	0	2,284
1795	4,040	1,437	0	0	5,477	0	0	0	0	0	5,477
1796	2,415	756	0	0	3,172	0	0	2,883	0	2,883	6,055
1797	600	843	0	0	1,443	0	0	913	0	913	2,356
1798	727	3,179	0	0	3,906	0	0	289	0	289	4,195
1799	632	836	0	0	1,467	6	0	645	0	651	2,118
1800	727	1,909	0	0	2,636	8	0	4	0	12	2,648
1801	2,232	6,836	0	0	9,068	0	0	0	0	0	9,086
1802	1,705	1,422	0	0	3,127	47	0	191	0	238	3,365
1803	941	253	0	0	1,195	0	0	6	0	6	1,201
1804	2,054	14,255	0	0	16,310	199	0	1,640	0	1,839	18,149
1805	1,858	7,635	0	0	9,492	0	0	845	0	845	10,337
1806	1,972	8,375	0	0	10,347	0	0	360	0	360	10,707
1807	2,038	6,802	0	0	8,841	1,084	0	0	0	1,084	9,925
1808	2,912	5,774	0	0	8,686	504	0	0	0	504	9,190

Sources: PRO, CUST 3 and CUST 17.

Note: Totals may not sum exactly owing to rounding of the individual entries.

Gum exports doubled again in the decade of the 1830s to 2,000 tons per year.[14] This second doubling took place despite the newly discovered preparation of dextrine in France. Dextrine was less than half the price of gum, but it was difficult to conserve and was not suitable for all the uses to which gum arabic was put.[15] Desert exports continued strongly, but at least by the turn of the twentieth century, Sudan had replaced the western Sahara as the most important world supplier of gum arabic.[16]

At least by the mid-eighteenth century, the British and the French were the primary shippers of gum arabic from the western Sahara, but industries in Great Britain and France did not use the majority of the gum. A 1783 estimate of gum consumption in France put it at one-sixth of the gum exported from Senegal,[17] and approximately the same percentage of use in France was estimated in the 1830s. Of the gum shipped from Saint-Louis du Sénégal in 1832, for example, only 18 percent was retained for use in France; the remainder was exported to other countries, from whence it was often reexported.[18] This diffuse demand allowed for an exception in French colonial commercial policy. In the nineteenth century, gum arabic was the only product which could be exported from Saint-Louis on non-French ships.[19] And because gum arabic could be carried by ships flying other than the French flag, gum functioned as a currency in the Saint-Louisian export trade, where it was sometimes used as payment for goods coming from Paris or London.[20]

This gum trade from the southwestern Sahara played a more important role in the economic history of West Africa than many historians have realized. From the late seventeenth century until the 1870s, gum arabic was the single most important product traded by the Europeans who stopped along the gum coast of the western Sahara or traded at the mouth of the Senegal River. And gum was the only product shipped from West Africa for which there was but a single source of supply. Although in West Africa generally the export trades in agricultural and arboreal products did not come into their own until the illegalization of the Atlantic slave trade in the early nineteenth century, the gum trade was important from an early period and took on even greater importance when the Atlantic slave trade began to collapse after 1790. By the 1820s the economic livelihood of the colony of Saint-Louis du Sénégal rested uneasily upon the trade in gum arabic.

Our awareness of the early importance of the gum trade has been slow to emerge for two reasons. First, the trade is difficult to quantify. Exports of gum arabic took place both from small trading ports along the desert coast to the north of Senegal and from Saint-Louis. Export records do exist for Saint-Louis, although they are incomplete, but exports from the coast went largely unrecorded. Second, Philip Curtin's Senegambian economic history, which focussed on the whole of Senegambia, brought together export data from the trades along the Senegal and Gambia rivers and from Gorée and the *petite côte* (the Atlantic coast from Gorée south to the Gambia River). Of the Senegambian points of export, large quantities of gum arabic passed only through Saint-Louis at the mouth of the Senegal River, and thus gum exports appeared less significant when aggregated with the slave trades from these other points of exportation.[21]

When the geographic field of analysis is narrowed to the desert-edge zone of the Senegal River valley and its hinterlands, the gum trade assumes a new importance. Even excluding gum exports from the desert coast, the value of gum arabic, measured by the price of goods paid to the African supplier, exceeded the value of the export trade in slaves from the Senegal River valley in the late seventeenth century. The value of slave exports surpassed that of gum by at least 1718, and then gum again became the principal export from about 1790 until the 1870s, when it was surpassed by the value of peanut exports.

Table 5.3. Estimates and returns of exports from the Senegal River valley (excluding the gum coast) in pounds sterling, 1687–1797

Year	Gum		Slaves	
	Quantity (metric tons)	Value (£ sterling)	Number	Value (£ sterling)
1687	200	914	100	340
1693	294	1,342	200	448
1718	2,200	2,723	650	3,419
1750	1,028	3,557	1,050	15,120[a]
1784	339	15,135	1,500	41,280[b]
1793–97[c]	339	9,594	—	—

Sources:

Slave exports from Saint-Louis are estimated roughly from Curtin, *Economic Change*, vol. 1, page 162, Table 4.2. His table "Consolidated Capacity Estimates" is not intended to be interpreted as estimates of the numbers of slaves actually exported, and whenever actual time series were checked against capacity estimates, the time series fell short in the eighteenth-century slave trade by 25–50 percent. But even allowing for a possible shortfall in this range, the general relationship between the two trades is unchanged.

Gum exports and values for gum and slaves are taken from Curtin, *Economic Change*, vol. 2, 96–97, Table A 15.5, and 98–99, Table A 16.5.

After 1783, the gum trade handled by the French on the river declined; the gum then went to Portendick.

[a] This value is for 1753 rather than 1750.

[b] This value reflects the annual average for 1769–78.

[c] The quantity and value shown are annual averages for 1793–97.

The importance of gum arabic becomes even more apparent when the prices for gum on the European market are considered together with the prices on the African market. The European data are sparse, but they provide evidence of the wide disparity between the prices paid for gum to Bidan suppliers and the prices on the European markets, that is, evidence of the great profitability of the trade for the Europeans.[22] The large profits to be won from the gum trade help explain the "gum wars" fought between European trading groups along the western Saharan coast through the first half of the eighteenth century.[23]

Table 5.4. Prices of one metric ton of gum arabic in pounds sterling, 1710–1827

	London* or France†	Saint-Louis to desert supplier	Saint-Louis sale to négociants** or F.O.B.‡
1710[a]	88*		
1718[b]		3.40	
1723[b]		5.45	
1739[b]		6.06	
1745[b]		3.46	
1776[b]		23.31	
1783[b]		44.62	
1786[c]	137†		
1788[b]		30.36	
1803[d]	160–180		52–60**
1810[e]			90–95‡
1823–27[b]		69.57 (annual average)	

Sources:

[a] PRO, CO 267/18, Observations on the Trade to Africa, with Proposals to Extend and Improve the same for Benefit of the West India Islands and consequently Great Britain and Ireland, dated Barbadoes 1710, Robert Vaughan and Thomas Carney.

[b] Curtin, *Economic Change*, vol. 1, 217, footnote 4.

[c] Silv. Meinrad Xavier Golberry, *Travels in Africa* (London, 1802), vol. 2, 25.

[d] Herbin de Halle, *Statistique générale et particulière*, 98.

[e] PRO, CO 267/33, Extract of a Letter written from Lieutenant Colonel Maxwell to Lieutenant Colonel Torrens, Government House, Senegal, 10 March 1810.

Table 5.5. Printers' wholesale purchase price of gum arabic in Europe, 1741-1803

	France	England	Hamburg	Holland
	Cost per pound	Cost per long hundredweight		
1741[a]		32-33s		
1743[a]		31s		
1744[a]		30s		
1749[a]		52s		
1749-50[a]			30-32s	
1750[a]		5£ 17s 6p		
1751[a]		11£ 10s; 12£ 7s	5£	
1752[a]			6£ 1s, 10£	7£ 10s
1758[b]	20-22 sous			
1780-1800[c]	30 sous			
	40 sous			
	up to 3 francs			
1795[d]	up to 60 sous			
1801[b]	5 francs			
1803[c]	40-45 sous			

Sources:

[a] Great Britain, House of Commons, "Report from the Select Committee Respecting the Importation of Gum Senega."

[b] ANF C[6] 21, Notice historique sur la Compagnie du Senegal, 1801.

[c] Golberry, *Fragmens d'un voyage*, 253. Golberry estimated the average price over this 20-year period to be 44 sous.

[d] ANF C[6] 20, Memoire du Capitaine de Vau.; J. J. Eyriès Sur le Commerce de la Gomme Au Sénégal (1795).

[e] Herbin de Halle, *Statistique générale et particulière*, 98.

If these prices in London and France are roughly indicative of the market values of gum arabic in England and France in the eighteenth century, the value of the gum exported that century from the desert edge may have exceeded that of the trade in slaves from the Senegal River valley, even in the 1780s, at the height of the Atlantic slave trade from this region. Indeed, this was the opinion of contemporary observers.[24]

The Idaw al-Hajj and the "Origins" of the Gum Trade

During the course of the late sixteenth-century or early seventeenth-century crisis in the Adrar brought on by warfare and drought, one of the dominant zwaya groups, the Idaw al-Hajj, migrated from Wadan to the Trarza, and in the seventeenth century, the modern chapter in the gum trade began. According to Idaw al-Hajj tradition:

About 400 or 500 years ago the Ulad al-Mokhtar came to this region. The first to come was the father of the Ulad al-Mokhtar, who was named Najib. He settled in the village named Tigumatin. There he found a woman who was very heavy.[25] Her name was Hafsa Mint Mahmsidigh. She was of the Id Agvudya grouping of the Tandgha . . .

Najib had three sons by Hafsa. Their names were Atfagha Awback, Al-Amin, and Al-Wavij. One son, Al-Amin Wuld Najib, was a scholar, and he travelled to the Maghrib where he devoted himself to writing books. One day he left the Maghrib for the Straits of Gibraltar with two companions from the western Sahara in order to buy some high-quality writing paper. On the way there both of his companions fell ill. But Al-Amin Wuld Najib remained in good health because his mother Hafsa had given him some gum arabic, and told him to eat three pieces before each meal, and Al-Amin followed her counsel. Once there he encountered some Europeans,[26] and after eating with these Europeans Al-Amin took out a piece of gum which had been ground and mixed with sugar. The gum piqued the curiosity of the Europeans. Al-Amin told them that he had brought the gum with him from Mauritania. They asked him to return with them to Mauritania by ship to show them where to find the gum, but Al-Amin refused. Instead he gave them a letter for his brother Atfagha Awback. He instructed the Europeans to sail their boat up the Senegal River until they came to a large dune. According to Al-Amin's instructions, the camp of Atfagha Awback would be behind the dune.

The Europeans made several copies of Al-Amin's letter, and then they sailed to the Senegal River and then up the river to the dune. When word reached camp, Hafsa suggested to Atfagha Awback that he go see what the Europeans wanted. He mounted a donkey and headed out, and when he was nearing the river, the Europeans sighted him with their field glasses and then fired off a round of gunshots to indicate their location.[27] When Atfagha Awback arrived, the Europeans showed him a spurious copy of the letter and asked him if it was the handwriting of his brother. He said that it was not. At last they showed him the original letter, and he identified the handwriting as that of his brother. And in this manner the parties assured themselves of the authenticity of the letter and its recipient. After a long debate, Atfagha Awback signed an accord with the Europeans for the sale of gum. This accord granted to the descendants of Najib the right to receive a tax payment from the captain of each boat which came to trade for gum. This tax was called *kubl*.

The first individual to trade gum to the Europeans was Atfagha Awback Wuld Najib, but the responsibility for dealing with the Europeans did not remain in his hands. When his brother Al-Amin had first set off for the Maghrib, Al-Amin's wife had been pregnant with a son, Al-Mokhtar; and these trade responsibilities passed to this son upon his maturity. The direct descendants of Al-Mokhtar Wuld al-Amin Wuld Najib continued to exercise authority in Trarza gum affairs up until the early nineteenth century.[28]

This Idaw al-Hajj tradition overstates the originality of their claim to beginning the Atlantic sector export trade in gum arabic. It is clear, for example, that the Portuguese had exported some gum arabic from Arguin along the Atlantic coast of the western Sahara from at least the early sixteenth century, before the Idaw al-Hajj migration to the Trarza.[29] And even as late as the seventeenth century, the gum trade along the Atlantic coast seems to have taken place under the direction of the Ulad Dayman, closely linked to the Trarza emiral grouping, rather than the Idaw al-Hajj. But by the late seventeenth century, the Idaw al-Hajj had emerged as the zwaya grouping with the most influence in the gum trade along the Senegal River.

The internal political organization of the Trarza Idaw al-Hajj was different from that of the other zwaya groups in the western Sahara. It had a single politico-commercial head who was known as the *shamsh*.[30] This title was derived from Shams al-Din, the name of an ancestor of the Idaw al-Hajj in the period before the migration to the Trarza. The date of the first exercise of this position of authority is not known, but the earliest European notice of this title dates from 1686 when La Courbe recorded his voyage to Lake Cayar.[31]

In the late seventeenth century, the principal gum market, known as the Escale du Désert or Serinpaté by the French, was located on the north bank of the Senegal River, near the town of Ngurbel, which was the capital of Waalo. The brak of Waalo was clearly more powerful than the shamsh at the time of La Courbe's voyage, but by about 1697 pressure from the Bidan forced the brak to move Ngurbel to the south bank of the river.[32] By 1724, the shamsh and other Idaw al-Hajj were collecting taxes from the French at Saint-Louis which were three times greater than those of the brak.[33] By the middle of the eighteenth century, the Idaw al-Hajj had established their own gum market, known as the Escale des Darmankours, in close proximity to the Escale du Désert.

The shamsh's prime responsibilities included the gum negotiations with the Europeans at Saint-Louis. These negotiations took place in two parts. The Saint-Louis traders arrived at the river markets to settle the amount of tax to be paid to the Trarza emir. The Trarza emir often took part in these negotiations himself, with the shamsh at his side. When the issue of tax for the emir was settled, the traders entered into bargaining with the shamsh and other Idaw al-Hajj over the price per measure of gum that would be in force and the size of the measure that would be used. In the course of the actual gum sales, small deviations from the established price and measure were common fare, but in a broad sense the shamsh set one important determinant of the gross volume of foreign goods that entered the Trarza.

Prices on the seacoast were generally about 25 percent higher than those on the river, but the price differential mostly reflected the higher costs of transporting the gum to the coast. The transport premium to the Atlantic littoral was offset by the fact that the Europeans did not need to employ intermediaries for extensive periods of time to purchase the gum, as they did in the river trade. The European traders simply anchored in a bay and took on the gum by means of small boats. Zwaya gum caravanners were free to transport their gum to either market, and they waited for price quotations both from the river and from the Atlantic markets before embarking on caravan.[34]

Over time the gum trade spread through the Gibla, and many zwaya groups began to take part. The Idaw al-Hajj continued to exercise influence primarily in the Trarza gum trade.[35] In other desert areas different zwaya groups held local authority; for example, the Ulad Sasi played an important role in the Brakna gum trade. But during the eighteenth century the Idaw al-Hajj set the prices for gum at the Trarza markets on the Senegal River and along the Atlantic coast, and they effectively determined the price of gum at the Brakna market as well.

Competition between the Atlantic Coast and Riverside Sectors

The European and Afro-European traders based at Saint-Louis du Sénégal were chronically anxious about the gum trade conducted by rival European powers on the Atlantic coast of the western Sahara. In the eighteenth century, the French took active measures to eliminate competition from the coastal stations. After retaking the island of Arguin from the Dutch in 1721, the French went on to destroy the newly built Dutch fort at Portendick in 1727, all in an effort to force the gum trade down to the river.[36] But this initiative did not enjoy full success. At Portendick, trading ships from other European national groups, particularly the British, continued to anchor off the coast and to communicate with the mainland with trading skiffs. This competition remained the bane of the Afro-French traders at Saint-Louis du Sénégal, who never knew just how much gum was available in the desert to trade in any given year.

An additional problem for the Europeans in control of Saint-Louis du Sénégal was that until the gum boom of the nineteenth century the trade in gum arabic at Portendick generally began after the river gum trade ended. Trade at Portendick started at the beginning or middle of July and continued through August. The existence of lagged, alternative markets thus strengthened the desert traders' market position both along the river and along the Atlantic coast. They could always make good on their threats to carry their gum to Portendick, and this increased the commercial pressure on the river traders to bring in as much as possible. The river trader's fear of competition from other European nations trading at Portendick showed up in concern about the quality of their own trade goods as well as about the prices that Europeans might be willing to pay farther up the coast. And even along the coast, the desert traders maintained a strong market position. If prices were not to their liking, the desert traders could simply bury their gum in the sand and head back into the interior after the beginning of the rains.[37] The desert route to Portendick, however, was not without its difficulties for the desert traders. In addition to the problems of increasing aridity, which worked against the long-term viability of Arguin and Portendick, this route left the caravans open to attack from the independent warrior groups to the north of the Trarza who roamed the coast.[38]

Illustration 5.1. View of Saint-Louis.

Illustration 5.2. A Negro and a Moor belonging to a gum caravan.

The Afro-European trading diaspora based at Saint-Louis was in some considerable measure dependent on the gum trade. The desert traders understood this vulnerability and used it to their advantage. The Bidan were able to move in and out of various commercial sectors in response to changing market conditions and at times to abandon the gum sector almost entirely. Perhaps the most striking eighteenth-century example of this dates from the 1740s, when the Bidan gained control of the regional grain trade. The desert traders then refused to sell the Europeans grain except in exchange for cloth. The Europeans were forced to meet this intensified desert demand for cloth; cloth flooded into the regional market; and this in turn meant that desert people no longer needed to harvest gum in order to get cloth. This spelled trouble for the French, who proposed to their directors that food be imported to the colony to break the hold that the desert people had over them.[39]

All in all, the effect of competition and the increased demand for gum arabic in Europe on gum prices was powerful enough.[40] The terms of trade trended strongly in favor of the desert traders over the course of the eighteenth century.

Table 5.6. Estimated net barter terms of trade, 1718–1849 (value of one metric ton of gum arabic expressed in guinée cloths)

	Guinées	Index
1718	2.63	100
1723	4.85	184
1739	6.03	229
1745	3.44	131
1776	14.30	544
1783	27.98	1,069
1788	31.88	1,212
1823–27	51.50	1,958
1830	41.12	1,563
1833	63.05	2,397
1838	70.61	2,685
1849	50.25	1,911

Sources: Gum prices for 1718 to 1823–27 are in pounds sterling, from Curtin, *Economic Change*, vol. 1, 217, footnote 4. Gum prices for 1830–49 are estimated from Curtin, *Economic Change*, vol. 2, Table A15.14. Guinée prices before 1776 are rough estimates based upon Curtin, *Economic Change*, vol. 2, Table 15.11, which provides an import price index for the 1730s and is included only to estimate general magnitude. Guinée prices from 1776 to 1849 are from Table 5.8 in this book; see also Curtin, *Economic Change*, vol. 2, Table A15.13. The guinée price for 1788 is unavailable; the 1787 price was used as a substitute. The guinée price for 1825 was used for an average gum price in 1823–27.

In 1765, following the British seizure of Senegal, efforts were made to open up yet another market for gum to the south, when desert traders arrived at Gorée and offered to reestablish the gum trade with the French there.[41] Apparently little resulted from this initiative.[42] But by the early 1770s, the new French governor Boniface began once again to encourage the overland transport of gum through Kajoor; a warehouse was to be set up at Dakar.[43] But this also never met the expectations of the French; and negotiations with the Darmankour foundered.[44]

Another initiative was soon launched by Abbé Demanet, who in 1773 began to use Gorée as a staging ground for the gum trade out of Portendick, on the Atlantic coast of the western Sahara.[45] He succeeded in trading 500 tons of gum arabic at Portendick, and he did so by inducing the Darmankour chief, Mazamba Jakhumpa, to extend a line of credit to the Compagnie de Guyane. Demanet then left for France with his gum ships. The administrator for the company who replaced Demanet paid off a part of the debt, expressed good faith, and pledged to honor the outstanding bills, but succumbed to disease; the next administrator claimed that he had no authority to honor the debt. Governor Boniface made efforts to force the company to meet its financial obligations, but in vain. Thereafter, the weight of time and the fact that the Compagnie de Guyane had disbanded and reformed with different shareholders meant that the remaining debt would not be fully paid. Ultimately, the Darmankour chief received another payment of goods in the amount of 20 slaves, but this was apparently only a fraction of what he was owed. The outcome was disastrous for Mazamba Jakhumpa. He held off his desert creditors as long as possible, but then was driven into exile, most probably in Kajoor.[46] Thus the largest extension of credit during the eighteenth century had been by desert traders to Europeans, rather than the reverse. The high turnover in European personnel, conjoined with some bad faith, meant that the Europeans had proved themselves bad credit risks.

The Heyday of the Trade in Gum Arabic

With the withering away of the export slave trade after 1790, Saint-Louis became increasingly dependent upon the gum trade, and the colony's commercial activity became concentrated on the lower Senegal. This dependence was cause for alarm because the European and métis traders had little control of the supply of gum, which could fluctuate greatly from year to year; and after the French reoccupation of Senegal in 1817, the colonial administration attempted to diversify the sources of the colony's wealth. The administration underwrote efforts to create plantations in the floodplain bordering the lower Senegal River in the years 1819–31, but after years of repeated failure the sponsors of this initiative were ready to abandon it. By 1830, virtually all commercial activity of the colony focussed on the gum trade.[47]

From 1817 until the late 1830s, Saint-Louis sustained a period of intensive growth. As Wolof from Waalo and Kajoor moved to participate in the flourishing colony, the population more than doubled, from 6,000 to 13,000, and the number of family dwellings *(habitations bâties)* jumped from 50 to 1,500. By 1837, the colony boasted more than 300 buildings *(maisons)* in the colonial architecture of the period. In the two decades between 1818 and 1837, the total annual commercial activity of the colony had increased sixfold, from 2 million to 12 million francs.[48]

The new commercial opportunities of the 1830s attracted Frenchmen with capital: the class of *négociants* increased from 4 or 5 in 1818 to 30 in 1837. The number of Afro-European *habitants* who directly took part in the gum trade also increased sharply in the same period from 40 to 150. And in a short intense bout of commercial activity between 1833 and 1839 the number of riverboats working the gum trade doubled from 80 to 160. The lure of commercial opportunities extended far beyond those who had any capital to invest. The glimmer of an easier-won subsistence drew farmers away from their fields and artisans away from their crafts. By the end of the 1830s, 3,000 persons were winning their living directly or indirectly from the gum trade.[49]

During this period of growth, the colony of Saint-Louis experienced difficulties in integrating supply and demand both for the gum itself and for guinée, the indigo-impregnated cloth from south India against which gum was exchanged. The traditionally distinct sectors of the gum trade, one on the river itself and one at the town of Saint-Louis du Sénégal, came under increasing pressure from the French and Afro-European capitalists at Saint-Louis.

At the top of the commercial order were the négociants, a small group of French who represented mainland French commercial houses or were themselves the owners of Saint-Louisian import-export houses or both. They were few in number, but they were the most highly capitalized, and they imported goods directly from overseas. They held a monopoly on the importation of guinée from India and France, and this gave them considerable power in the river trade. Below the négociants on the ladder of capital were the *marchands détaillants*, who handled the merchandising of guinée and other goods in Saint-Louis, and the *licenciés*, who were, for the most part, small shopkeepers and owners of commercial stalls. Marchands détaillants and licenciés had smaller operations than did the négociants, but they were much more numerous, and they too played a significant role in the capitalization of the river trade.

Beyond the domain of the import-export houses and wholesalers lay the domain of river transport and sales, and here there was also a commercial hierarchy. At the top were the *traitants*, métis of some financial means who owned their own boats and worked the river ports along the lower and middle Senegal. Distinctions of wealth and capital among the traitants found expression in the size of their riverboats, the size of their loans received from the merchant community, and their volume of sales at the river markets. A very few of the wealthiest traitants traded directly with France (as the négociants did), but the large majority borrowed guinée from the Saint-Louisian merchants for use in the gum trade and repaid these debts at the end of the trade season. Many of the traitants had slaves to help man their riverboats; others hired river sailors known as *laptots* for this purpose. Some laptots were free Africans from Waalo, Kajoor, Fuuta, and Galam, but others were the slaves of the traitants or, between 1823 and 1848, individuals bought under an indentured labor system called *engagement à temps*. During the off season some of the free laptots moved in and out of a larger pool of African *marigotiers*, who conducted a petty trade in the river side-channels in skiffs and canoes when not occupied by farming or fishing.[50]

Trade in two sectors, one in Saint-Louis and one upriver, yielded profits in the gum trade. Merchants in Saint-Louis sold the guinée in a unit called the pièce de guinée (about 16.5 meters by 1 meter) to the traitants, using a system of deferred payment, lending the guinée out for the course of the gum season in return for a set quantity of gum per pièce de guinée payable at the end of the season. This system of delayed payment secured the négociants' profits in normal years. If they received guinée F.O.B. at 20 francs per piece, and if the current price of gum at Saint-Louis was 2 francs per kilogram, the négociants could sell their pièce de guinée to the traitants at the price of 15 kilograms of gum, thus assuring themselves a gross profit margin of 50 percent to cover costs and to afford themselves a reasonable net profit. For the merchants, this system shifted the risk of doing business onto the traitants. Gum harvests were undependable, and when the harvest was poor, competition among the traitants at the river markets was fierce, driving the price of gum up. But good harvests often followed poor ones, and traitants generally made good on their gum debts, even if bad seasons forced delays in repayment.

Traitants' profits came from the differential between the Saint-Louis price of guinée and the higher prices upriver. Traitants often spent months at the river markets waiting for caravans to arrive, and they ran up considerable expenses feeding their crew, paying their crew's salaries, paying taxes, maintaining their boats, and entertaining the Bidan caravanners whose gum they wanted to buy. These costs ran about a quarter to a third of the Saint-Louis price of guinée, and thus, if a pièce de guinée cost them 15 kilograms of gum in Saint-Louis, the traitants needed to sell the guinée at the river markets for 20–22.5 kilograms in order to cover the costs of doing business.[51]

The Petite Traite

Traditionally, the colony of Saint-Louis had traded on both the upper and lower portions of the Senegal River. Before the 1790s the trade to Gajaaga on the upper river had been important, because most of the slaves and gold for export had been bought in this region. The upper river was navigable with boats larger than skiffs or canoes only during the season of high water, from the end of July until the first of January, and then generally only one round trip per season was feasible. Before 1820 this Gajaaga trade had been the exclusive province of the Compagnie de Galam, which had been capitalized by the négociants of Saint-Louis and granted monopoly rights to trade up river during the high water season. After the illegalization of the Atlantic slave trade, trade from Gajaaga became much less significant in the overall trade from Saint-Louis.[52] Before 1820, marigotiers and a few traitants had traded for grain on the upper Senegal during the low-water season from January through July, but these off-season excursions had had little importance. After a few years of experimentation, in 1824 the colonial government lifted trade restrictions on the upper Senegal during the high-water season, and traitants and marigotiers boated up the high water on the river to trade for grain, dried fish, beans, mats, and other local artisanal crafts among the villages along the river and side-channel waterways in much the same way that this brokerage took place on the lower river. Particularly important was the trade in grain. Gajaaga was a prime cereal-producing zone, and the waalo cereal harvests, which had once been a secondary trade of the Compagnie de Galam, entered into trade on the lower Senegal.

This trade in grain on the lower Senegal intensified during the 1830s, when European demand for gum doubled. The increased demand caused the primary gum season to double to six months, from the first of February through the end of July, and a minor gum harvest and gum trade began to take place in the period from November until the end of January. Traitants and marigotiers traded grain from the upper Senegal, additional grain from Fuuta, and small quantities of goods such as tea, sugar, rice, and cloth from Saint-Louis to the Bidan and their slaves during the early gum harvest.[53] Because the gum quantities traded in the early season were small, compared with those of the main gum trade later in the year, the Afro-Europeans spoke of this trade as the *petite traite*.

By the 1840s and 1850s the Bidan in the Gibla were importing grain from Fuuta and the upper Senegal on a regular basis from the marigot traders. The desert peoples' preference was to sell the first gum harvest to the small boat traders from Galam. For their part, the French wanted to outlaw this "contraband" trade. The marigotiers and laptots argued strongly in its favor, holding that if they did not carry this trade, the desert people would simply trade directly with farmers in Fuuta.[54] The logic of the trade lay in the fact that the desert populations found that they could meet their cereal needs more easily by trading for grain than by growing it; the gum trade in no way interfered with or competed for the allocation of labor during the agricultural season. This gum-for-grain trade was facilitated by the great increase in the value of gum arabic that had been passed on to desert traders (see Table 5.6). And the millet trade along the river apparently brought grain to the desert less expensively than did the overland trade to Kajoor. By the 1850s, the gum and grain trades had become directly linked: desert traders took the imported guinée into Kajoor to trade for millet.

In good years the volume of gum that entered into the petite traite probably averaged about 10 percent of the gum weighed by customs in Saint-Louis.[55] But the petite traite had a larger importance to the zwaya and their slaves. This early-season grain trade supplemented the diet of the zwaya, and it decreased their slaves' and haratins' dependence upon wild seed grasses, which they often used to augment a diet of scarce animal products and cultivated grain. From the 1830s, Bidan in the Gibla who participated in the petite traite began to consume more grain, helping to bridge the hungry winter months before the caravans would head south to buy the newly harvested waalo grain in late spring. As the gum trade season expanded, more boats began to work the river, and this intensification of river traffic facilitated the exchange of other goods along the river. Some villages began to specialize in the production or marketing of such goods as straw mats, beans, or calabashes. But the real motor behind this intensified exchange was the new industrial demand for gum.

The Grande Traite

From the first of January or the first of February until the end of July, zwaya transported the bulk of their gum arabic south to the river for the official season of the gum trade known as the *grande traite*. Along the Senegal River this gum was off-loaded from animal caravans, weighed and sold, and transferred to riverboats. The sale of the bulk of this gum arabic took place at three designated markets along the lower and middle Senegal. These gum markets themselves were modest affairs. They had no building infrastructure other than thatched huts, and the traitants anchored their boats on the river and often lived on their boats during the season of trade. These seasonal markets were called *escales* (French: ports of call) rather than *marchés*, the usual term for the year-round markets of Saint-Louis, Europe, and the larger towns of the African interior. The three escales along the lower and middle Senegal reflected the balance of political authority along the river region. Two escales were in the Trarza region: the Escale du Désert, controlled by the Trarza emir, and the Escale des Darmankours, controlled by the shamsh. The Darmankour cleric also served as cross-cultural broker between the Wolof of Waalo and the Trarza hassani. In the Brakna the single central escale was called the Escale du Coq, and at least by the early nineteenth century it was under the joint control of the Brakna emir and his Tukulor minister from Fuuta. Gum was traded upriver as well as on the lower and middle reaches of the Senegal. But the quantities traded along the upper river were small and irregular until the expansion of the gum trade from the 1850s. There, the Idaw Ish were the warrior group with the most influence in the upper-river gum trade.

During the gum season the zwaya caravanners and brokers and the traitants lived close to each other at the escales. The traitants often spent tedious weeks or even months at a stretch waiting for the gum caravans to arrive, negotiating, and giving gifts. Over time, distinctive features of trade developed.

Traitants acted as hosts at the escales, providing food and gifts to the caravanners and brokers and to the emirs and their representatives and their entourages. Individual traitants paid salaries to cross-cultural *maitres de langue*, whose job it was to intercept the gum caravans in the desert, to deliver the caravan to the traitant, and to begin the process of negotiating the sale of the caravan's gum, but the maitres de langue's best efforts were not binding upon the caravanners. Opportunities for chicanery were rife, and the traitants provided a flow of gifts such as blankets, grain, cloth, tea, and so forth, in an effort to win the favor of the caravanners. Once the gum arrived in the market, the caravanners stockpiled it, and the traitants, upon concluding a purchase, had to pay the caravanners to carry the gum to the weighing scales and then to the boats.[56]

The traitants' largest costs of doing business at the escale, however, were the payments to the Bidan political authorities, which were collectively called *coutumes*. The regime of coutumes varied somewhat by escale and by year, but the essential features did not. Each traitant gave a collection of goods and foodstuffs to the political authorities at the escales and paid a tax according to the tonnage of his boat and a tax on each half ton of gum traded. The payments in goods and foodstuffs were tiresome for the traitants, particularly if the gum was slow to arrive at the escales, but they were not a major expense. The tax on boat tonnage, however, was another matter. The Bidan authorities levied this tax regardless of the size of the harvest, and thus it fell particularly heavily in bad years, when there was insufficient gum and the traitants lost money or were in danger of doing so. Traitants lobbied for its removal off and on throughout the 1830s and 1840s. They wanted to substitute a simple tax on gum traded that would be less injurious during bad seasons. But one party's injury was the other party's insurance, and the Bidan were reluctant to relinquish this tax because it assured them of revenue even in years of poor gum harvests. The Darmankours finally acceded to the traitants' request in 1847,[57] but by this time very little gum travelled to their escale. At the other escales the tax on boat tonnage remained a point of contention into the 1850s. The tax on gum traded seems to have remained constant at one pièce de guinée per half ton.[58] This tax probably cut into the profits of the caravanners rather than those of the traitants. In the absence of this tax, the gum caravanners in the bustle of escale competition probably could have commanded a gum price equal to that of the escale price plus the tax on gum traded.[59]

By the 1830s, as more and more individuals moved into gum trading, the increased competition at the escales came to threaten the traitants' collective interests. They borrowed heavily to secure guinée for the gum trade, and their ability to obtain future credit (and thus their continued commercial existence) depended upon their being able to deliver gum to their creditors and to turn a profit. Bidan traders, in contrast, operated under no such pressure. As more individuals entered the traitant class, competition became stiffer at the escales, and the Bidan became adept at exploiting their market position.

One response to the threat of excessive competition at the escales, beginning in about 1830, was to get the colonial government to declare a binding, minimum price floor for guinée (measured in metricized livres of gum) at the escales.[60] This price control was called a compromise (*compromis*) because it implicitly called on the traitants to view their fortunes collectively and to eschew both the risks of potentially ruinous competition and the possibility of great personal gain in favor of a modest, regulated profit. When the traitants presented a united front to the caravanners, the traitants realized a small but adequate margin of profit. But the compromise reduced the traitants to mere porters of gum, and they threw off the trade constraints whenever they saw the glimmer of greater potential profits.

The traitants themselves sometimes demanded the imposition of price controls after a particularly bad trade season. A common pattern was for the controls to hold in the first few weeks or even months of the trade, but when the harvest appeared to be better than the previous year, the traitants would begin to seek their own maximum advantage in the lively, brawling marketplace of the escale, and the general restraint needed to enforce the price controls fell apart. Traitants were by nature optimistic, and because neither the size of the gum harvest nor the timing of its arrival at the escale could be known with accuracy, traitants were rarely able to resist the immediate gain made possible by the caravanner who offered to sell his entire caravan load of gum to a single traitant at a price above the official one. The zwaya understood well the traitants' commercial position, and they tried to break the compromise by threatening to take their gum back into the desert and rebury it until the next season, or to take it to different markets, or simply to send word into the interior that an unreasonable compromise was in effect and thereby stop all caravan traffic to the escales.[61]

The zwaya could also turn to more profitable trades if the colonial government forced their gum profits too low, but their most potent threat was simply to withhold their gum from the French and sell it to the British. This threat of engaging other markets, even in the first half of the nineteenth century, was not without substance. Zwaya could take their gum caravans overland to the Gambia, but the quantities transported overland were small because the distance was great and the threat to their animals loomed large, and most of the gum traffic that did travel overland originated in groves to the northeast of the escales, in the Tagant, the Assaba, and the Gidimaxa. A more substantial threat to the river trade along the lower Senegal came from the British at Portendick.

By the early nineteenth century, Portendick was not an attractive location for a gum escale. By this time, the journey from the gum groves to the coast was longer than the journey from the gum groves to the river escales, and the coast was so barren that only camels could be used for the caravans. Even stockpiling the gum and waiting to trade was onerous because there was little potable water in the area surrounding Portendick. And from the marine perspective, Portendick was no more attractive. The coast was treacherous; there was no natural harbor; and the British were forbidden by international agreement to build any trading establishments on the coast.[62]

These disadvantages, however, were not sufficient to close down the escale. In 1819, three years after losing Saint-Louis to the French, the British were able to capitalize on the conflict between the French and the Trarza. Desert caravans transported the entire gum harvest to Portendick and thereby temporarily severed the commercial lifeline of the colony. That same year the Trarza emir, Amar Wuld Mokhtar, sent a representative to Bathurst, and the governor of the Gambia agreed to renew the annual payment of coutumes to the emir. British trade at Portendick took place regularly throughout the 1820s, and in 1825 private traders organized as the English Company of Portendick took over the tax payments themselves. Data are incomplete, but it appears that during the 1820s Portendick was able to attract intermittently about 10 percent of the gum that otherwise would have been marketed at the river escales. During the 1834 Franco-Trarza war, gum collected from the Trarza travelled again to Portendick, and the British, according to French reports, introduced arms to the Trarza hassani through this coastal trade. To shut off the gum trade and the flow of arms, in 1835 the French set up a blockade of Portendick, seized some British trading vessels, and set off an international legal dispute, and in 1836 at the resolution of the Franco-Trarza conflict they lifted the blockade. British trade resumed at Portendick in 1837, but only for a single year. According to John Gray, no trade took place between 1838 and 1842, and between 1842 and 1847, the trade took place only fitfully.[63] After 1819, Portendick may have

Table 5.7. The gum trade at Portendick, 1693–1846

	Number of metric tons
1693[a]	979
1785[b]	181
1786[b]	181*
1787[b]	181
1800[c]	272–317*
1801[d]	226*
1803[e]	266*
1819[f]	Trarza take entire harvest to Portendick
1821[g]	5–6
1822[h]	75
1823[i]	125
1824[j]	200–300
1828[k]	110–115
1830[l]	0
1834[m]	300
1836[n]	30
1837[o]	100
1838[p]	virtually no trade
1844[q]	0
1845[r]	very little
1846[s]	300–350

Sources:

[a] ANF C⁶ 2, La Courbe, Mémoire sur le commerce de Guinée, cited by Curtin, *Economic Change*, vol. 2, 64–65.

[b] Golberry, *Travels in Africa*, vol. 1, 182.

[c] Pelletan, *Mémoire sur la colonie française du Sénégal et ses dépendances*, 21.

[d] ANFSOM, DFC Sénégal, carton 83, no. 115, Rapport sur les établissements français d'Afrique, adressé le 8 juillet 1817 . . . M. Schmaltz, 13 mai 1818.

[e] Herbin de Halle, *Statistique générale et particulière*, 113.

[f] ANS 2 B 5, Gouverneur au Ministre, 27 mai 1820.

[g] ANS 2 B 6, Gouverneur au Ministre, 29 mai 1821.

[h] ANS 2 B 7, Gouverneur au Ministre, 14 juillet 1822.

[i] Marty, "Tentative commerciales anglaises," 292, 295.

[j] ANS 2 B 8, Gouverneur au Ministre, 11 avril 1823.

[k] ANS 2 B 13, Gouverneur au Ministre, 11 septembre 1828.

[l] ANS 2 B 14, Gouverneur au Ministre, 25 août 1830.

[m] ANS 2 B 16, Gouverneur au Ministre, 2 septembre 1834.

[n] ANS 2 B 17, Gouverneur au Ministre, 17 octobre 1836.

[o] ANS 2 B 17, Gouverneur au Ministre, 17 juin 1837 and 8 juillet 1837.

[p] ANS 2 B 17, Gouverneur au Ministre, 10 août 1838.

[q] ANS 2 B 22, Gouverneur au Ministre, 24 mai 1844.

[r] ANS 2 B 24, Gouverneur au Ministre, 26 mai 1845.

[s] ANFSOM, Sénégal XIII, dossier 28, Extrait d'une lettre adressé le 31 juillet à M. le Directeur des colonies par M. Larcher, chef du service judiciaire à Saint Louis.

* Annual estimate.

caused commercial damage to the traitants only during the periods of Franco-Trarza conflict, but the psychological effect was more continuous. The threat of turning the gum caravans toward Portendick was one more point of leverage for the gum merchants at the escales.

The Supply of Guinée

Another major factor plaguing the gum trade was the supply schedule for guinée. Zwaya traders had established their preference for guinée in the eighteenth century, and on occasion the Bidan had simply refused to accept inferior substitutes. By 1821, the wider structure of demand was changing in the interior. Not only the Bidan but Wolof and Tukulor from Waalo, Kajoor, and Fuuta were coming to demand guinée over their earlier preferences for coral, amber, and other types of cloth.[64]

Orders for guinée from India took one or two years to arrive in the colony, and because négociants had no way to predict accurately the size of future gum harvests, they generally based the size of their orders on past experience. The mismatching that resulted from large orders of guinée arriving in Saint-Louis during years of poor harvests could have been diminished if the négociants had been willing to stockpile it for a season or two at a time. But there were several factors working against this. The price of guinée F.O.B. fluctuated from year to year, and the négociants were wary of warehousing the cloth for an entire season, both because they were unwilling to invest time and money in cloth capital that sat unproductively in moist warehouses risking losses from water rot and because they were fearful of being caught holding expensive guinée next year if a less expensive shipment should arrive at port. Few traitants were wealthy enough to hold stocks from one season to the next, and they were likewise wary of incurring losses owing to fluctuating prices. The result was that the merchants tended to dump guinée on the market during the year of its arrival, and this caused considerable price fluctuation within the colony from year to year and even within a single trade season, in spite of the long-term trend toward ever-lower prices for guinée.

A shipment of cloth arriving in midseason, after the traitants had already taken out their loans, was a strong temptation for the négociants to break with established practice and send agents to the escales to sell it directly to the gum merchants. This practice, of course, undercut the traitants' market position and encouraged default on their loans, but the négociants hoped for immediate profits from the sale of their new cloth and figured that eventually the traitants would make good on their debts.

An example from the 1820s is instructive. In early 1823, négociants sold guinée to the traitants at 45, 50, 55, and even 60 livres of gum, payable at the

Table 5.8. Prices of one pièce de guinée in French francs, c. 1776–1876

	F.O.B. cost	Cost to traitants	Cost to France and England
Before 1776[a]	19–20	—	—
1776–83[d]	50	—	—
1787[b]	25	—	—
1803[b]	50	—	—
1814[c]	—	—	40
1821[d]	51	—	—
1825[e]	35	—	—
1830[f]	21–25	—	18–19
1831[g]	20	—	—
1832[g]	17.5	—	—
1833[g]	17.5	—	—
1834[g]	17.5	—	—
1835[h]	—	25	—
1836[h]	—	25	—
1837[h]	—	23	—
1838	16–17[i]	20[h]	—
1839[h]	—	15	—
1840	12[j]	15[h]	—
1843[k]	13–14	—	—
1844[l]	13	—	—
1849[m]	13.5	—	—
1876[n]	—	—	5.8–9.5

Sources:

[a] Golberry, *Travels in Africa*, vol. 1, 192.

[b] Herbin de Halle, *Statistique générale et particulière*, 101.

[c] Geoffrey de Villeneuve, *L'Afrique ou histoire, moeurs, usages, et coutumes des Africains*, vol. 1, 92.

[d] ANS 2 B 6, Gouverneur au Ministre, 8 août 1821.

[e] ANS 2 B 24, Gouverneur au Ministre, 23 decembre 1844.

[f] ANS 2 B 14, Gouverneur au Ministre, 15 avril 1830.

[g] ANFSOM, Sénégal XIII, dossier 25, Copie d'une lettre adressé à M. le Ministre de commerce par M. Deves de Bordeaux, 16 août 1834.

[h] ANFSOM, Sénégal XIII, dossier 25, Observations sur le commerce du Sénégal et plus particulièrement sur la traite de la gomme aux escales du Fleuve; soumises à Monsieur de St. Hilaire, Conseiller d'état, Directeur des colonies, par M. Gallois-Montbrun, Conseiller Ve. President de la cour d'appel au Sénégal, aujourd'hui conseiller à la cour royale de Pondicherry, février 1840.

[i] ANS Q 18, Du commerce en général et de la traite en particulière . . .

[j] Dezert, "Du commerce de la gomme," 942.

[k] ANS 2 B 22, Gouverneur au Ministre, 28 decembre 1843.

[l] ANS 2 B 24, Gouverneur au Ministre, 23 decembre 1844.

[m] ANFSOM, Sénégal XIII, dossier 29, Habitants à M. le Gouverneur, 22 octobre 1849.

[n] ANFSOM, Sénégal XIII, dossier 31, G. Deves, Pres de la Chambre de Commerce à M. le Gouverneur, 27 decembre 1876.

end of the season. During this season of the grande traite, a ship arrived from Bordeaux with an additional 13,000 pièces de guinée. Négociants bought the guinée inexpensively and sent their own representatives immediately upriver to the escales to sell it to the Bidan at 50–55 livres of gum, thereby ruinously underselling the traitants. The traitants avoided this minor catastrophe only by good fortune. Later in the year another ship laden with guinée sank near Saint-Louis, and the traitants bought up the water-damaged cloth and passed it on to the gum caravanners, who accepted it at full value without objection.[65]

The Commercial Crisis

This problem of the erratic supply of guinée stayed largely in the background until the late 1830s, when widespread enthusiasm for the future of the gum trade encouraged négociants to place larger orders for guinée than ever before. The importance of rainfall and desert wind to the overall supply of gum was poorly understood, and the supply of gum, owing to a succession of productive years, appeared to be rising solely in response to European demand. Guinée consumption had been increasing throughout the 1820s, and by 1830 the colony was using an estimated 50,000 pièces de guinée per year. But in 1837–40, the quantities increased considerably, and the arrival of 138,000, 240,000, 138,000, and 109,000 pièces de guinée in consecutive years threw the colony into a commercial crisis.[66] Compounding the difficulty was the fact that the first 1838 shipment arrived early in the year and sold at 10 francs per piece (less expensively than cloth in previous years), and then in September 1838 another large shipment arrived which was even less expensive, priced at 6 francs in France.[67]

This oversupply of guinée caused its price to drop immediately. Traitants who had bought cloth early in the season were in deep trouble. They had made commitments to repay their guinée debts in amounts of gum which would be impossible to realize at the escales. As in 1823, the négociants exploited the situation, sending traders up the river on behalf of their firms. This pressure not only forced the traitants into debt but also forced some of the newly arrived négociants, who were not as deeply entrenched in their market positions at Saint-Louis as were the older firms, out of the import-export trade and into the river trade in an effort to avoid losses.[68] During these years a dual system grew up in the river trade. Those traitants who began to work on behalf of the négociants as hired employees had a clear commercial advantage over the traditional traitants. The employee with secured wages could undersell the independent traitant without personal risk. The négociants of Saint-Louis, even if suffering small losses on the sale of cloth at the escales, could absorb them because the sale of cloth to the independent traitants brought profits, and because they had other financial resources from the sale of their gum to European markets.

This dual system made for furious competition at the escales. The traitants struggled for advantage and inflicted losses upon each other. By the end of the 1839 gum season, competition had driven the price of guinée at the escales below its price at Saint-Louis. The independent traitants were 2,237,000 francs in debt to their négociant creditors. The desert traders were in possession of unprecedented quantities of guinée, owing both to the size of the harvest and to the traitant competition. They were stockpiling guinée under their tents and even selling it back to the merchants at Saint-Louis at a profit.[69] So much guinée hit the African markets that it set off a round of inflation in the interior. By 1840, for example, the price of cattle, measured in guinée, had tripled in the course of a year.[70]

By the end of the 1839 gum season the colony was in serious straits. Clearly something had to be done. Attempts to reinstate a price floor for guinée at the escales and to create a privileged gum association in 1840 and 1841 were only partly successful. They allowed for profits at the escales, but these attempts did nothing to retire any of the outstanding traitant debt.[71] In 1842, another trading association was created exclusively for the grande traite. The heavily capitalized négociants made large profits from the trade of their hired traitant employees, but the association enjoyed little success in bringing in the traitant debt.[72]

The crisis continued, and the Paris government stepped in. It promulgated the Royal Ordonnance of 15 November 1842. This edict reestablished the river trade as the exclusive domain of the independent traitants and restricted the European merchants and négociants and commissioned Europeans working with the commercial houses to the import-export sector and sales in Saint-Louis. It restricted membership on the list of approved traitants to those traitants who had engaged in the grande traite since at least 1836 (before the commercial crisis), and who were at least 21 years of age and inscribed on the official lists of Saint-Louis du Sénégal and dependencies. The Royal Ordonnance relegated the traitants who did not meet these criteria to the status of "aide-traitant," and many of the disenfranchised left the grande traite to find work in the less prestigious marigot trade. The Royal Ordonnance also contained provisions for control of the trade by the colonial government, giving the governor the right to decree a minimum tonnage for the boats making the gum trade, to set the rate of exchange of guinée versus gum at the escales, and to prohibit the extension of further credit to the gum traders and caravanners. But the heart of the measure was a mechanism to extinguish traitant debt. Five percent of all gum coming down the river to Saint-Louis was to be warehoused by the

Table 5.9. Prices of one kilogram* of gum arabic in current French francs, in Saint-Louis and in France, 1785–1859

	Saint-Louis	France
1785[a]	1.36–1.81	3.63–4.08
1786[b]	—	3.63
1800[c]	1.81	—
1801[c]	3.27	—
1802[c]	1.81	—
1803	1.81[c]; 1.09–1.36[d]†	3.63–4.08[d]†
1804[c]	1.81	—
1805[c]	1.81	—
1806[c]	1.81	—
1807[c]	1.36	—
1808[c]	0.91	—
1815[c]	0.54	—
1816[c]	1.36	—
1832[e]	0.50‡	—
1836[a]	1.60	2.00
1837[f]	1.40	—
1838	1.40[f]; 0.90[a,g]	1.30[a,g]
1839[f]	1.40	—
1840	1.99[f]; 1.20[h]	—
1841	1.20[f]; 1.30[i]	—
1842[f]	1.22	—
1843[f]	1.40	—
1844[j]	2.50	—
1845	2.25[k]; 2.20[l]	—
1846	2.20[m]; 2.20[l]	—
1849[n]	1.00	—
1850[n]	2.00	—
1858[l]	0.60	—
1859[l]	0.60	—

Sources:
    [a] ANS Q 18, Du commerce en générale et de la traite de la gomme en particulière.
    [b] Golberry, *Travels in Africa*, vol. 2, 25.
    [c] ANFSOM, DFC Sénégal, carton 83, no. 115, Rapport sur les établissements français d'Afrique. . .
    [d] Herbin de Halle, *Statistique générale et particulière*, 98.
    [e] ANS 2 B 15, Gouverneur au Ministre, 12 octobre 1832; ANS 2 B 14, Gouverneur au Ministre, 12 octobre 1832.
    [f] ANFSOM, Sénégal XIII, dossier 27, Notesannexes à l'état de commerce de Saint Louis (Sénégal) pour l'année 1843.
    [g] ANS 2 B 17, Gouverneur au Ministre, 10 août 1838.
    [h] ANS 2 B 18, Gouverneur au Ministre, 5 février 1840.
    [i] ANS 2 B 18, Gouverneur au Ministre, 11 septembre 1841.
    [j] ANS 2 B 24, Gouverneur au Ministre, 12 novembre 1844.

Table 5.9. Prices of one kilogram* of gum arabic in current French francs, in Saint-Louis and in France, 1785–1859 (*continued*)

ᵏ Bouët-Willaumez, *Commerce et traite*, 23.

ˡ ANFSOM, Sénégal IV, dossier 45, Moniteur du Sénégal et dépendances, 27 decembre 1859.

ᵐ ANFSOM, Sénégal XIII, dossier 28, Compte Rendu des Résultats de la traite de la gomme aux trois escales du Fleuve pendant l'année 1846.

ⁿ ANS Q 22, M. Valantin aux habitants du Sénégal, 14 août 1851.

* Prior to 1832, prices were figured for nonmetric livres. These prices have been adjusted for kilograms.

† These price ranges of gum were cited without reference to a specific year; they are assumed to be for 1803.

** The price for 1806 applies to the first nine months of that year. The price for the last three months of 1806 was the same as that for 1807. The drop in price was due to a shortage of specie in the colony. The price of gum in London (not shown above) was said to be half the normal price.

‡ This price was said to be a recent decrease from 2.0 francs; a proportional decline was noted in France.

government until the end of the gum season, at which time it was to be apportioned equally to each traitant. Creditors, however, had the right to the sales proceeds of the gum belonging to debtors.

In 1843, the colonial administration began efforts to reform trade practices at the escales. One initiative forbade the traitants from bearing arms at the escales. Another tried to prevent illegal gum sales. Many zwaya caravanners and traitants had an economic interest in avoiding the escale taxes in order to realize greater profits. But the Trarza and Brakna emiral groups and the Darmankour clerics shared a common interest in restricting trade to the escales in order to collect taxes, and the French, in the midst of commercial crisis, wanted to shut off the contraband trade and keep the price as low as possible. They also forbade the extension of further credit to the zwaya and tried to regulate the giving of gifts and even the salaries of the maitres de langue. In addition, the French forbade the payment of tax on gum traded to the Bidan in advance of its sale, and thus broke with the older custom by which traitants made individual agreements with the local escale authority for the delivery of specified quantities of gum. Under the reform scheme, the commandant of the escale oversaw the traitants' three equal payments made at the start of the gum season, during the trade, and at the end of the season.[73]

For several years in the early and mid-1840s, the Royal Ordonnance of 15 November 1842 appeared to be working well. Between 1844 and 1846 nearly half of the traitant debtors had cleared their debts, and by 1846 fully half of the traitant debt had been repaid.[74] But this success owed more to the unprecedentedly high prices for gum on the Saint-Louis markets, which were double the prices of preceding years[75] and which had been brought about by the poor gum harvests of 1842, 1843, and 1844, than it did to the design of the scheme. Some traitants roundly abused the provision that allowed for the distribution of the revenue from the sale of 5 percent of the total gum traded to all the registered traitants: traitants dropped out of the trade altogether but stayed on the list and collected their share of the gum sale revenues.[76]

In 1847 and 1848 traitant debt began to rise again, and by 1849 it was clear that the payment scheme was unworkable. It was then amended by a republican initiative which opened the official list of traitants to members of the entire indigenous population of Saint-Louis du Sénégal and dependencies who were inscribed on the population roles, 21 years of age or over, and not paying patents as négociants or marchands.[77] But this 1849 initiative held only briefly, from 1850 through 1852, which were years of poor trade. In 1851 the escales did not even open at the beginning of the season, and most of the trade took place at other points along the river.[78] Early in 1853, an administrative order fundamentally changed the rules of the river trade. It abolished price-fixing and the exclusive privilege of the commercial houses to buy gum from their traitant debtors; it allowed traitants to buy and sell freely among themselves; and it opened participation in the gum trade to all. Almost immediately, the commercial houses began to establish bases of trade upriver. This was the end of traitant hegemony on the river.[79]

In 1848, the French administration suppressed the exclusive trade rights of the Compagnie de Galam, and by 1853 gum exports from the upper river had trebled.[80] General Faidherbe's military campaigns from 1854 to 1858 further advanced the cause of "free trade." Earlier warfare had involved only one gum-selling region at a time, and then, the French had withheld tax payments from the emiral group they were fighting, and gum had generally flowed to the neighboring escale. But during the broader 1854–58 war, the French came to regard any tax payment to the enemy as an act of concession. The divergent interests of the hassani and zwaya were clearly exposed. The Trarza emir ordered the flow of gum to the escales to cease, but the zwaya ignored him.[81] At the end of the war, the colonial administration abolished the traditional tax and set a flat 3 percent value tax to be paid to the Gibla emirs.[82] They acceded uneasily to the new balance of power along the lower and middle Senegal.

A new revolutionary economic process was already beginning among the Black African farming communities. Although the value of peanut exports from the Senegal River region would not consistently surpass the value of gum exports until the 1870s,[83] Black African farmers were planting the seeds of change, and the beginning of a new era was at hand.

The gum trade would remain an important commercial sector for the sahelian people of the Gibla well into the twentieth century. And from the 1850s onward the gum trade would assume increasing significance for the Bidan in the Assaba, Gidimaxa, and Gorgol regions. But, following the French conquest of the lower Senegal, peanut production began to expand rapidly in Senegambia, and the regional economic center of export production shifted south to the peanut basin.

Conclusion

Beginning in the early seventeenth century, the climate of the western sahel and northern savanna lands began a long-term and dramatic trend toward increasing aridity. This had a profound impact because it required farming peoples in the northern savanna who had been practicing rainfed agriculture, either to move south into more humid lands or to transform their styles of life. A similar crisis confronted the herding peoples of the desert frontier who were forced to choose between moving south as the desert-edge pasturelands for sahelian cattle withered or accepting a life based on camel herding, which was suited to the more arid environment. In broad overview, the increasing aridity caused the expansion of the great camel zone, pushed the sahelian cattle zone ever farther to the south, and rolled back the zone of rainfed agriculture.

Early in this period of a radically altering ecological environment, groups in the desiccating sahel began to forge a new ethnic identity—to call themselves the Whites. The emergence of this desert-edge ethnicity was the result of many transformations in identity among formerly Arab, Berber, Wolof, Soninke, Fuutanke, and Bafur groups. The new political and social orders within this world of White ethnicity were varied and unstable for some time; groups sought to exploit the myriad of desert-edge microenvironments and forged accommodations with each other and with the Black farming groups to the south. Over time, two hierarchic and parallel systems of social relations in the sahel—one headed by warriors and one headed by clerics—emerged from these transformations, and these parallel systems evolved along with the southward movement of the southern frontier of the western Sahara.

This desertification of the sahel was accompanied by an increase in localized political violence when competition for scarcer resources intensified and new economic patterns came into being. Along the northern edge of the savanna and along the Senegal River, hassani established tribute relations with Black villagers. The White warriors accomplished this through the exercise of political terror and the continual threat of further violence. In essence, Black African farmers gave up a substantial percentage of their agricultural surplus in exchange for protection services. This purchased protection, however, was principally effective in staving off incipient violence from those hassani who benefitted directly from this system of extortion. Emiral authority was often challenged by leaders of fractions of the emiral families, and when this happened, political violence could be directed against the villagers who paid tribute in grain. And the hassani protection contracts did not extend south of the desert-edge grouping of tribute-paying villages. There, desert warriors from within and without the emiral fractions raided to gather slaves, not food.

The zwaya economic systems were based principally on commerce rather than the orchestration of political violence, and over time an increasing interdependence based on ecologically specialized trade developed between Blacks and Whites. The evolving patterns of production and exchange differed significantly along the southeastern and southwestern borders of the sahel. Following the late sixteenth-century collapse of the older system of trans-Saharan trade based in the eastern Adrar, the salt trade along the deep trade axis extending southeast from the plateau regions grew to great importance with the settlement of major towns in the western Adrar and in the Tagant. Over time these settled communities became increasingly dependent upon imported grain. Caravans left annually from each major town to take on salt at the great Ijil deposits in the northern Adrar and to trek into the savanna.

Across the southwestern frontier, the salt trade from the desert did not assume the same importance, because coastal salt deposits closer at hand could provide for much of the needs of the Black and White communities. Additionally, along the southwestern frontier, there were no oasis communities in the desert to be supplied with grain; the demand for imported food was concentrated among the pastoral communities themselves. By the turn of the eighteenth century, the increasing aridity encouraged some Whites to cross the frontier and settle in order to exploit the richer pastures in Black lands. Other Whites intensified their commercial activity in the savanna. They exported grain back into the desert in exchange for animal transport and brokerage services, and by the mid-eighteenth century most of the internal trade in the northern savanna was in the hands of the Whites.

During the period under study, a large number of Black African captives from the savanna moved north through both hassani and zwaya networks to replenish the slave systems which flourished in the sahel, the full desert, and in North Africa. One important conduit was predatory raiding by desert warriors. Many of these attacks were small-scale and involved the abduction of a few women and children; but other raids could involve the destruction of an entire village. The hassani enjoyed the advantages of surprise, stealth, and speedy retreat, and agricultural communities could do little to protect themselves from these depredations, subject as they might be to even worse retaliation.

Most Black captives moved north in caravans, however, after having been sold by savanna merchants to sahelian merchants. In this commercial sector, a major conduit was the horse-for-slave trade. Typically, Black African aristocracies purchased horses from desert traders in exchange for the slaves that their forces gathered in cavalry raids. This trade predated the Atlantic slave trade, persisted throughout the era of the Atlantic slave trade, and survived into the twentieth century. The horse-for-slave trade was driven by a dynamic of high mortality: horses introduced from the desert were decimated by trypanosomiasis in the savanna, and the mortality of slaves in the desert and on the trans-Saharan crossing was likewise high. Another major conduit, particularly along the southeastern frontier, was the salt-for-slave trade. There, captives had been gathered through warfare and pillage among rival states and communities in the western savanna, and they were sold to desert traders carrying salt from the plateau regions. Salt in a higher-quality form than vegetable ash was in constant demand in the savanna regions, and the demand was infinitely renewable. Over time, as the savanna lands retreated to the south, and as political violence rendered savanna livestock herding—itself an important source of animal products high in salt—more precarious, the demand for salt probably increased.

Over the period 1600–1850 the northward transfer of captive, laboring populations had differential impacts throughout the sahel. In the plateau regions, the importation of these populations allowed for the large-scale oasis cultivation of grain, melons, and dates. In the sahelian herding zones, slaves simply augmented the laboring work force. And along the southern edge of the sahel, slaves and freed slaves could be settled in agricultural communities to increase the grain supply available to the clerical groups from caravan commerce. Across these subregions, the presence of a sizable slave and freed slave population meant that there was a significant increase in leisure among the more noble, slave-owning White groups. Among the clerical groups, this slave labor helped to underwrite the high literacy rate which distinguished the Bidan from virtually all other nomadic populations.

Thus, over the period 1600–1850, the desertification of the western sahel brought about an increase in regional exchange across the desert frontier, and this increase was rooted, in good measure, in new patterns of political violence. With the dissolution of Jolof in the mid-sixteenth century, the collapse of Songhai in the late sixteenth century, and the retreat of the Fuutanke of Grand Fulo, participation in political violence was opened broadly to large numbers of warrior groups throughout the sahel and savanna. The increase in political violence generated from within the savanna and launched across the desert edge produced large numbers of slaves, many of which were absorbed into the new slave societies that formed along the western sahel and in the western Sahara. These slave populations were built up in marginal lands and were sustained by slave imports. The flow of slaves was unidirectional. Desert-edge warfare between rival hassani or zwaya groups did not generate new slaves in the same way that warfare between rival Black groups regularly did in the savanna because Whites would not enslave other Whites. Whites would enslave only Blacks. A transformation in sahelian slavery had taken place, and the new ideology of Black and White ensured that the gulf between masters and slaves could not be easily bridged.

During the era of the Atlantic slave trade, the influence of European traders on the Atlantic coast did not bring about either a large decline in the trans-Saharan trade or a truly major reorientation of desert trade toward the Afro-European settlement of Saint-Louis du Sénégal and away from the Maghrib. There was no victory of the caravel over the caravan. The political violence of the seventeenth, eighteenth, and early nineteenth centuries did, of course, result in the export of large numbers of Black Africans into the Atlantic slave trade. But even at the height of the Atlantic slave trade during the first half of the eighteenth century, the number of slaves generated along both the southwestern and southeastern frontiers and sent north to sahelian, Saharan, and Maghribine markets may well have been larger than the number of slaves which entered the Atlantic slave trade. Horses traded from the sahel (and North Africa) were more critical to the political economy of savanna enslavement than the alcohol, cloth, and inferior firearms which entered through the Atlantic sector.

Like the Bidan communities along the desert edge, the Afro-European community at Saint-Louis du Sénégal did not produce enough grain to supply its needs. The growing population of the Afro-European settlement drew its food supply principally from the surrounding states and represented a substantial and concentrated demand for grain in the regional market; and this urban demand became increasingly important over time. Yet for the period under study, the demand for cereal at Saint-Louis du Sénégal was hardly dominant. During the era of the Atlantic slave trade, the Saint-Louisian demand was considerably inferior to the demand from the desert-edge sector and was probably inferior even to the demand for grain to feed the cavalries of the Black African states. Here, as in the slave sector, the Atlantic demand was substantial but far from determinant.

Following the collapse of the Atlantic slave trade in the late eighteenth century and its illegalization in the early nineteenth century, the trade in gum arabic grew rapidly and took on new importance for the Afro-European trading community at the mouth of the Senegal River. Africans flocked to Saint-Louis to seek new opportunities in the trade. The new entrants introduced fierce competition. Larger volumes of gum and guinée cloth flowed through the gum escales along the Senegal River, and the terms of trade moved strongly in favor of the desert people. The booming gum arabic trade funnelled new wealth into the Gibla and intensified the grain trade along the lower Senegal. New patterns in the regional grain economy began to emerge. Cereals from the upper river, as well as from Waalo, Fuuta, and Kajoor, began to flow into the Gibla.

In the 1850s the French embarked on the military conquest of the lower Senegal, marking the beginning of colonial rule for Senegambia. In the aftermath of the conquest, the French attempted to limit the influence of the desert warriors to the region north of the river. They eventually were successful in circumscribing hassani authority, and over time French policy gradually changed the balance of authority between desert-edge warriors and clerics. The French imperial policy took the Senegal River as the boundary between the sahelian herders and the Black African farmers and thereby established the border of the modern-day states of Senegal and Mauritania. The desert frontier had become fixed in colonial law, although the desertification of the western Sahara continued.

Many contemporary historians concerned with the economic history of the precolonial western sahel have chosen to circumscribe their fields of study along the lines of precolonial states or contemporary national boundaries and have paid scant attention to the economic impact of desert peoples and the evolution of the regional economy under the force of progressive desiccation. Most have held that the trans-Saharan trade died down after the opening of the Atlantic trade. One result has been the elaboration of an "Atlantic thesis": the idea that the actions of Europeans in the Atlantic sector of commerce were the determinant force for economic change along the western sahel.

This study has argued that the evolution of the regional economy along the western sahel took place in large measure independently of the Atlantic sector. It has argued that in the core sectors of the regional exports of foodstuffs and slaves it is possible to make comparisons between the relative importance of the Atlantic sector (which opened onto the larger Atlantic world) and African sector (the sahelian, Saharan, and North African markets), and that the African sector was the more important of the two. And thus it concludes that the history of the desert frontier over the period 1600–1850 was not principally determined by the dynamics of a European-dominated world system. The more profound roots of poverty, political violence, and enslavement in the western sahel are to be found in the pervasive ecological crisis of the precolonial centuries.

Notes
References
Index

Notes

Chapter 1. Ecological Change and the Emergence of the Desert Frontier, 1600–1850

1. To the north of the Tropical Continental is a Mediterranean system of winds. It is characterized by its dryness and stability, and it influences the weather of the northern half of the Sahara. The arid Sahara today is thus sometimes described as a climatic divide between the tropical rainfall regime of West Africa and the cool, winter-season rainfall regime of the semiarid Mediterranean littoral. For further information, see G. Smith, MBE, "Climate," in J. L. Cloudsley-Thompson (ed.), *Sahara Desert* (Oxford, 1984), 20–23.

2. In recent decades of the twentieth century, the ITD has not penetrated as far north—for reasons that are not well understood—and the decreasing rainfall has been directly responsible for the drought which has stricken the desert, sahel, and savanna regions since the late 1960s. At the present state of knowledge, it can only be said that it seems likely that the northward extension of the ITD has been progressively shortened over the past several centuries, for reasons that cannot be established with certainty. On West African climate, see Derek F. Hayward and Julius S. Oguntoyinbo, *Climatology of West Africa* (London, 1987); and Oyediran Ojo, *The Climates of West Africa* (London, 1977).

3. For the earliest periods see, Alayne Street and Françoise Gasse, "Recent Developments in Research into the Quaternary Climatic History of the Sahara," in J. A. Allen (ed.), *The Sahara. Ecological Change and Early Economic History* (Cambridgeshire, England, 1981), 7–28; and Patrick J. Munson, "A Late Holocene (c. 4500–2300 BP) Climatic Chronology for the Southwestern Sahara," in J. A. Coetzee and E. M. Van Zinderen Bakker, Sr., (eds.), *Palaeoecology of Africa and the Surrounding Islands* (Rotterdam, 1981), vol. 13, 53–62; S. K. McIntosh and R. J. McIntosh, "West African Prehistory (from c. 10,000 to A.D. 1000)," *American Scientist* 69 (1981), 602–613; Roderick McIntosh, "Pulse Model: Genesis and Accommodation of Specialization in the Middle Niger," *JAH* 34 (1993), 181–220.

4. Sharon Elaine Nicholson, "A Climatic Chronology for Africa: Synthesis of Geological, Historical, and Meteorological Information and Data" (unpublished Ph.D. dissertation, University of Wisconsin, Madison, 1976), esp. 75–81, 251–254; and S. E. Nicholson, "Climatic Variations in the Sahel and Other African Regions during the Past Five Centuries," *Journal of Arid Environments* 1 (1978), 3–24.

5. See George E. Brooks, *Western Africa to c. 1860 A.D., a Provisional Historical Schema Based on Climate Periods* (Bloomington, 1985); George E. Brooks, "A Provisional Historical Schema for Western Africa Based on Seven Climate Periods (ca. 9000 B.C. to the 19th Century)," *Cahiers d'études africaines* 101–102, 26-1-2 (1986), 43–62; George E. Brooks, *Landlords and Strangers: A History of Western Africa, 1000–1630* (Boulder, 1992), chapter 1.

6. Duarte Pachero Pereira, *Esmeraldo de Situ Orbis*, translated and annotated by Raymond Mauny (Bissau, 1956), 41.

7. For early map examples, see "Carte de la Coste de l'Afrique depuis le cap Blanc jusques a la Riviere de Gambie, presenté a Mon. de Pontchartrain ministre et secretaire destat, controlleur general des finances" (no cartographer attributed, n.d. [c. 1690s]; "Carte très détaillée des Païs compris puis le Cap Blanc jusqua la Rivière de Sierelione" (no cartographer attributed, n.d. [c. 1692]); "Partie Occidentale de l'Afrique ou se trouve La Barbarie . . . ," by N. de Fer (n.d.); and "Partie de l'Afrique Françoise ou du Senegal," by Martin Jean (1729), all in the collection of the Bibliothèque Nationale, Paris. The maps "Carte de la Coste de l'Afrique . . ." and "Partie de l'Afrique Françoise . . ." label the Moor village Caragoli (Sarakolle?).

By the 1740s, the gum groves were no longer depicted close to the St. John River. See, for example, "La Guinee de meme que la plus grande Partie du Pais des Negres . . . ," by Heritiers d'Homan (1743), also in the collection of the Bibliothèque Nationale.

8. Melchior Petoney, "A Relation Sent by Melchior Petoney to Nigil de Moura at Lisbon, from the Iland and Castle of Arguin . . . ," in Richard Hakluyt (ed.), *The Principal Navigations Voyages Traffiques & Discoveries of the English Nation* (London, Toronto, and New York, 1927), vol. 5, 43–44. The term "*cattell*" as used in Petoney's text carries a broad meaning of "livestock."

9. H. T. Norris, "Znaga Islam during the Seventeenth and Eighteenth Centuries," *Bull. SOAS* 32 (1969), 497, footnote 2.

10. Claude Jannequin, *Voyage de Lybye au royaume du Sénégal le long de Niger* (reprint: Geneva, 1980), 44.

11. Jannequin, *Voyage de Lybye*, 68.

12. Michel Adanson, "A Voyage to Senegal, the Isle of Goree, and the River Gambia," in John Pinkerton (ed.), *A General Collection of the Best and Most Interesting Voyages and Travels in All Parts of the World* (London, 1814), vol. 16, 626–630.

13. H. T. Norris (trans. and ed.), *The Pilgrimage of Ahmad, Son of the Little Bird of Paradise: An Account of a Nineteenth Century Pilgrimage from Mauritania to Mecca* (Warminster, England, 1977), 53.

14. On the chronology of drought in Senegambia, see Philip D. Curtin, *Economic Change in Precolonial Africa: Senegambia in the Era of the Slave Trade* (Madison, 1975), vol. 2, 3–7; and Charles Becker, "Notes sur les conditions écologiques en Sénégambie aux 17e et 18e siècles," *African Economic History* 14 (1985), 167–216.

The Senegal River flooded the riverside lands in 1754 and produced a good crop in the flood zone. But flow of the Senegal River was (and is) governed by rains which fall in the highlands of the Fuuta Jalon in Guinea, far to the south in another ecological zone, and thus offers no indication of the conditions of rainfed agriculture in the sahel. In 1753, for example, a year of abject drought, the Senegal River rose exceptionally and washed away part of the French fort at Gajaaga along the upper reaches of the river valley and flooded half of Saint-Louis du Sénégal (see Curtin, *Economic Change*, vol. 2, 4).

15. Becker, "Notes sur les conditions écologiques," 191-193.

16. Hayward and Oguntoyinbo, *Climatology of West Africa*, 93 95; and Office de la Recherche Scientifique et Technique Outre-Mer, *République du Sénégal. Précipitations journalières de l'origine des stations à 1965* (Paris, 1976); for comparison with nineteenth-century observations, see A. Borius, *Recherches sur le climat du Sénégal* (Paris, 1875), 182; Le Frère Constantin, "Observatoire du Saint-Louis du Sénégal (École Secondaire). Observations météorologiques. Moyennes conclus de 23 années d'observations," *BCEHSAOF* 13 (1901), 437-473. Le Frère Constantin, who was familiar with the work of Borius but apparently did not have access to his data for the years 1861 and 1863-64, calculated a mean rainfall for Saint-Louis of 433 millimeters for the years 1862, 1868-70, 1873-82, 1892-99. Total annual rainfall over these years showed great interannual variation, ranging from a low of 141 millimeters in 1863 to a high of 673 millimeters in 1881.

Data on desert rainfall are available for only about 120 years or so, but since the earliest collections, annual rainfall appears to have been diminishing (1873-1972) (see Charles Toupet, *La sédentarisation des nomades en Mauritanie centrale sahélienne* [Lille, 1977], 168-172; and his article "L'évolution du climat de la Mauritanie du môyen age jusqu'au nos jours," in *La désertification au sud du Sahara* [Dakar, 1976], 56-63 [Colloque de Nouakchott, 17-19 decembre 1973]).

17. "Ce que l'on appelle Mil au Senegal est appellé Mahis à l'Amerique, bled de Turquie en France, grand Turc en Italie." Labat then goes on to mention two sorts of "*mil*," large and small, adding that the facts about this cultigen are too well known to bear repeating (Jean Baptiste Labat, *Nouvelle relation de l'Afrique occidentale* [Paris, 1728], vol. 2, 165). His use of the terms "*gros Mil*" and "*petit Mil*" has confused historians, because nineteenth- and twentieth-century observers have used the terms "gros mil" for sorghum and "petit mil" for millet. Later in his text, Labat writes: "Le gros mil qu'on appelle en France bled de Turquie, à l'Amerique Mahis, & en Italie grand Turc, fait la principale partie de la nourriture des Negres" (Labat, *Nouvelle relation*, vol. 3, 314). In the seventeenth and eighteenth centuries, "mil" was the French term used to describe maize, as were the other variants advanced by Labat. The French were unfamiliar with millets and sorghums (see Fernand Braudel, *The Structures of Everyday Life* [New York, 1981], 164).

18. A. G. Pruneau de Pommegorge, *Description de la Nigritie* (Paris, 1789), 31.

19. Frédéric Carrère and Paul Holle, *De la Sénégambie française* (Paris, 1855), 74 and 104-105. The disappearance of maize from Waalo is inferred; it is not among the listed crops.

20. In the late twentieth century, maize remains a staple coarse grain in southern Senegambia (see James L. A. Webb, Jr., *The Gambia in Graphs: A Summary of the National Agricultural Statistics*, Technical Report No. 3, USAID Project No. 625-0012 [Dakar, 1986]).

21. Jean-Pierre Carbonnel, "Analysis of the Recent Climatic Evolution in Burkino Faso (Upper Volta)," *Natural Resources Forum* 9, no. 1 (1985), 53-64.

22. Peter Hutchinson, *Rainfall Variations in the Gambia since 1886* (Republic of

the Gambia: Ministry of Water Resources and Environment, Department of Water Resources, 1982).

23. Chambonneau, "Relation du Sieur Chambonneau, commis de la compagnie de Sénégal, du voyage par luy fait en remontant le Niger (juillet 1688)," *Bulletin de géographie historique et descriptive* 2 (1898), 316.

24. Labat, *Nouvelle relation*, vol. 2, 165.

25. Francis Moore, *Travels into the Inland Parts of Africa* (London, 1738), 134–135.

26. Adanson, "A Voyage to Senegal, the Isle of Goree, and the River Gambia," 619.

27. James L. A. Webb, Jr., *Rainfall and Risk in the Gambia River Basin: Implications for Investment Planning*, Technical Report No. 1, USAID Project No. 625-0012 (Dakar, 1986). This study examined the statistical record for 18 rainfall stations in the Gambia River basin (see Appendix 2: "Selected Descriptive Statistics").

28. The camel with the single hump, the *Camelus dromedarius*, was introduced into the western Sahara from Asia in the first millenium C.E. For a general study of the camel in arid lands, see Richard W. Bulliet, *The Camel and the Wheel* (Cambridge, Mass., 1975). Because of its superior survival capabilities in the desert environment, the dromedary emerged as the principal domesticated species of the central western Sahara, filling a role which had apparently earlier belonged to the horse (Robin Law, *The Horse in West African History* [Oxford, 1980], 2).

29. Knut Schmidt-Nelson, *Desert Animals: Physiological Problems of Heat and Water* (Oxford, 1964), 63, 92.

30. Emile Baillaud, *Sur les routes du Soudan* (Toulouse, 1902), 42; Curtin, *Economic Change*, vol. 1, 280. See also E. Ann McDougall, "Camel Caravans of the Saharan Salt Trade: Traders and Transporters in the Nineteenth Century," in Catherine Coquery-Vidrovitch and Paul E. Lovejoy (eds.), *The Workers of African Trade* (Beverly Hills, 1985), 99–122.

31. Camels could also serve as reservoirs of fluid for caravaners. When traversing a long stretch of arid desert, it was not unknown for caravaners to cut out the tongues of a few camels to prevent them from regurgitating the fluid in their stomachs; these camels could then be killed as needed and would provide a minimum of 30 liters of fluid. (Alioun Sal, "Voyage de M. Alioun Sal, sous-lieutenant indigène à l'escadron de spahis du Sénégal [1860]," in Jean Ancelle [ed.], *Les explorations au Sénégal et dans les contrées voisines depuis l'antiquité jusqu'au nos jours* [Paris, 1886], 211).

32. Some desert areas became too dry to support livestock herding. In the Empty Quarter of east-central Mauritania, for example, the pasturage is generally insufficient to support domesticated animal life, even herds moving in transit. On the Empty Quarter, see Théodore Monod, *Majâbat al-Koubra. Contribution à l'étude de l'"Empty Quarter" ouest saharien* (Dakar, 1958); and Théodore Monod, "Majâbat al-Koubra (supplément)," *Bull. IFAN*, série A, 23 (1961), 591–637.

33. Moore, *Travels*, 90. Camels also figured in an extraordinary purchase of a horse, probably by the damel of Kajoor (see Pruneau de Pommegorge, *Description de la Nigritie*, 16–17).

34. By the mid-twentieth century, taurin were found below the western savanna, in a zone extending south from 14° north latitude to the coast (Georges Doutressoule, *L'élevage en Afrique occidentale française* [Paris, 1947], 89).

Zebu cattle are found today throughout the savanna and sahel between 14° and 18° north latitude. This longitudinal division between the taurin and zebu zones is not absolute; mixed herds of the two varieties are found in a band approximately 100 kilometers wide straddling the 14th parallel. But this division at the 14th parallel also marks approximately the present-day northern limit of trypanosomiasis. The zebu is particularly susceptible to the disease and cannot survive to the south of this line.

35. The introduction of the zebu into the western Sahara may be encoded in the story of Bubazzul and the founding of Tigumatin. The zebu moor male has short horns, and this may be the animal called *tequemad* in Berber. See below, chapter 2.

36. In the twentieth century, Bidan herders have raised both the zebu gobra and the zebu moor, but the zebu gobra is a relative newcomer to the desert fringe. Fuulbe herders introduced it into Mauritania from the savanna in the twentieth century, after the French pacification of desert groups encouraged the movement of these herders (and Wolof and Tukulor cultivators) northward into the desert fringe.

By the mid-nineteenth century, the breed zebu moor exhibited a great sexual dimorphism. The mature female weighed only 250 kilograms, making it well suited to limited desert pasturage. The mature male weighed 350–400 kilograms and was well suited for desert-edge transport. Both the zebu moor ox and zebu gobra ox were considered good draft animals. Desert herders used the zebu moor ox particularly for the transport of gum arabic along the desert fringe (Héricé [négociant du Sénégal], "Note sur le commerce des boeufs du Sénégal avec les antilles françaises," *RC*, 2e série, 11 [1853], 467–473). By the mid-twentieth century (and perhaps as early as the mid-nineteenth century), not only was the zebu moor cow lighter in weight than the zebu gobra cow, and thus required less forage, but it was a better milk producer as well (Doutressoule, *L'élevage en A.O.F.*, 77–189, esp. 93–100).

37. Interview with Muhammad Ahmad Wuld Mshiykh, 22 February 1981, at Nouakchott, 10.

38. Louis Léon César Faidherbe, "Renseignements géographiques sur la partie du Sahara comprise entre l'Oued Noun et le Soudan," *Nouvelles annales des voyages*, 6e série, 5e année (août 1859), 131.

39. For a recent study of the movement of Arab groups into the desert, see H. T. Norris, *The Arab Conquest of the Western Sahara* (Harlow, Essex, 1986).

40. The juxtaposition of Whites and Blacks has a long history in literary Arabic (see Catherine Taine-Cheikh, "La Mauritanie en noir et blanc. Petite promenade linguistique en hassaniyya," *Revue du monde musulman et de la Méditerranée* 54, no. 4 [1989], 94–95). The use of the term "Bidan" in the western sahel goes back at least to the middle of the fourteenth century, when the North African world traveller Ibn Battuta mentioned a "mosque of the Whites" at Gao on the middle Niger River (Nehemiah Levtzion and J. F. P. Hopkins [eds.], *Corpus of Early Arabic Sources for West African History*, trans. J. F. P. Hopkins [Cambridge, 1981], 300, cited by John O. Hunwick [ed. and trans.], *Shariʿa in Songhay: The Replies of al-Maghīlī to the Questions of Askia al-Ḥājj Muḥammad* [Oxford, 1985], 11).

41. H. T. Norris, "Future Prospects in Azayr Studies," *African Language Review* 9 (1970–1971), 99–109.

42. By the mid-twentieth century, Berber was spoken only in certain subregions of the Trarza (see Paul Dubie, "L'îlot berberophone de Mauritanie," *Bull. IFAN* 2 [1940], 316–325).

43. The general term for Blacks in desert Arabic is "al-Kwâr," possibly derived from the term for village. For a discussion of the terminology in Hassaniyya referring to Blacks, see Taine-Cheikh, "La Mauritanie en noir et blanc," 100–103.

44. Elias Saad, *Social History of Timbuktu* (Cambridge, 1983), 27–33 and 71. On Awdaghust, see E. Ann McDougall, "The View from Awdaghust: War, Trade and Social Change in the Southwestern Sahara, from the Eighth to the Fifteenth Century," *JAH* 26, no. 1 (1985), 1–31.

According to Rainer Oßwald, crucial cultural influences flowed into the western Sahara from the Niger bend region. Oßwald has argued that the "Moorish" literature of the western Sahara, which began to blossom in the sixteenth century, was stimulated by Berber scholars who were based at the towns of Timbuktu and Jenne along the southern edge of the Sahara and who were strongly influenced by their intercourse with North Africa. In the development of a clerical culture in the western Sahara of the fifteenth and sixteenth centuries, these east-west connections were probably more important than those with North Africa (see Rainer Oßwald, *Die Handelsstädte der Westsahara* [Berlin, 1986], 280–311 and 479–504, in particular his "Graphik zur Entwicklung des Gelehrtentums und der arabischen Literatur in der Westsahara").

For a thorough study of the Niger bend in the seventeenth century, see Elizabeth Hodgkin, "Social and Political Relations on the Niger Bend in the Seventeenth Century" (unpublished Ph.D. thesis, Centre for West African Studies, Birmingham University, 1987).

45. Jean Boulègue, *Le Grand Jolof* (Paris, 1987).

46. On Grand Fulo, see Jean Boulègue, "Un empire peul dans le Soudan occidental au début du XVIIe siècle," in *La parole, le sol, l'écrit: 2000 ans d'histoire africaine* (Paris, 1981), tome 1, 699–706.

47. H. T. Norris, *Saharan Myth and Saga* (Oxford, 1972), Manuscript A, "The Ancient History of the Mauritanian Adrar and the Sons of Shams al-Din by ʿAbd al-Wadud b. Ahmad Mawlud al-Shamsadi (d. 1944/5)," 131. Here, Shamsadi relates the account of Mokhtar Bin Ahmad Bin al-Amin al-Munnari al-Shamsadi. Norris does not provide any information to date the original account. He notes that Mokhtar Wuld Hamidun had some knowledge of the original author's family, the Ulad Mannura of the Ulad Bu ʿAbdalla clan, which apparently disappeared (changed their tribal affiliation?) during the nineteenth century.

48. Norris, *Saharan Myth and Saga*, Manuscript B, "A History of the Western Sanhaja, by Shaykh Sidiya Baba (d. A.D. 1924) of the Ulad Abyayri," 168.

49. Oumar Ba, "Des sites historiques au Brakna (Mauritanie)," *Notes africaines*, no. 118 (1968), 60–62; Oumar Ba, "Des sites historiques au Tagant (Mauritanie)," *Journal de la Société des africanistes* 17, no. 2 (1973), 245–246; Oumar Ba, "Des sites historiques au Tagant (Mauritanie)," *Notes africaines*, no. 138 (1973), 40–41; F.-M. Colombani, "Le Guidimaka. Étude géographique, historique, et religieuse," *BCEHSAOF* 14 (1931), 394–395.

50. According to one account, the Bambara had been living at Walata with a fraction of the Limhajib. The Bambara left when other fractions of the Limhajib arrived to settle in Walata:

> At the time of the arrival of the Limhajib, the Bambara refused them water. And it was thus that the chief of the Limhajib gave his student three grains of earth and told him to throw them in the well one after another. When he threw the first piece, the well overflowed and thus they provisioned themselves with water. When he threw the second piece, the water became red as blood. And the last grain permitted the transformation of the red water into earth. The Bambara asked immediately for water provisions to allow them to go see their chief in Mali. And this is why the Bambara left Walata, leaving behind their village set in the area of the dam at Walata.

(Interview with Bati Wuld Mbuya, at Walata, 20 December 1981, 6.) The dating of this out-migration is problematic and unresolved. The "Bambara" of the tradition may refer simply to sedentary agriculturalists who inhabited the region in an earlier period. That said, it should be noted that F.-M. Colombani recorded an oral tradition to the effect that the founders of Walata were Marka (Bambara-speakers) (Colombani, "Le Guidimaka," 393).

51. Bidan settlement in the plateau regions, of which the founding of Rashid is one example, is treated more fully in chapter 3, below.

52. Nicholson, "A Climatic Chronology," 80.

53. Toupet, *La sédentarisation des nomades*, 163; J.-H. Saint-Père, *Les Sarakollé du Guidimakha* (Paris, 1925); Colombani, "Le Guidimaka," 365–432.

54. Interviews with Mokhtar Wuld Hamidun, 6 May 1982, at Nouakchott, 8, and Muhammad Laghdaf Wuld Sidi Muhammad, 19 December 1981, at Nema, 12. See also chapter 2, below. Many Bidan are reluctant to divulge what they know about the Black origins of some of the Bidan families. The ideology of Bidan society insists upon Arab and Berber origins. But, according to Mokhtar Wuld Hamidun, even at the heart of the Ulad Dayman, one of the most distinguished of the old Berber tribes of the Tashumsha, there are groups who are remembered as having previously been of Peul and Tukulor ethnicity—the Ahl Ndibnan and the Ahl Behenin, respectively.

55. Interview with Mohamdi Wuld Dahud, 17 February 1982, at Tidjikja, 2. For a history of this Berber group, the Idaw Ish, see Pierre Amilhat, "Petite chronique des Id ou Aich, heritiers guerriers des Almoravides sahariens," *Revue des études islamiques* 11 (1937), 41–130.

56. The two outstanding examples of this adaptation were the Kunta groups of the Tagant and Adrar and the Ahl Sidi Mahmud of the Assaba.

57. The use of the terms "emirate" and "emir" is a convenience and a historical convention. These quasi-states, where the control of the dominant warrior group was often intermittent and uncertain, do not seem to have considered themselves as emirates. In the Trarza, for example, the head of the Ulad Ahmad Bin Daman was generally referred to as sultan until the middle of the nineteenth century.

58. See for example, ANFSOM, Sénégal IV, dossier 14, Coutumes annuelles, 1785. This document provides great detail on the annual taxes and includes the surprising information that the Trarza emiral entourage, when visiting Saint-Louis du Sénégal, required a daily ration of wine.

59. On the political organization of the emirates, see Abdel Wedoud Ould Cheikh, "Herders, Traders and Clerics: The Impact of Trade, Religion and Warfare on the Evolution of Moorish Society," in John G. Galaty and Pierre Bonte (eds.), *Herders, Warriors, and Traders. Pastoralism in Africa* (Boulder, 1991), 211–217; Pierre Bonte, "The Constitution of the Emirate and the Transformations of Systems of Production in the Adrar (Mauritania)," *Production pastorale et société*, no. 16 (printemps 1985), 33–53.

60. On the nature of Bidan society, see Ismaël Hamet (ed. and trans.), *Chroniques de la Mauritanie sénégalaise* (Paris, 1911), 27–55; Harry T. Norris, *Shinqiti Folk Literature and Song* (Oxford, 1968), particularly chapter 2, "West Saharan Society," 12–30; Charles C. Stewart, with E. K. Stewart, *Islam and Social Order in Mauritania: A Case Study from the Nineteenth Century* (Oxford, 1973), 54–65; Francis de Chassey, *L'étrier, la houe, et le livre* (Paris, 1977); Constant Hamès, "Statuts et rapports sociaux en Mauritanie précoloniale," *Études sur les sociétés des pasteurs nomades*, Cahiers du centre d'études et de recherches marxistes, no. 133 (1977), 10–21; Ahmed-Bāba Miské, "Al-Wasīt (1911). Tableau de la Mauritanie à la fin du XXe siècle," *Bull. IFAN*, série B, 30 (1968), 117–164.

61. *Muallimin* were metal, leather, and wood workers. They generally lived in the camps of powerful patrons, in small groups of one or more families, and found marriage partners among the greater muallimin community dispersed throughout the western Sahara. They were a small part of the overall Bidan community, but they made fundamental contributions to desert material culture. Among their manufactures were riding saddles, blankets, pillows, mats, rifle covers, shoes, book covers, smoking pipes, and metal ornamentation for teapots. When warrior groups adopted rifles and gave up the use of spears in the eighteenth, nineteenth, and twentieth centuries, these desert workers' expertise in the reparation and fabrication of firearms became critical. The other casted group was the *iggawin*, who were praise-singers. They lived in the camps of the hassani lineages, and they sang of the exploits and valor of their warrior patrons. They were in integral part of hassani camp life. The oral literature and songs of the Bidan are discussed by Harry T. Norris in his *Shinqiti Folk Literature and Song* (Oxford, 1968).

62. For a recent study of the history of caste in West Africa, see Tal Tamari, "The Development of Caste Systems in West Africa," *JAH* 32 (1991), 221–250.

63. A similar pattern of nomadic dominance took shape in the eastern Niger bend region. As Elizabeth Hodgkin notes in her study of the Niger bend region in the seventeenth century:

> For the period of the seventeenth and eighteenth centuries, the single sharp drought of 1639–42 may have brought a general Tuareg migration southward and begun Tuareg dependence on the river and the riverain population, but in the form of sudden, separate descents rather than a continuous presence. It was the prolonged crises of the first half of the eighteenth century, when the cycle of drought became to some extent self-perpetuating, that brought major changes to the relations of production, setting up a form of pillage economy dominated by the Tademeket and Iullemmeden Tuareg on the eastern Niger Bend.

(Hodgkin, "Social and Political Relations on the Niger Bend in the Seventeenth Century," 431.)

64. Interviews with Mokhtar Wuld Hamidun, 6 May 1981, 1–3, and 17 December 1980, 2–3; both at Nouakchott; and with Shaykh Wuld Banda, 6 January 1981, at Keur Macène, 2–3.

65. For details about the taxes paid in the late nineteenth century by the Soninke to the Bidan, see Colombani, "Le Guidimaka," 416–418.

66. James Riley, *An Authentic Narrative of the Loss of the American Brig Commerce . . .* (New York, 1813), 162. This reminiscence of Sidi Hamet was taken down by James Riley 9 or 10 years after the event, through the assistance of an interpreter who translated into Spanish what Riley was unable to understand in Arabic. It may conflate observations from more than one region of the desert edge into a single account. Sidi Hamet had travelled along a coastal route from Wad Nun before turning east and heading for Timbuktu. The journey east from the Atlantic coast had taken two moons; on the return trip Sidi Hamet presumably found himself in the Assaba or western Hawd. The observation about white men slaves refers to European and American shipwrecked sailors who were enslaved in the desert, much as Riley himself had been. These white slaves seem to have been concentrated along the Atlantic coast. For an overview of their enslavement and ransom, see Oliver Vergniot, "De la distance en histoire. Maroc-Sahara occidental: Les captifs du hasard (XVIIe–XXe siècles)," *Revue du monde musulman et de la Méditerranée* 48–49, nos. 2–3 (1988), 96–125.

67. See, for example, the account offered by a Trarza historian which idealizes the workings of the Trarza emirate:

> Inside the Trarza emirate [within the emiral grouping], there were never attacks to "steal" Blacks but only to collect taxes. There were many slaves and they were very important to the way of desert life. People [zwaya from the Trarza under the influence of the emiral grouping] didn't buy "stolen" slaves, nor ones taken illegally by force. It was bandits and tyrants who invaded the Black villages in zones not controlled by a strong emir.

(Interview with Muhammad Salim Wuld Baggah, 28 December 1980, at Medherdhra, 15.) These bandits and tyrants could be members of a larger emiral grouping who were trying to establish their independence, as well as hassani groups from outlying areas.

68. PRO, CO 267/29, 1 January 1811, Answers to the Questions proposed to Lt. Colonel Maxwell, Lieutenant Governor of Senegal and Goree by his Majesty's Commissioner for Investigating the Forts and Settlements in Africa.

69. Slavery in the desert remains an important topic awaiting fuller treatment. Slavery in the western savanna has received rather more attention (see particularly Claude Meillassoux, *The Anthropology of Slavery*, trans. Alide Danois [Chicago, 1991]; Claude Meillassoux, "État et conditions des esclaves à Gumbu [Mali] au XIXe siècle," in Claude Meillassoux [ed.], *L'esclavage en Afrique precoloniale* [Paris, 1975]; Claude Meillassoux, "Female Slavery," in Claire C. Robertson and Martin A. Klein [eds.], *Women and Slavery in Africa* [Madison, 1983], 49–66; Martin Klein and Paul E. Lovejoy, "Slavery in West Africa," in H. A. Gemery and J. S. Hogendorn [eds.], *The Uncommon Market: Essays in the Economic History of the Atlantic Slave Trade* [New York, 1979]; Martin A. Klein, "Women in Slavery in the Western Soudan," in Claire C. Robertson and Martin A. Klein [eds.], *Women and Slavery in Africa* (Madison, 1983), 67–92; Martin Klein, "The Demography of Slavery in Western Soudan," in Dennis D. Cordell and Joel W. Gregory [eds.], *African Population and Capitalism* [Boulder,

1987; rpt., Madison, 1994], 50–61; and Martin A. Klein, "The Slave Trade in the Western Sudan during the Nineteenth Century," in Elizabeth Savage [ed.], *The Human Commodity. Perspectives on the Trans-Saharan Slave Trade* [London, 1992], 39–60).

On precolonial desert slavery, see Alison Jones Webb, "Nineteenth Century Slavery in the Mauritanian Sahara" (unpublished M.A. thesis, The Johns Hopkins University, 1984). On desert slavery in the colonial period, see E. Ann McDougall, "A Topsy-Turvy World: Slaves and Freed Slaves in the Mauritanian Adrar, 1910–1950," in Suzanne Miers and Richard Roberts (eds.), *The End of Slavery in Africa* (Madison, 1988), 362–390. On contemporary desert slave culture, see Aline Tauzin, "Le gigot et l'encrier. Maitres et esclaves en Mauritanie à travers la littérature orale," *Revue du monde musulman et de la Méditerranée* 51, no. 1 (1989), 74–90. For an investigation of the nature of slavery in contemporary Mauritania, see John Mercer, *Slavery in Mauritania Today* (Human Rights Group: Edinburgh, Scotland, 1982).

70. Saugnier and Brisson, *Voyages to the Coast of Africa* (reprint: New York, 1969), 99.

71. For a study of slave conditions in a more recent period, see El-Keihil Ould Mohamed El Abd, "Colonisation française et mutations sociales en Mauritanie: Cas de l'esclavage en milieu maure 1900–1960" (unpublished mémoire de Maitrise, Université de Nouakchott, 1986–1987).

72. This view is expressed forcefully in Carrère and Holle, *De la Sénégambie française*, 225–226: ". . . those newly enslaved are bound under a terrible yoke; their lives count for nothing; burdened with the heaviest labor, they are not given enough to eat. Quaking from both the terror inspired by a master without pity and the pain of gnawing hunger, those who have escaped tell extraordinary stories of cold cruelty." See also Carrère and Holle, *De la Sénégambie française*, 259; and ANFSOM, Sénégal II, dossier 4, Note sur le Sénégal, M. Carrère, 9 janvier 1854.

Following the abolition of slavery in the French colony of Saint-Louis du Sénégal in 1848, the Whites were at some pains to make sure that their own slaves did not flee there seeking refuge. The story current in the desert was that the French took their slaves away to France and ate them. According to mid-nineteenth-century observers, this belief was widely shared among Black Africans. Some African laborers, contracted for years at a time, refused food on their way to Saint-Louis, hoping to arrive thin and haggard and therefore not be eaten first (Carrère and Holle, *De la Sénégambie française*, 313).

73. For an insightful historical analysis of the influence of West African diet and disease on Caribbean demography, see Kenneth F. Kiple, *The Caribbean Slave: A Biological History* (Cambridge, 1984).

74. Slaves who performed years of faithful service might be repaid through favors and small gifts. The young Black women who became the sexual partners of their White masters could hope that their masters would acknowledge paternity of the male offspring of these unions, because a child thus acknowledged might be freed from direct servitude—and the mothers might be freed as well.

According to Trarza oral tradition, Amar Wuld Kumba, one of the Ulad Ahmad Bin Daman who had a Wolof mother, is said to have been mocked by one of the Trarza praise-singers who said, "If you become emir—and you will never become emir because you are Black—do with me what you want and even forbid me to drink water if you like." Amar Wuld Kumba did become emir (c. 1795 to c. 1800), and the griot was punished with a vengeance (interview with Mokhtar Wuld Hamidun, 11 April 1981, at Nouakchott, 3). This Trarza emir is referred to by his matronym (Kumba is the name of his Wolof mother), indicating that his identity is drawn from both inside and outside the Bidan world.

There was no formal intermediate status between White and Black. The mulatto Bidan children, however, were often held in lower regard that the offspring of an all-Bidan union. In cases where the White father was either unknown or unwilling to admit patrimony, the male child had slave status, as he would have had if his father had been a slave. That said, the Bidan held that the best warriors were of mixed ethnic background (Carrère and Holle, *De la Sénégambie française*, 226).

75. Masters had three ways to liberate a slave: once and for all, as an act of charity; conditionally, upon the master's death, by decreeing that the master's heirs would have no further claim upon the slave; or upon the payment of a certain number of fixed monthly payments to be made to the master by the slave (interview with Mokhtar Wuld Hamidun, 25 June 1981, at Nouakchott, 3).

76. There were benefits of freedom, to be sure: freed slaves lived separately from their masters and could marry without their masters' permission, and they were on surer social footing to resist excessive demands by other nobles.

Chapter 2. The Southwestern Frontier

1. Denise Robert-Chaleix, "Nouveaux sites médiévaux mauritaniens: Un aperçu sur les régions septentrionales du Bilad as-Sudan," in *L'histoire du Sahara et des relations transsahariennes entre le Maghreb et l'Ouest Africain du Moyen-Age à la fin de l'epoque coloniale* (Bergamo, Italy, 1986), 46–58.

2. Boulègue, *Grand Jolof*, 13–14.

3. Paul Marty, *L'émirat des Trarzas* (Paris, 1917–18), 1–18. For an overview of Arab immigration into the western Sahara, see Norris, *Arab Conquest*, 26–47.

4. J. A. Le Brasseur, "Détails historiques et politiques, mémoire inédit (1778) de J. A. Le Brasseur," presented and brought to publication by Charles Becker and Victor Martin in *Bull. IFAN*, série B, 39 (1977), 96. This northern penetration is likely the reason why the largest seasonal lake in the Trarza, known today as Lake Rkiz, was known to the seventeenth-century French as Lac Cayar (Kajoor).

5. The desert marabouts were paid a slave and 20 *têtes de pagnes* for the performance of this ritual (R. Rousseau, "Le Sénégal d'autrefois. Étude sur le Cayor. Cahiers de Yoro Dyâo," *BCEHSAOF* 16 [1933], 258–260). Interestingly, the name of the Bidan marabout in Wolof oral tradition is Mokhtar Mbaye, said to be of the "Takhradjeute Dohïche" (Takradjent Idaw Ish). The name suggests the mixed Berber and Black African background of the desert grouping.

6. Although there appears to be no linguistic evidence to support the idea of a movement of Hausa-speaking peoples to the western Sahara, the link between Hausaland and the western Sahara in this period of the fifteenth to sixteenth century is not at all implausible. The Sanhaja and Masufa Berber groupings played at least some role in the Islamization of the Hausa states; scholars are known to have cultivated connections over very great distances; and it is likely that east-west connections were more important to the intellectual life of the western Sahara during this period than were those across the desert to North Africa (Oßwald, *Handelsstädte*, 283–284).

7. Abd el Wedoud Ould Cheikh, "Nomadisme, Islam, et pouvoir politique dans la société maure précoloniale (XI–XIXe siècles)" (unpublished thèse de doctorat de sociologie, Université de Paris V, 1985), 224. This version was collected at the site of the present-day Tigumatin. For an additional account of the founding of Tigumatin (in Berber) rendered by the same individual, see Tape 345 in the IMRS Collection, an interview with Shaykh Wuld Mokhtar Demba, recorded in 1976. In other accounts, Bubazzul is credited with descent from the Prophet Muhammad (interview with Mokhtar Wuld Hamidun, 6 May 1982, at Nouakchott, 7).

8. This third point is made by Ould Cheikh, "Nomadisme, Islam, et pouvoir politique," 224–225.

9. Interview with Mokhtar Wuld Hamidun, 6 May 1982, at Nouakchott, 7.

10. The name Fall does not seem to be related etymologically to the Pulaar names Tall or Sall, at least from a linguistic point of view. Although Tall is pronounced with a long vowel (ta:l), as is Fall (fa:l), Sall is pronounced with a long vowel and a geminate consonant (sa:ll). In addition, the Black African Fall are not speakers of Pulaar. Interestingly, the Wolof Falls as well as the Diagnes of northern Senegal are greeted today with the titles Fall Naar and Diagne Naar, respectively.

The term "Gannaar" probably includes the old prefix "gaa" or "ga" in Wolof, which means "the country of, the place of" and which is still found in terms such as Gànjaay, a village in the Saluum, which would mean "the place of the Njaay" (in French orthography: Gandiaye), and Ganjool, a village near Saint-Louis du Sénégal. Gannaar would thus mean "the country of the Naar." In Wolof, "naar" means "native speaker of Arabic" (personal communications from the linguist Dr. Omar Ka, 5 February 1991 and 21 March 1991).

11. Mbul was also the name of the capital of Kajoor, according to Wolof tradition, founded during the reign of Amari Ngone Sobel. The name is said to derive from the *Celtis australis* tree, known in Wolof as *bul*. (Rousseau, "Le Sénégal d'autrefois," 261).

12. The term "Gannaar" in the Trarza refers to the land surrounding Tigumatin. According to Mokhtar Wuld Hamidun, there was at one time a town called Gannaaret somewhere in the region. In addition, the Wolof use the term "Gueni-nar" to refer to a Bidan who is a stranger (from Mauritania). Today, the Bidan use the term "Ahl Gannaar" to refer to all blacks who claim sharifian descent through Bubazzul (interview with Mokhtar Wuld Hamidun, 6 May 1982, at Nouakchott, 7; see also Albert Leriche and Mokhtar Ould Hamidoun, "Notes sur le Trarza: Essai de géographie historique," *Bull. IFAN* 10 [1948], 471–472). A late seventeenth-century Frenchman identified Gannaar as a village on the coast above Saint-Louis (Jean Barbot, *A Description of the Coasts of North and South Guinea* [London; 1732], 532). One scholar has suggested that the term "Gannaar" has its roots in the name of the ancient Libyan tribe known as Canarii (Canarians) by Pliny (Tadeusz Lewicki, "Gannar—Le nom Wolof de la Mauritanie," *Paideuma* [Mitteilungen zur Kulturkunde] 35 [1989], 177–179).

I have not found any reference to Tigumatin in any European account or on any European map, but the evidence from these sources concerning Mbul and Gannaar is suggestive. Neither Gannaar nor Mbul appears on the early maps of the region in possession of the British Museum Library Map Room, the Library of Congress Map Collection, the Royal Geographical Society, or the Bibliothèque Nationale (Paris), the four major collections which I have consulted. In the seventeenth century the geographer

John Ogilby credited Mbul (Mboll) as the site of the palace of the king of Kajoor and an adjoining town which housed the servants and attendants of the court (John Ogilby, *Africa* [London, 1670], vol. 2, 342), and seventeenth-century cartographers placed Mbul roughly in the region of Njambuur, or central Kajoor. This would locate Mbul approximately 100 kilometers south of the site of Tigumatin in the south-central Trarza. The same cartographers credit Gannaar as a town and locate it properly to the north of the Senegal River, but too close to the seacoast. Gannaar disappears from European maps by about 1700, whereas Mbul continues to be located in or near Njambuur (see particularly the King's Topographical Collection CXVII, 1–35, available in the British Museum Library Map Room). The seventeenth-century maps referred to above are undated but filed after the sixteenth-century maps and before the eighteenth-century maps; in addition, they are dated to the seventeenth century by cartographic style and general geographic knowledge (see in particular, "Totius Africae Accuratissima Tabula," by Frederico de Wit of Amsterdam; "Accuratissima Totius Africae Tabula in lucem producta," by Iacovum de Sandart of Nuremberg; and untitled maps by Io. Baptista Homanno and A. F. Zuneri. Eighteenth-century maps with relevant geographic information are "Partie Occidentale de l'Afrique," by N. de Fer [1700], and an untitled map dated 1737 by Ioh. Matthia Husio, M.P.P.O.).

Many possible interpretations of these data might be advanced, but in light of the oral data from the Trarza, the most likely hypothesis appears to be that the creation of Tigumatin brought about the definitive decline of the desert-edge town of Mbul. The prestige associated with the name may have encouraged Amari Ngone Sobel, the ruler of Kajoor from 1549 to 1593, to use the name of this town when he founded his new capital in Kajoor.

13. Interview with Mokhtar Wuld Hamidun, 11 April 1981, at Nouakchott, 13.

14. Jean Boulègue, "La participation possible des centres de Pir et de Ndogal à la revolution islamique sénégambienne de 1673," in Jean Boulègue (ed.), *Contributions à l'histoire du Sénégal* (Paris, 1987), 119–125. According to two different accounts by the same author, Latsukaabe Fall died in June 1719, either on the 9th or 13th of the month (ANF C⁶ 6, Du Sénégal le 26 août 1720 [signature illegible]; and ANF C⁶ 6, Observations sur l'adition ou suplement au Memoire general que Mr Brüe mon predecesseur ma remis lors de son depart pour France, 1 août 1720).

15. Norris, *Saharan Myth and Saga*, 156, note H.

16. The Ahl Gannaar are credited with spiritual power in the Trarza region. The following account is of an historical episode from the late eighteenth century offered by Mokhtar Wuld Hamidun:

> The first war the Ulad Ahmad Bin Daman were ever in was against the Ulad Daman. The latter had killed some innocent members of the Ulad Ahmad Bin Daman. Their chief Ali al-Kori Wuld Amar Wuld Ali Shandhora was found with the Ahl Gannaar. So Ali al-Kori left to see an Ahl Gannaar man named Ndara Sghair, known for his saintliness. He asked him to make his enemies stay in the same place so he could send an army after them. The man assured him that they would not leave the place of attack until his army was ready. At last Ali al-Kori raised a large army and met the guilty party at the place. The attack ended with the defeat of the Ulad Daman.

(Interview with Mokhtar Wuld Hamidun, 6 May 1982, at Nouakchott, 7–8.)

17. Leriche and Ould Hamidoun, "Notes sur le Trarza," 471–472. This claim to Berber foundations of Mbul is interesting, in that Mbul seems to have been under Wolof control until the religious movement that brought about the foundation of Tigumatin. That the town of Tigumatin is said to have been built during the era of the founding of Wadan and Tishit is an effort to convey the meaning that the town and its role are ancient.

18. Tigumatin is not mentioned in the account of Al-Yadali concerning the jihad of Nasir al-Din (discussed below). Mokhtar Wuld Hamidun has suggested that Tigumatin ceased to exercise its role as a center of commerce in the Trarza sometime before this jihad (see also Leriche and Ould Hamidoun, "Notes sur le Trarza," 471–472).

19. The location of Tigumatin is remembered today in the Trarza, but the town itself has disappeared without a trace; banco and thatch, the usual materials of desert-edge dwellings, deteriorate without regular maintenance.

20. Interview with Mokhtar Wuld Hamidun, 27 April 1982, at Nouakchott, 6. The fact that Wad Nun traders are represented as sellers of meat near Tigumatin is curious. One would not suppose that long-distance caravan traders would be linked with the sale of meat. One possibility is that this may be a reference to the trade in livestock (more specifically, hides) that shows up in the export records of Saint-Louis from the late sixteenth century (see below, note 33).

21. Carson I. A. Ritchie, "Deux textes sur le Sénégal (1673–1677)," Bull. IFAN, série B, 30 (1968), 338. Interestingly, Chambonneau mentions a prophecy of long-standing among the Blacks that predicted a reform movement like that of Nasir al-Din. It is likely that this prophecy was influenced by the earlier religious movement that produced the Ahl Gannaar on the fringes of the Wolof world ("Deux textes," 352).

22. Philip D. Curtin, "Jihad in West Africa: Early Phases and Interrelations in Mauritania and Senegal," JAH 12 (1971), 14–18.

23. See in Hamet, Chroniques, the account of Muhammad al-Yadali, "Amr El Oualy Nacer Eddine (Historie du Saint Nacer Eddine)," 164–218, esp. 175–176.

24. "Shurbubba" was a rallying cry of the zwaya participants in this desert-side phase of the conflict.

25. Hamet, Chronicles, 175–185. For a near contemporary view of this jihad by a scholar from Walata, see Norris, Arab Conquest, 41–42.

26. Ritchie, "Deux textes," 352.

27. Interview with Mokhtar Wuld Hamidun, 17 December 1980, at Nouakchott, 10.

28. The French governor Chambonneau's text entitled "L'histoire du Toubenan" was published in Ritchie, "Deux textes," 289–353. Muhammad al-Yadali's text appeared in Hamet, Chroniques, as "Amr El Oualy Nacer Eddine (Histoire du Saint Nacer Eddine)," 164–218. Chambonneau's account deals exclusively with the jihad of Nasir al-Din and makes no mention of Shurbubba. Al-Yadali's rendering includes both the savanna and desert-side phases of the conflict. Harry T. Norris argued that, in the eyes of Al-Yadali, the jihad originated in Nasir al-Din's vision of a religious community that would transcend tribal and ethnic divisions, although elsewhere Norris notes that it may have been precipitated by a need to check Wolof raiding for slaves, and still elsewhere that the motives for the jihad are not clear and may have become confused during the course of the conflict (Norris, "Znaga Islam," 510, 515, 518). Philip Curtin, while not explicitly postulating one or more causes of the warfare, seems to have taken the

position that the warfare arose from conflicts within desert society (Curtin, "Jihad in West Africa," 11–24).

29. Boubacar Barry, *Le royaume du Waalo* (Paris, 1972), see esp. 135–159. Abdel Wedoud Ould Cheikh has objected to Barry's formulation on the grounds that hassani were in control of the trading post of Arguin toward the middle of the seventeenth century, and on this basis he has characterized Barry's opposition of hassani and zwaya interests as oversimplified (see Ould Cheikh, "Herders, Traders and Clerics," 208–209).

30. See below, chapter 4.

31. ". . . Ce grand Marabou ou Bourguly [Wolof: master of prayer] envoya son frere avec suitte en ambassade a deffunt N. de Muchins pour lors *Messieurs*, votre Commendant en ces Pays, L'assurer qu'il vouloit faire avec lui, la mesme Amitie, que les Roys dont il occupoit les places, avoient tuoiours euc avec les Commendans des Blans, qu'il n'avoit rien perdu qu'au Contraire il pouvoit venir et envoyer par tous ses pays en traite avec autant ou plus d'assurance que par le passe, qu'il le prioit aussi d'en agir de mesme pour lui et ses gens . . ." (Ritchie, "Deux textes," 341).

32. Barbot, *A Description of the Coasts of North and South Guinea*, 25. Genehoa, appearing in early Arabic sources as Ganawa or Janawa or Qinawa, was the Berber name for the Sudan. It is perhaps derived from the Berber *"ignawen"* (pl. of *"agnaw,"* which means *"mule"*) (Levtzion and Hopkins, *Corpus*, 447).

33. John Barbot also noted that the French at Saint-Louis du Sénégal provisioned themselves with meat from desert sources, rather than from the Black African states (see Barbot, *A Description of the Coasts of North and South Guinea*, 62, 46).

The documentary evidence collected by Philip Curtin on the export of hides from Saint-Louis du Sénégal during this period bears on this change. Although the early sources do not mention the ethnic identity of the herders who raised the animals whose hides entered the export trade, the numbers themselves are suggestive. From an average of 6,000 or 7,000 hides exported annually in the late sixteenth century, the number of exported hides rose dramatically in the seventeenth century to 35,000 or 40,000 by the 1660s. It is likely that these hides came both from the desert steppe and from the savanna zone below the river. According to Trarza oral tradition the town of Tigumatin had a wide beaten track leading to it, so numerous were the animals going to market. If this tradition refers not only to the horse trade but to the cattle trade as well, it would suggest that some of the hides of the animals which desert people herded to market in Tigumatin were exported through Saint-Louis. Thus it may well be that desert people dominated not only the slave trade in Senegambia but also played a significant role in the Atlantic sector, well before the sustained growth of the gum trade. In any event, following the "war of the marabouts," hide exports fell by two-thirds and remained low into the 1720s (La Courbe, *Premier voiage du Sieur de la Courbe fait à la coste d'Afrique en 1685* [Paris, 1913], 132–133; Curtin, *Economic Change*, vol. 1, 218–221, and vol. 2, appendix 2, "Hides," 65–67; interview with Mokhtar Wuld Hamidun, 27 April 1982, at Nouakchott, 7).

34. La Courbe, *Premier voiage*, 132–133.

35. Labat, *Nouvelle relation*, vol. 3, 86–88.

36. ANF C^6 7, lettre de 18 decembre 1723 par M. Du Milay. The author complained that the trading colony at Saint-Louis was nearly without beef, because Ali

Shandhora, the Trarza chief, had stopped the Bidan from trading with them. The French were forced to trade with the Blacks and the (very limited) demand from Saint-Louis was depleting their herds; cattle were becoming rare in their lands.

37. Doumet, "Mémoire inédit de Doumet (1769). Le Kayor et les pays voisins au cours de la seconde moitié du XVIIIe siècle," presented and commented upon by Charles Becker and V. Martin, *Bull. IFAN*, série B, 36 (1974), 47. Today, there are few cattle kept in the Wolof areas, in contrast with the Sereer in the Siin and Saluum regions to the south of Kajoor and Bawol and the Tukulor of Fuuta, who practice mixed economies of cereal production and livestock herding. The cattle that the Wolof do own they tend to consign to Fuulbe herdsmen (Curtin, *Economic Change*, vol. 1, 25–28). This custom likely dates from the ecological practices engendered by the peanut revolution of the late nineteenth and twentieth centuries.

38. Most of the Idaw al-Hajj settlements in Senegal date from the reign of Lat-sukaabe Fall, the damel of Kajoor from 1695 or 1697 to 1719 (see Henri Gaden, "Légendes et coutumes sénégalaises; cahiers de Yoro Dyâo," *Revue d'ethnographie et de sociologie* 3 [1912], 201–202). The dates of the damel's reign are taken from Mamadou Diouf, *Le Kajoor au XIXe siècle* (Paris, 1990), annexe 3, "Liste des 'Damel' du Kajoor." There they settled primarily in villages between Louga-Guewel and Kebemer. The names of the villages were Ngalil, Ngoumbelle, Nterbeti-Khadi, Muslaje, Ndak-houmpe, Nkeliman, Gadyel, and later, Wadan (interviews with Ahmad Baba Wuld Shaykh, March 1982, at Nouakchott, 10–11; and with Mokhtar Wuld Hamidun, 17 December 1980, at Nouakchott, 2; Gaden, "Légendes et coutumes sénégalaises," 201–202).

The town of Wadan in Njambuur was founded about 1827 (L. Flize, "Le Ndiam-bour et le Gadiaga," *RC*, 2e série, 17 [1857], 392).

For more on the Idaw al-Hajj, including Idaw al-Hajj oral tradition concerning their involvement in the war of the marabouts, see James L. A. Webb, Jr., "Shifting Sands: An Economic History of the Mauritanian Sahara, 1500–1850" (unpublished Ph.D. dissertation, The Johns Hopkins University, 1984), chapter 2.

39. According to Mokhtar Wuld Hamidun, the meaning of the terms referring to the Idaw al-Hajj groupings varies according to the following usage. The name Darman-kour is sometimes restricted to refer only to the Idaw al-Hajj settlements in Senegal. Other terminology for these groups is as follows. The descendants of Wavij Wuld Najib in Senegal are known collectively by their Wolof name Sugufara. Sometimes the meaning of the name Sugufara is expanded to include all Idaw al-Hajj in Senegal. The sub-divisions of the Darmankour/Sugufara are called Goumbella (which is said to be derived from the Berber group name Tamguna), Ndakhoumpa, Sadi, Teftel, Tandina, Hamar, Sabara, and Ture. The names Sugufara and Ndakhoumpa are said to be Wolof in origin. Sadi, Teftel, Tandina, and Hamar are remembered as the names of groups which consti-tuted the original grouping of the Idaw al-Hajj at Wadan (interview with Mokhtar Wuld Hamidun, 17 December 1980, at Nouakchott, 2).

Trarza Idaw al-Hajj tradition stresses the fact that Idaw al-Hajj did not marry outside the *qabila* (tribe): "In the old days, the Idaw al-Hajj only married among themselves. If a man married outside of his tribe he was bound up with iron chains. It wasn't until recently that the Idaw al-Hajj started to marry outside of the tribe. This situation is rare today. The Idaw al-Hajj were always limiting themselves when it came to marriage" (interview with Ahmad Baba Wuld Shaykh, March 1982, at Nouakchott, 11). The name Darmankour was also rendered as Darmancour, d'Armankour, d'Armancour, Darmancourt, or Darmanko by the Europeans.

40. Gaden, "Légendes et coutumes sénégalaises," 201–202.

41. Ogilby, *Africa*, vol. 2, 346.

42. La Courbe, *Premier voiage*, 99.

43. Labat, *Nouvelle relation*, vol. 2, 169.

44. ANF C^6 10, Du Senegal Messieurs des Directeurs de la Compagnie des Indes, 7 juillet 1726. The author of this document complained that most of the grain had been gotten from the Moors, who insisted on payment in amber for both grain and cattle. The price of grain from Kajoor had gone up 750–875 percent, and it had to be paid for in coral.

45. ANF C^6 13, lettre de 24 février 1752, dc la Brüe et al.

46. Pierre David, *Journal d'un voiage fait en Bambouc en 1744*, ed. André Delcourt (Paris, 1974), 210; ANF C^6 12, Rapport au Senegal, 1 juin 1746.

47. ANF C^6 14, Mémoire dated 13 May 1754, unsigned. By the 1750s this had thrown the gum trade into a crisis. For further information, see chapter 5 below. Doumet also indicates the importance of Bidan commerce in Kajoor in the 1760s:

> Les Mores font tout le commerce de ce royaume . . . Le roy Damel fait son séjour à vingt lieües environ dans les terres et dans un eloignement presqu'egal du Sénégal et de Gorée; cette résidence s'appêlle Arboul. Les Maures y vont par caravannes et y conduisent des chameaux, chevaux et ânes, chargés de toutes les marchandises qui peuvent etre à l'usage ou à la bienséance de Damel. Ces differentes marchandises parviennent aux Maures de la traite de gomme qu'ils font avec les Anglais dans la rivière du Sénégal; et c'est sur eux que roule tout le commerce de l'intérieur du roiaume. . . Ils achetent pareillement tout le mill de l'intérieur de ces païs, traversent jusques aux villages situés sur la côte, vis à vis de Gorée, y changent leur mill pour du poisson sec, qu'ensuite ils vont revendre dans les parties les plus éloignées du bord de la mer. (Doumet, "Mémoire," 43).

48. As a British trader in the 1760s estimated: "For they draw the greatest part of their support from the South Side of the River, and our Vessells have daily opportunities of ruining them by Stopping their Caravans and Pillaging them of their Corn and Merchandise . . ." (PRO, T 70/37, John Barnes to the Committee, 9 July 1764).

49. For estimates of the grain demand from Saint-Louis and Gorée and from slave ships, see James F. Searing, *West African Slavery and Atlantic Commerce: The Senegal River Valley, 1700–1860* (Cambridge, 1993), 81–85, 140. Searing stresses the importance of the grain demand from the Atlantic settlements during the eighteenth century. He does not attempt an estimate of the sahelian demand for imported grain during this period.

50. Colonial studies of equine dietary requirements found that horses needed five kilograms of grain per day (six kilos when travelling), in addition to some six kilos of hay or straw, for maintenance (see two documents in ANFSOM, Sénégal XVI, dossier 41: Ministère de la Marine et des Colonies, no. 80, Rapport sur l'alimentation des chevaux de Guerre au Sénégal, 21 decembre 1887; and Rapport au nom de la commission chargée de suivre les essais sur l'alimentation par le Mil et le Maïs comparés à l'Orge, par Duchemin et al.). Jacques Meniaud estimated that four kilos of grain were necessary to complement the nutrition gained from grazing on wild seed plants, peanut

stalks, and niébé stalks; the male horses received better nutrition than the females (see Jacques Meniaud, *Le Haut-Sénégal-Niger* [Paris, 1912], tome 2, 116). C. Pierre, discussing the general condition and maintenance of horses in French West Africa, states that horses graze between the months of June and November; during the dry season, if their owners are able, the horses are fed with millet and peanut hay (C. Pierre, *L'élevage dans l'Afrique occidentale française* [Paris, 1906], 45). G. Doutressoule states that only riding mounts were fed with grain; the daily ration for horses at work ranged between three and four kilos of grain and four and five kilos of hay; maintenance rations were considerably lower (Georges Doutressoule, *L'élevage au Soudan Français* [Paris, 1948], 286–287). He also indicates that male horses were better fed than females (*L'élevage en A.O.F.*, 66). For more on the cavalries of the Senegambian states, see chapter 4 below. If one assumes that the horses of the Black African nobility were fed with grain at the lower figure of four kilos per day (horses of the commoners presumably would have received far less), approximately 650 horses owned by the nobility of the Black African states of the middle and lower regions of the Senegal River (Fuuta, Waalo, Kajoor, and Bawol) would have consumed annually an amount of grain equivalent to the peak demand for grain from Saint-Louis, Gorée, and the slave ships during the era of the Atlantic slave trade.

51. PRO, T 70/37, John Barnes to the Committee, 17 February 1765. Even as late as 1848, the French at Saint-Louis would describe both Saint-Louis and Gorée as particularly dependent upon Kajoor (ANS 2 B 27, Governeur Baudin au Ministre, 12 février 1848).

52. For further information on the relationship of the grain trade and the gum trade, see chapter 5 below.

53. La Courbe, *Premier voiage*, 175; Barry, *Waalo*, 170.

54. ANF C⁶ 6, Du Sénégal le 4ème mai 1720, André Brüe.

55. Bibliothèque Nationale, Fonds français, MS 24222, Journal de André Brüe, folio 335. According to a Wolof oral tradition collected by Amadou Bamba Diop (which does not appear in the chronicle of Yoro Dyâo), a desert army, bolstered by Wolof forces, invaded Kajoor searching for Latsukaabe Fall (see Amadou Bamba Diop, "Lat Dior et le problème musulman," *Bull. IFAN*, série B, 28 [1966], 493–539). Jean Boulègue has suggested that this invasion took place at the latest at the beginning of 1720 and perhaps in 1718 or 1719 (Jean Boulègue, "La traite, l'état, l'Islam. Les royaumes wolof du quinzième aux dix-huitième siècle" [unpublished doctorat d'État, Université de Paris I, 1986], 522).

56. According to Le Brasseur, Ali Shandhora travelled up the coast of the western Sahara to Morocco disguised as a griot (Le Brasseur, "Détails historiques," 90–91). The Moroccan sultan gave the Trarza emir gifts which since that time have symbolized emiral authority in the Trarza: a copper tam-tam, a white turban, and most distinctively, a pair of white trousers (*sirwal*), a color of pant which the Trarza emir alone has the right to wear. At the conclusion of the war, Ali Shandhora reestablished his personal authority in the Trarza region, cutting off the head of the Ulad Dalim chieftain who had presumed to make advances to the Trarza emir's wife during his absence in the Maghrib (Marty, *L'émirat des Trarzas*, 68–69).

The Moroccan expeditionary forces, for the most part, seem to have returned to the Maghrib at the end of their campaigns, but a major exception was the Moroccan army sent to aid Ali Shandhora. Some of these forces dispersed after the defeat of the Brakna, when Ali Shandhora attempted to impose taxes on them and incorporate them into the Trarza emirate. Others made a place for themselves in the Bidan world. One group entered the large Ulad Barikallah confederation to the north of the Trarza, where groups who claim these Moroccans as their descendants reside and are known today as the Shorfa of the Ulad Barikallah. Another group, the Rhalla, remained warriors, paying tribute to the Trarza emir and nomadizing on the northern fringes of the Trarza. Yet another group, the Lutaydat, stayed in the Trarza but gradually lost their identity as warriors. They came to specialize in caravan transport services in Waalo and Kajoor, at first in the grain trade and later in the peanut trade, all the while maintaining a status as half-tributaries of the Trarza emir (see interviews with Muhammad Salim Wuld Baggah, 29 December 1980, at Medherdhra, 9; and with Mokhtar Wuld Hamidun, 19 December 1980, at Nouakchott, 5; Marty, *L'émirat des Trarzas*, 70; Capt. M. Vincent, "Voyage d'exploration dans l'Adrar," *Revue algérienne et coloniale* [octobre 1860], 450).

Although the sultan is not known to have sent armies into the southwestern Sahara after the 1720s, the Trarza debt to the sultan was long remembered. The Trarza emir continued to pay symbolic tribute to the Moroccan sultan as late as 1914 (Marty, *L'émirat des Trarzas*, 70).

For intrigues which threatened to derail Ali Shandhora's plans, see ANF C⁶ 6, lettre de 28 mars 1721.

57. At least by the early nineteenth century, this army marched under a military banner, very much on the European model (see ANFSOM, DFC Sénégal, carton 84, no. 241, La Barre du Sénégal, M. Bodin). According to Trarza oral tradition, these freed slaves (and their descendants) are said to have remained exceptionally faithful to the Trarza, to the degree that the emirs are said to have had more confidence in the slaves whom they freed and retained as servants than in their White tributaries (interview with Mokhtar Wuld Hamidun, 27 April 1982, at Nouakchott, 9–10).

58. Searing, *West African Slavery*, chapter 2.

59. For more on the Moroccan invasions along the southeastern frontier, see chapter 3 below.

60. The Moroccans were also looked upon as potential allies by members of the Black aristocracies in dissidence against the ruling authorities. In 1733, for example, Guiogomaye, the brother of the damel, threatened to lead the Moroccans into Kajoor (ANF C⁶ 10, Rapport du 30 août 1733).

61. ANF C⁶ 7, lettre de M. de la Rigaudere, 3 mai 1722. The forces of Waalo, Kajoor, and Bawol apparently teamed up to march in pursuit of the northern invaders.

62. Oumar Kane, "Les maures et le Futa-Toro au XVIIIe siècle," *Afrika Zamani*, no. 2 (1974), 79–104. For accounts of political violence between the Brakna and Fuuta Tooro, see Siré Abbas Soh, *Chroniques du Fouta sénégalais* (Paris, 1913), 38–42.

63. Boubacar Siré, the siratigi of Fuuta installed by the Bidan in 1718, sent his son to the Moroccan sultan in 1720 to dissuade him from sending reinforcements to the Trarza. The siratigi warned of Wolof strength, arguing that following the marriage of a daughter of the damel to the brak the Wolof states of Waalo, Kajoor, and Jolof were capable of putting 50,000 men in the field and would defeat the Moroccan forces. His fear was that the Moroccan troops would march first through Fuuta, already severely

pillaged, and would then carry out the design of Ali Shandhora to depose the brak and to establish Trarza hegemony in the Waalo. This anticipated by some 50 years the final onslaught of desert forces on Waalo (ANF C⁶ 6, lettre de 28 mars 1721).

64. A. Delcourt, *La France et les établissements français au Sénégal entre 1712 et 1763* (Dakar, 1952), 143.

65. Searing, *West African Slavery*, 80–81.

66. Frederic Shoberl (ed.), *The World in Miniature. Africa, Containing a Description of the Manners and Customs, with Some of the Historical Particulars of the Moors of the Zahara, and of the Negro Nations between the Rivers Senegal and Gambia* (London, 1827), vol. 2, tome 1, 35–39. This account appears to conflict with the list of damels and their reigns compiled by Yoro Dyâo and amended by Colvin (see Diouf, *Kajoor*, annexe 3, "Liste des 'Damel' du Kajoor"; PRO, CO 267/12, Stoupan de la Brüe, Delacombe, Duranger, danglez [a translation from the French done by the English], 6 April 1757). The buur ba Jolof's success was considered a threat to the European slave trade. As the letter notes, "Nothing could happen more preducial [*sic*] to the Interest of the Company's trade, in Gorée than that revolution of Cayor. This king of Yolof is Maraboux, and subsequently sells no slaves to the Christians. He, besides, makes no use of Brandy."

67. This anecdote also conveys the scorn with which the Bidan have viewed the practice of Islam in Senegal. Muslims, of course, do not believe that Allah was born of a mother, and the declaration attributed to the damel's mother underlines her ignorance of Islam (interview with Mokhtar Wuld Hamidun, 17 December 1980, at Nouakchott, 10).

68. Interviews with Mokhtar Wuld Hamidun, 11 April 1981, at Nouakchott, 1–2; and with Ahmad Baba Wuld Shaykh, March 1982, at Nouakchott, 17–18; Marty, *L'émirat des Trarzas*, 80.

Another historical anecdote underlines the obligations that the damel of Kajoor incurred to the Trarza chieftain: "Sidi al-Mokhtar Wuld Haddi wanted to marry a Brakna princess who wanted as dowry a lizard made of gold. Sidi al-Mokhtar went to Kajoor where the blacksmiths made for the princess the lizard she desired" (interview with Mokhtar Wuld Hamidun, 17 December 1980, at Nouakchott, 10). I could find no further precise information in Mauritania on this right to pillage. It is likely that the damel simply designated villages which were politically troublesome to be destroyed by the Trarza warriors.

Mamadou Diouf has written that the right of pillage was one of the expressions of the authority and sovereignty of the damel. According to Diouf, this pillage took place on the borders of the Kajoor kingdom, although he presents no direct, supporting evidence for this assertion. Two-thirds of the booty pillaged on command of the damel is said to have been remitted to him, as compared with only half of the goods seized in warfare (Diouf, *Kajoor*, 290, 71).

Faidherbe noted in the 1850s that the Ulad Sharqi Wuld Haddi (and the Ahl Tunsi, another branch of the Trarza emiral grouping) were known in Senegal as Khandoussa, the name of an insect which is said to devour the weakest ("nom d'un insecte qui passe pour en dévorer de plus petits") (Faidherbe, "Notice sur la colonie du Sénégal et sur les pays qui sont en relation avec elle," *Nouvelles annales des voyages de la géographie, de l'histoire, et de l'archaeologie*, 6e série, 5e année, 1 [1859], 83, footnote 1).

69. Curtin, *Economic Change*, vol. 2, 4–5. This drought appears not to have affected the desert groups as severely as it did the riverine and savanna states, because it went unrecorded in the desert chronicles. Faidherbe gives the dates of substantial Trarza military interventions as 1760–61 (see his "Notice historique sur le Cayor," *BSG* [1883], 548).

70. Philip D. Curtin, "Nutrition in African History," *Journal of Interdisciplinary History* 14 (1983), 379; and Curtin, *Economic Change*, vol. 1, 13–23.

71. Dominique Harcourt Lamiral, *L'Affrique et le peuple affrican* [*sic*] (Paris, 1789), 238, 240–241.

72. PRO, T 70/37, John Barnes to the Committee, 17 February 1765.

73. Barry, *Waalo*, 199–218.

74. Paul Marty (trans.), "Poème historique d'Abou Bakr Ibn Hejab, le Dîmani," *BCEHSAOF* 4 (1921), 253.

75. Barry, *Waalo*, 199–218.

76. Historians have disputed the purported complicity and incitement of Governor O'Hara in the 1775 Trarza raids on Waalo (see Curtin, *Economic Change*, vol. 1, 126, footnote 11; and Boubacar Barry, *La Sénégambie du XVe au XIXe siècle. Traite négrière, islam, et conquête coloniale* [Paris, 1988], 110–113). My research has turned up a curious letter that antedates the 1775 attack on Waalo. A 1773 letter from Boniface at Gorée states that O'Hara was intriguing against the Trarza because they would not agree not to trade with the French at Gorée. O'Hara is reported to have advanced 300 slaves to a marabout who was interested in waging war to purify the practice of Islam in the region. Boniface reported that this marabout was going to make war against the brak and the damel (ANF C⁶ 16, lettre de Gorée, 22 octobre 1773, Boniface). In addition, an unsigned French report from 1803 expresses doubt that the English were responsible for the destruction of Waalo (ANFSOM, DFC Sénégal, carton 83, no. 105, Des Peuples qui habitent les Côtes du Sénégal et les bords de ce Fleuve, Des Royaumes sur la côte de Gorée, Cayor, Baol, Sin et Salum, 1803).

77. PRO, T 64/376B, An Account of the Quantity of Gum Senegal and of the Number of Slaves, exported from any of His Majesty's Dominions in Africa, between 1st January 1763, and 1st of January, 1777. . .

78. ANFSOM, DFC Sénégal, carton 82, no. 75, Mémoire sur la traite de la gomme au Sénégal, août 1783, M. Eyries.

79. "At that time the Moors used to come from the north, they came to plunder the property of the blacks. They did not consider the black people to be human beings, they would kidnap children and enslave them, take away cattle, they simply did that continually. At that time praying was not common" (Moustapha Kane and David Robinson (eds.), *The Islamic Regime of Fuuta Tooro* [East Lansing, 1984], the account of Seegaa Nan, "Sileymaani Baal and Abdul Kaader," 37).

80. Pommegorge, *Description de la Nigritie*, 51.

81. Oumar Kane, "Les maures et le Futa Toro au XVIIIe siècle," *Cahiers d'études africaines* 54, 16–2 (1974), 237–252; David Robinson, "The Islamic Revolution of Futa Toro," *IJAHS* 8 (1975), 185–211; and his *Chiefs and Clerics* (Oxford, 1975), 12–13. For oral tradition concerning this conflict, see in Kane and Robinson, *Islamic Regime*, the account of Mammadu Njaani Mben, "The Toorobbe and the Deeniyadkoobe," 26–33.

The success of the revolution in Fuuta Tooro emboldened the Fuulbe reformers. Abdulkader, the new ruler of the Fuuta Tooro, wrote a letter to the Trarza emir demanding a gift of five saddled horses in order to aid in the expansion of the holy war. The Trarza emir tore up the letter. The Fuulbe, in A.H. 1200 (1786/87 C.E.), attacked the Trarza and killed the emir. According to Soh's account, the Brakna hassani were reduced to paying tribute to Fuuta in order to retain their independence (Soh, *Chroniques du Fouta sénégalais*, 47–49).

82.   A putative history linking the Idaw al-Hajj (the Darmankour) with the Brakna emiral group was first written down by Golberry in 1785. It was repeated by others (see Silv. Meinrad Xavier Golberry, *Fragmens d'un voyage en Afrique* [Paris, 1802], tome 1, 220–223; R. Geoffrey de Villeneuve, *L'Afrique ou histoire, mœurs, usages, et coutumes des africains* (Paris, 1814), 22–24; Shoberl, *World in Miniature*, vol. 1, tome 1, 25–26; Kane, "Les maures et le Futa Toro," *Afrika Zamani*, 82–83).

83.   Flize, "Le Ndiambour et le Gadiaga," 391–392.

84.   ANFSOM, DFC Sénégal, carton 83, no. 115, Rapport sur les établissements français d'Afrique, adressé le 8 juillet 1817, M. Schmaltz. The brak paid an annual tribute of 100 cattle and in return received a horse (ANS 2 B 6, Gouverneur au Ministre, 15 juillet 1821). As Lieutenant Colonel Maxwell pointed out, "Most of the Negroe Princes pay a tribute to the Moors to induce them not to pillage. The Kingdom of Damel pays a hundred cattle annually and is pillaged notwithstanding" (PRO, CO 267/29, 1 January 1811, Answers to the Questions proposed to Lt. Colonel Maxwell, Lieutenant Governor of Senegal and Goree by his Majesty's Commissioner for Investigating the Forts and Settlements in Africa). By the 1850s, this Kajoorian tribute had increased to 200 cattle (see Carrère and Holle, *De la Sénégambie française*, 121; on Jolof: ANS 2 B 20, Gouverneur au Ministre, 23 octobre 1842). Eunice Charles has suggested that the Jolof tribute of 100 cattle per year began to be paid at some point after the visit of the explorer G. Mollien to Jolof in 1818 (Eunice Charles, *Precolonial Senegal: The Jolof Kingdom 1800 to 1890* [Boston, 1977], 30–31).

85.   Convention entre le commandant pour le roi et administrateur du Sénégal et dépendances et Mohammed Kharabat Chems, chefs [*sic*] de la tribu des d'Armankours, 30 juin 1819 (reproduced in Marty, *L'émirat des Trarzas*, 392–395).

86.   Paul Marty, "Tentatives commerciales anglaises à Portendick et en Mauritanie (1800–1826)," *Revue de l'histoire des colonies françaises*, 2e trimestre (1922), 265–302.

87.   This control was not, however, uncontested. In the 1840s, political violence generated from within the Trarza emiral family spilled over into Kajoor. Hamit Shay, a member of the emiral family, led pillaging expeditions into the Wolof state in 1841 and 1842. The forces of the damel were reported to have been thoroughly defeated; in addition, the son and nephew of the damel were killed, and many prisoners of war were taken (ANS 2 B 19, Gouverneur au Ministre, 18 juillet 1841; ANFSOM, Sénégal IV, dossier 19, extrait, conseil général de Saint Louis, séances de 20 septembre 1841 et 27 septembre 1841; ANFSOM, Sénégal, dossier 19, Extrait d'un rapport adressé au Ministre de la Marine par le Gouverneur du Sénégal sur la situation de la colonie au 1er janvier 1842; Convention entre le gouvernement du Sénégal et Hamet Schey, prince de la tribu des Trarza, 13 août 1842).

For an overview of political events in Kajoor during this period, see Diouf, *Kajoor*, 145–150. Diouf, however, does not provide any perspective on the long history of Trarza influence in Kajoor and writes as if the political violence of the early 1840s was new.

88. Interestingly, however, the quantity of gum sold along the river does not seem to have diminished during the intermittent Franco-Trarza conflict of 1831–35.

89. Interview with Muhammad Salim Wuld Baggah, 29 December 1980, 8. According to Mokhtar Wuld Hamidun the warrior involved was named Bu Zafra.

90. Anonymous, "Sénégal. Affaires politiques et militaires," *RC*, 2e série, 16 (1856), 349; Anonymous, "Sénégal. Affaires politiques," *RC*, 2e série, 18 (1857), 135; Anonymous, "Sénégal. Situation politique de cette colonie," *RC*, 2e série, 17 (1857), 170–171.

91. ANFSOM, Sénégal IV, dossier 45, Traité de Paix avec Mohamed el-Habib (1858). Dimar was the only Fuutanke region to pay tribute to the Trarza (Carrère and Holle, *De la Sénégambie française*, 133). Earlier, the buur ba Jolof had entreated the French to build a fortified trading post at Mérinaghen, offering to put up half the capital himself, to furnish labor and the transport of materials (ANS 2 B 30, Gouverneur Protet au Ministre, Régime politique no. 285, 2 juillet 1851). The principal problem for the French was the hegemony of the Trarzas over Waalo and the chaos that emanated from that region. In 1852, the French governor brought the political leaders from the Trarza and Waalo and from Fuuta and the Brakna together for talks. The Trarza emir showed up with 12,000–15,000 supporters, camped on the northern bank of the river. The Brakna emir and the almami of Fuuta camped on the southern bank. Neither grouping was willing to make contact with the other (ANS 2 B 30, Gouverneur Protet au Ministre, 8 juin 1852). The annual razzias of the Bidan in Kajoor apparently ended in 1854 (Faidherbe, "Notice historique sur le Cayor," 529).

92. Interview with Muhammad Salim Wuld Baggah, 29 December 1980, at Medherdhra, 5.

93. See, for example, the correspondence for the 1860s and 1870s between the heads of Trarza emiral factions and French colonial governors in ANS 9 G 2.

94. I discuss the use of currency along the southwestern frontier in chapters 4 and 5, on the horse and slave trade and the gum arabic trade, respectively, and along the southeastern frontier in chapter 3.

95. Stewart, *Islam and Social Order*, 109–122.

Chapter 3. The Southeastern Frontier

1. Raymond Mauny, "L'expédition marocaine d'Ouadane vers 1543–1544," *Bull. IFAN* 11 (1949), 129–140; Michel Abitbol, "Le Maroc et le commerce trans-saharien du XVII siècle au début du XIX siècle," *Revue de l'occident musulman et de la Méditerranée* 30 (1980), 5–19; Jamil M. Abun-Nasr, *History of the Maghrib* (Cambridge, 1975), 212–214. Following the collapse of Songhai, Moroccan armies settled in the Timbuktu region, where they stayed, intermarried, and adopted many features of Black African culture. They began to form a new ethnic group known locally as the Arma. For a study of Timbuktu in the century after the Moroccan conquest, see Hodgkin, "Social and Political Relations on the Niger Bend in the Seventeenth Century."

2. Abitbol, "Le Maroc et le commerce trans-saharien," 5–19.

3. On the movement of the Idaw al-Hajj to the Trarza, see Webb, "Shifting Sands," chapter 2.

4. For information about the dispersion of the Tadjakanet and the emergence of the Kunta, see Thomas Whitcomb, "New Evidence on the Origins of the Kunta— 1 & 2," *Bull. SOAS* 38 (1975), 103–123 and 403–417; ᶜAbdal-ᶜAziz ᶜAbdallah Baṭrān, "Sidi al-Mukhtar al Kunti and the Recrudescence of Islam in the Western Sahara and the Middle Niger, c. 1750–1811" (unpublished Ph.D. thesis, University of Birmingham, England, 1971); H. T. Norris, *Saharan Myth and Saga*, see his translation of the text by Shaikh Sidiya, "A History of the Western Sanhaja," 195–200.

5. According to oral tradition, this early movement of Kunta to Wadan was peaceful, and the Kunta and the Idaw al-Hajj lived in close relations with each other in the eastern Adrar in the seventeenth century (interview with Mokhtar Wuld Hamidun, 6 May 1982, at Nouakchott, 2).

6. Saad, *Timbuktu*, 13.

7. According to oral tradition, conflict broke out at Shinqiti when groups there tried to replace the imam of the town's mosque who was one of the Smassid (descendants of Bubazzul) with a man from the Laghlal (Oßwald, *Handelsstädte*, 474).

8. Within the Adrar, rainfall was far from evenly distributed; the western regions fared better than the eastern regions. In the second half of the twentieth century, for example, Atar received twice the annual rainfall that Shinqiti received, even though both are at the same latitude (Toupet, *La sédentarisation des nomades*, 25).

9. Ahmed Ennasiri Esslaoui [Es Slawi], *Kitab Elistiqsa* [Kitab al-Istiqsa], trans. Eugène Fumey in *Archives marocaines* [Paris, 1906], tome 9, 76–77.

10. On the basis of weak and conflicting evidence, Allan Meyers, one of the authorities on the Moroccan slave armies, disputes the contention that recruits for the slave armies were taken from Black Africa (see Allan Meyers, "Class, Ethnicity, and Slavery: The Origins of the Moroccan ᶜAbid," *IJAHS* 10 [1977], 427–442; Allan Meyers, "Slave Soldiers and State Politics in Early ᶜAlawi Morocco, 1668–1727," *IJAHS* 16 [1983], 39–48). Ralph Austen, however, has painstakingly assembled other evidence which convincingly demonstrates that large numbers of Black Africans were taken across the desert as slaves during the decades when the Moroccan slave armies were active (1670s–1780s) (see Ralph Austen, "The Mediterranean Islamic Slave Trade Out of Africa: A Tentative Census," in Elizabeth Savage [ed.], *The Human Commodity. Perspectives on the Trans-Saharan Slave Trade* [London, 1992], 214–248).

11. The sultan of Morocco at this time also received Khenata, the daughter of the Brakna chieftain, as a wife (Abū al-Ḳāsim Ahmad ibn ᶜAli ibn Ibrāhīm al-Zayānī, *Le Maroc de 1631 à 1812*, ed. and trans. O. Houdas [Paris, 1886], 31–32; Ahmed Ennasiri Esslaoui [Es Slawi] *Kitab Elistiqsa* [Kitab al-Istiqsa], tome 9, 76–77).

12. Gaston Boyer, *Un peuple de l'ouest soudanais. Les diawara* (Dakar, 1953), 39.

13. Thora G. Stone, "The Journey of Cornelius Hodges in Senegambia, 1689–90," *English Historical Review* 39 (1924), 93. Curtin cites this document and credits the expedition as Moroccan (see Curtin, *Economic Change*, vol. 1, 51, footnote 5). On the Arab nomadic forces, see Norris, *Arab Conquest*, chapter 6.

E. Ann McDougall has interrogated the Hodges text, brought to light problematic aspects of it, and suggested other possible identifications of Tarra (McDougall, "The Quest for Tarra: Toponomy and Geography in Exploring History," *History in Africa*

8 (1991), 271–289). Yet upon a close reading of these materials, I find that the proposed alternative identifications loom more problematic than the identification of Tarra with Jarra. McDougall's preferred alternate identification is the town of Togba in the Tagant. The name Togba, however, has no etymological link with Tarra; it was apparently not a walled city as was Tarra; it was not east-northeast of Hodges' location; and it was far too small to be considered a large town, with a granary capable of storing only 20–30 tons of grain and thus capable of supporting only a very modest population. The principal reason that McDougall rejects the identification of Tarra with Jarra is that she finds Hodges' location of Jarra in the "Ye Moores Countrey" very problematic. Hodges probably meant that the town was within the hassani field of influence, particularly during the dry season, when it was possible for desert warriors to penetrate into the savanna lands. As is indicated above in the text of this chapter, the town of Jarra had fallen under desert domination by the time of Mungo Park's journey in the late eighteenth century.

14. Curtin, *Economic Change*, vol. 1, 53.

15. ANF C^6 9, Memoire concernant l'elevation d'un fort dans le pays de Foute Riviere du Senegal, 7 avril 1726, Demion. The survival rate of children as young as six or seven on a trans-Saharan caravan may have been considerably lower than that of older children. The Moroccan preference for children might explain how Black Africans became sufficiently socialized to be incorporated into the sultan's slave armies.

16. ANF C^6 10, Rapport du fort Saint Joseph en Galam, 7 mars 1731, par M. Begue (?—name imperfectly legible).

17. Boyer, *Un peuple*, 40.

18. Mungo Park, *Travels in the Interior Districts of Africa: Performed under the Direction and Patronage of the African Association, in the Years 1795, 1796, and 1799* (reprint: London, 1910), 84.

19. Interviews with Sidi Abdallah Wuld Zayn, 11 February 1982, at Tidjikja, 1; and Muhammad Wuld Imam Wuld Abd al-Qadir, 12 February 1982, at Tidjikja, 1. Although the Idaw Ali foundation story collected by the historian Abdallah Wuld Youba Wuld Khalifa holds that there were no people in the area of Tidjikja when the Idaw Ali founded their town, with the exception of some Ulad Talha (a fraction of the Idaw Ish), etymological confusion over the meaning of the term "Tidjikja" strongly suggests earlier habitation. Wuld Khalifa suggests three different roots for the term: one in Hassaniyya ("the well of the herds"), one in Berber ("the flowers of millet"), and yet another in Azayr whose meaning is lost (see Abdallah Ould Youba Ould Khalifa, "Les aspects économiques et sociaux de l'Oued Tijigja: De la fondation du ksar à l'independance" [unpublished thèse de doctorat, Université de Paris I, 1990–91], 225–228; for his discussion of the foundation myths of Tidjikja, 239).

20. There is some dispute about the foundation date for Rashid. Pierre Amilhat dates the founding of Rashid to 1722 or 1723 (Amilhat, "Petite chronique," 63 and 116). E. Ann McDougall, following Charles Toupet and Ahmed Lamine ech-Chenguiti, gives the date as 1765 (McDougall, "The Economics of Islam in the Southern Sahara: The Rise of the Kunta Clan," *Asian and African Studies* 20 (1986), 53, footnote 20). At any event, the settlement of Rashid seems to have been part of a larger pattern of the establishment of a substantial Kunta presence in the Tagant and the Hawd. According to an oral account, other Kunta groups (for example, the Ulad Busaif in the Aftut and

the Ulad Sidi Haiballah in the Tamurt en Naaj) had established zones of grazing along these south-central and southeastern regions even before the settlement at Rashid (interview with Sidina Wuld Hamid Zayn, 14 February 1982, at Rashid, 8).

21. Interview with Khalifa Wuld Jarullah, 9 February 1982, at Mudjeria, 9.

22. Amilhat, "Petite chronique," 117.

23. According to Idaw al-Hajj oral tradition: "This war is said to have had a secret cause. The Kunta and the Idaw al-Hajj had beaten an army from Shinqiti which had arrived on donkeys. A man from Shinqiti, a certain Wuld Razga of the Idaw Ali, went to Mecca to ask Allah to bring about a war between the inhabitants of Wadan. And this was done" (interview with Abdallahi Wuld Yaya Buya, 24 April 1981, at Wadan, 1). This story, of course, emphasizes the power of the shaykh to intervene with the divine, attributing causation and divine sanction. The fact that donkeys were used is additional evidence of the more humid environment of the late eighteenth century compared with more recent times. Unfortunately, neither the wars nor the Idaw al-Hajj exodus can be dated exactly. Sidi Mahmud was a contemporary and friend of Muhammad Wuld Muhammad Shayn, the emir of the Tagant (Idaw Ish), who exercised his rule from 1788 to 1822 (Amilhat, "Petite chronique," 68–69).

24. Anne Raffenel, *Voyage dans l'Afrique occidentale* (Paris, 1846), 254.

25. Greater population densities also meant, among other things, new possibilities for more elaborate political structures. This may explain, in part, why an "emirate" began to form in the Adrar in the late eighteenth century.

26. "Al-aysh" is used here as a generic term. For specific preparations, see Mokhtar Ould Hamidoun, *Précis sur la Mauritanie*, IFAN-Mauritanie (Saint-Louis du Sénégal, 1952), 55–56.

27. This higher protein yield was due to the incomplete arrays of amino acids in both milk and sorghum that, when combined, complemented each other (see Frances Moore Lappé, *Diet for a Small Planet* [New York, 1975], particularly parts 1 and 2).

28. Stone, "The Journey of Cornelius Hodges," 92.

29. Xavier Guillard, "Un commerce introuvable: L'or dans les transactions sénégambiennes du XVIe au XVIIIe siècle," in *Contributions à l'histoire du Sénégal*. Cahiers du Centre de recherches africaines no. 5 (Paris, 1987), 61, tableau 3: "Variations de la parité sel/mil en Galam de 1700 à 1736." These price observations refer to crystal salt brought upriver to trade for grain. The fluctuations in price were attributed to mediocre grain harvests or to the Moors' flooding of the savanna grain markets with desert salt.

30. Park, *Travels*, 43.

31. As the Soninke proverb puts it: "When a Soninke is hungry, a Bidan is dead."

32. On vundi, interviews with Allahi Wuld Ba Hamid, 19 December 1981, at Nema, 3–4; with Bati Wuld Mbuya, 20 December 1981, at Walata, 1–2; and with Muhammad Wuld Imam Wuld Abd al-Qadir, 12 February 1982, at Tidjikja, 6–7.

33. Park, *Travels*, 116.

34. On the Bidan tent, see Johannes Nicolaisen, *Ecology and Culture of the Pastoral Tuareg with Particular Reference to the Tuareg of Ahaggar and Ayr* (Copenhagen, 1963), 293.

35. Interview with Ahmad Abd al-Rahman, 19 January 1981, at Shinqiti, 6–7.

36. This description of side panels is not mentioned by M. Bourrel in his "Voyage dans le pays des maures brakna (rive droite du Sénégal, juin–oct. 1861)," *Revue maritime et coloniale* (sept. 1861), 529. This may indicate that cloth side panels were not in use throughout the western Sahara in the mid-nineteenth century. Their use may have been most prevalent in the plateau regions and in the Hawd, regions which were in more direct contact with the cloth markets of western Mali.

The major innovation in the Bidan tent since the colonial conquest has been an interior ceiling cover of brightly colored cotton panels, which, in addition to providing more insulation, lends visual relief from the wearying sameness of the colors of the surrounding desert.

In addition to the khayma, the Bidan use a barrel-vaulted tent called a *benié*. A benié is a less-noble dwelling than a khayma, and it is used by haratin and slaves as a principal tent, or by Bidan as an adjunct to their main tent. This benié may be an older, Berber style of tent (see Nicolaisen, *Ecology and Culture*, 293; and Toupet, *La sédentarisation des nomades*, 212).

37. The definitive collection of the early Arabic sources is Levtzion and Hopkins (eds.), *Corpus.*

In recent years, E. Ann McDougall has undertaken extensive research on the role of salt in the western Sahara (see E. Ann McDougall, "Salts of the Western Sahara: Myths, Mysteries, and Historical Significance," *IJAHS* 23, no. 2 [1990], 231–257; E. Ann McDougall, "The Ijil Salt Industry: Its Role in the Precolonial Economy of the Western Sudan" [unpublished Ph.D. thesis, University of Birmingham, England, 1980], 51–60; E. Ann McDougall, "The Sahara Reconsidered: Pastoralism, Politics, and Salt from the Ninth through the Twelfth Centuries," *African Economic History* 12 [1983], 263–286; E. Ann McDougall, "Salt, Saharans, and the Trans-Saharan Slave Trade: Nineteenth Century Developments," in Elizabeth Savage [ed.], *The Human Commodity. Perspectives on the Trans-Saharan Slave Trade* [London, 1992], 61–88).

In analyzing the early Arabic sources on the salt trade, McDougall has argued the case that the Ijil salt deposit was in production centuries before the first positive identification of the mine by name in the early sixteenth century (McDougall, "Salts of the Western Sahara," 243–247). More exact identification of saline deposits under exploitation in the western Sahara generally becomes possible only with the availability of Portuguese accounts beginning in the early era of European maritime expansion. Fifteenth-century sources noted salt pits and lakes in the western Sahara; an early sixteenth-century account identified the rock salt mine at Ijil by name; seventeenth-century Brandenburg sources indicate an important export of crystal salt from a deposit near Arguin (Valentim Fernandes, *Description de la côte d'Afrique de Ceuta au Sénégal* [1506–1507], ed. and trans. P. de Cenival and Théodore Monod [Paris, 1938], 78–79; Gerald Roe Crone [ed. and trans.], *The Voyages of Cadamosto and Other Documents on Western Africa in the Second Half of the Fifteenth Century* [London, 1937], 21; Adam Jones, *Brandenburg Sources for West African History 1680–1700*, "Document no. 40, 1 October 1685—3 March 1686 Extracts from the Journal of Jan Engelse, Describing the Founding of the Brandenburg Trading Post at Arguin" [Weisbaden, 1985], 120–123).

38. This seems to have been the case, even while European purchases of gold in Asante in the coastal forest zone diverted a large volume of gold far to the south

(Hodgkin, "Social and Political Relations on the Niger Bend in the Seventeenth Century," 375–423; see also Guillard, "Un commerce introuvable," 31–75).

39. For the central Sudan, see Paul E. Lovejoy, *Salt of the Desert Sun* (Cambridge, 1985). In the western sahel, other major concentrations of salt lay along the Atlantic coast. In the twentieth century, a coastal deposit of bitter, poor-quality salt at Nteret in the Trarza was controlled by the emiral family, which left slaves there to dig the salt and a slave or freed slave on site to collect a tax known as *mkubal* from the regional caravanners, who used the salt for their own animals (except horses) or traded the salt south to Waalo and Kajoor or to the southeast. For further details on Nteret, see Capitaine d'Arbaumont, "Le sel en Mauritanie et au Soudan," mémoire no. 1246, 22 juillet 1949, CHEAM, Paris; interview with Muhammad Abdallahi Wuld Askar, 6 January 1981, at Keur Macène, 1–3; interview with Muhammad Ahmad Wuld Mshiykh, 22 February 1981, at Nouakchott, 5; interview with Mokhtar Wuld Hamidun, 17 December 1980, at Nouakchott, 4.

40. McDougall, "The Ijil Salt Industry," 1–12; Philip D. Curtin, *Cross-Cultural Trade in World History* (Cambridge, 1984), 15–37.

41. d'Arbaumont, "Le sel en Mauritanie et au Soudan," 2.

42. Some Kunta elements had earlier travelled east and established themselves along the old royal Saadian route to the Sudan—at Tuat, Gurara, and in the Azawad. There in the west-central Sahara the Kunta produced several holy men of great renown, and the religious prestige of the Kunta, bolstered by their position in the Tuat-Timbuktu trade corridor, drew other groups to them. The Kunta were able to establish their authority over their groups of new talamidh (students) by enforcing the payment of religious tithes and gifts to the Kunta religious leaders (Stewart, *Islam and Social Order*, 112–115; McDougall, "The Ijil Salt Industry," 117–123; McDougall, "The Economics of Islam," 45–60; interviews with Mokhtar Wuld Hamidun, 19 December 1980, 8 and 6 May 1982, at Nouakchott, 10; Baṭrān, "Sidi al-Mukhtar al Kunti and the Recrudescence of Islam," 45).

After their expansion into the western Sahara, the Kunta continued to handle the trade from the salt mines in the central Sahara. The Tawdeni mines lay in an extremely desolate part of the west-central Sahara, where conditions were considerably more arid than in the Adrar. Along the route to Ijil, however, there was adequate pasture for camels, and in the Adrar by the eighteenth century much of the population depended directly or indirectly upon the importation of cereals from the Sudan. As one would expect, this degree of dependence was quite marked compared with that of Tishit and the Tagant plateau region farther to the south. Two Moroccans who were familiar with the trans-Saharan route through the Adrar to Timbuktu credited Wadan with a population of 2,000 souls in 1788 and characterized the environs as sterile. Tishit by contrast had a population of 8,000–10,000 and was a relatively fertile territory capable of growing grain including rice and maize (presumably through oasis irrigation) (Bibliothèque Nationale, Fonds français, MS 6430, II, Venture de Paradis, "Notions sur le Sahara, qui m'ont été données par les nommés Ben Ali, et Abd-ul-Rahman, sujets de Maroc qu etoient à Paris en 1788").

43. D. S. Margoliouth, "Al-Tidjaniya," in H. A. R. Gibb and J. H. Kramer (eds.) *Shorter Encyclopaedia of Islam* (Ithaca, 1953), 593–595.

44. The Walata and Nema chronicles record warfare between the inhabitants of Shinqiti and Wadan in 1742/43 (Paul Marty, "Chronicles de Oualata et de Néma," *Revue des études islamiques* [1927], 353–426 and 531–575).

45. Other terminology is as follows. Caravans returning from Morocco were generally called Al-Akbar, the large or great caravan. Caravans travelling to Saint-Louis or to any point along the Senegal River were called Al-Guareb, the boat caravan. Caravans travelling into Mali or Senegal were called Al-Rafga, which means, simply, "the caravan," (interviews with Abdallahi Wuld Yaya Buya, 24 April 1981, at Wadan, 5; and with Dhabi Wuld Zaydan, 25 April 1981, at Wadan, 6).

46. Interviews with Muhammad Lamin Wuld Hallah, 19 January 1981, at Shinqiti, 10; and with Sidina Wuld Hamid Zayn, 14 February 1982, at Rashid, 3; Léopold Panet, *Première exploration du Sahara occidental: Relation d'un voyage au Maroc, 1850* (reprint: Paris, 1968), 96; d'Arbaumont, "Le sel en Mauritanie et au Soudan," 12–13.

47. Interview with Sidina Wuld Hamid Zayn, 14 February 1982, at Rashid, 7.

48. This particular famine was so severe that a large number of slaves and other persons died of hunger. Again, in A.H. 1281 (1864/65 C.E.), "a lot of slaves died" (Marty, "Chroniques de Oualata et de Néma," 370).

49. Saugnier and Brisson, *Voyages*, 110; Archibald Robbins, *A Journal, Comprising an Account of the Loss of the Brig Commerce of Hartford, Conn.* (Hartford, Conn., 1829), 159.

50. See, for example, the letter from Abdi Wuld Muhammad Wuld Mbuya Hamar to Dah Wuld Muhammad Wuld Mbuya (c. 1875) in the collection of Arabic-language documents photographed by Serge Robert held at the library of the IMRS.

51. Interview with Bati Wuld Mbuya, 20 December 1981, at Walata, 1.

52. Interviews with Didi Wuld Dahan, 14 February 1982, at Rashid, 1–2; and with Mohamdhi Wuld Dahud, 17 February 1982, at Tidjikja, 3; Charles Toupet, "Le ksar de Tichit," *La nature* 3274 (dec. 1959), 536–539.

53. Capt. M. Vincent in 1860 estimated that 20,000 camels took on salt at Ijil on an annual basis (see his "Voyage et expéditions au Sénégal et dans les contrées voisines. Voyage dans l'Adrar et retour à St.-Louis," *Le tour du monde* [1861], 52). In Al-Wasît it was mentioned that 32,000 camels loaded with salt left Shinqiti in a single day for the town of Zara, although this is probably an exaggeration (see Ahmad Baba Miské [ed.], *Al Wasît. Tableau de la Mauritanie au début du XXe siècle* [Paris, 1970], 115; see also the interview with Abdallahi Wuld Yaya Buya, 24 April 1981, at Wadan, 3–4).

54. Interview with Khalifa Wuld Jarullah, 9 February 1982, at Mudjeria, 15.

55. Interviews with Ahmad Abd al-Rahman, 19 January 1981, at Shinqiti, 3–7; and with Al-Hadrami Wuld Ubayd, 23 January 1981, at Atar, 1–2; Albert Leriche, "De l'origine du thé au Maroc et au Sahara," *Bull. IFAN* 15 (1953), 731–736.

56. For an exploration of some of the theoretical problems of multiple currency zones, see James L. A. Webb, Jr., "Toward the Comparative Study of Money: A Reconsideration of West African Currencies and Neoclassical Monetary Concepts," *IJAHS* 15 (1982), 455–466.

57. Interview with Bay Wuld Shaykhna Muhammadi, 20 December 1981, at Walata, 1; Alioun Sal, "Voyage de M. Alioun Sal," 204, footnote 1.

58. Interviews with Mokhtar Wuld Hamidun, 27 April and 6 May 1982, both at Nouakchott, 7 and 9, respectively; Paul Dubie, "La vie materielle des maures," in *Mélanges ethnologiques* (Dakar, 1953), 218.

59. For more on the military violence of the slave trade and its relationship to the desert horse trade, see chapter 4 below.

60. Capt. M. Vincent, "Voyage et expéditions au Sénégal," 493.

61. Richard Roberts, "Ideology, Slavery and Social Formation: The Evolution of Maraka Slavery in the Middle Niger Valley," in Paul E. Lovejoy (ed.), *The Ideology of Slavery in Africa* (Beverly Hills, 1981), 170–199; Richard Roberts, "Production and Reproduction of Warrior States: Segu Bambara and Segu Tukulor, c. 1712–1890," *IJAHS* 13 (1980), 389–419; Richard Roberts, "Long Distance Trade and Production: Sinsani in the Nineteenth Century," *JAH* 21 (1980), 169–188; and Richard Roberts, *Warriors, Merchants, and Slaves. The State and the Economy in the Middle Niger Valley, 1700–1914* (Stanford, 1987).

62. Boyer, *Un peuple*, 39–40.

63. For a variety of observations about violence launched by desert people across the western sahel, see Park, *Travels*, esp. 55–95.

64. James Riley, *Authentic Narrative*, 168.

65. Riley, *Authentic Narrative*, 169, 174.

66. Interviews with Muhammad Laghdaf Wuld Sidi Muhammad, 19 December 1981, at Nema, 4; and with Ahmad Abd al-Rahman, 19 January 1981, at Shinqiti, 10. This might be best understood as a commercial metaphor, emphasizing the large supply of captives and their inexpensiveness rather than an exact description of how this commerce took place.

67. It is not possible, at this time, to estimate the relative contributions to the desert slave trade from the upper Senegal River valley and the Malian savanna. Evidence is fragmentary. But it is clear that at least at times the upper Senegal was a major supply area. In the 1840s, for example, after the ending of the Atlantic slave trade and before the jihad of Al-Hajj Umar Tall, traders from Tishit were said to take many slaves from the upper Senegal to sell into the northern trades (see ANS 2 B 27, Gouverneur au Ministre, 26 février 1848).

68. Ralph Austen, in his recently published article "The Mediterranean Islamic Slave Trade Out of Africa: A Tentative Census," has updated his classic essay "The Trans-Saharan Slave Trade: A Tentative Census," in Henry A. Gemery and Jan S. Hogendorn (eds.), *The Uncommon Market: Essays in the Economic History of the Atlantic Slave Trade* (New York, 1979), 23–72. Austen estimated that only 6 percent of the slaves died en route to Morocco and 10 percent en route to Algeria, owing to the relative ease of reaching the southern Moroccan and Algerian markets from Black Africa compared with the markets of Tunisia and Libya, for which his estimates of slave mortality are 15 and 20 percent, respectively. He makes no estimate of the number of slaves consumed on the Saharan market.

69.   Adjusted numbers of Atlantic and trans-Saharan slave exports from
       below the southeastern desert frontier, 1700–1809

	Atlantic exports	Trans-Saharan exports
1700–1709	1,489	1,824
1710–19	2,429	1,824
1720–29	3,520	1,824
1730–39	3,833	1,824
1740–49	2,345	1,824
1750–59	2,017	1,824
1760–69	1,849	1,824
1770–79	1,639	1,824
1780–89	1,021	1,824
1790–99	1,227	1,824
1800–1809	1,206	1,824

Sources: Tables 3.1 and 3.2 above.

70. In 1980, the population of the Islamic Republic of Mauritania was estimated
to be approximately 1.3 million, of which roughly 25 percent, or 300,000, were Black
African populations (Wolof, Tukulor, Soninke); roughly 30 percent, or 400,000, were
slaves and haratin; and 45 percent, or 600,000, were White. One sociological trend
would suggest that the percentage of slaves and haratin within the total population might
have been higher in the earlier twentieth century: over the course of the twentieth century, some slaves and freed slaves have been able to change their ethnic identity, securing
through intermarriage the status of Black African or White for their offspring, although
it appears that this strategy of relinquishing the burden of an ignoble past has been more
difficult to employ successfully in Mauritania than in Senegal or Mali. On the other
hand, the population groups of slaves, haratin, and Black Africans are documented
to have had higher fertility rates than Whites in the late twentieth century, and this would
suggest that the percentage of slaves and freed slaves within the total population would
have been lower at least in the earlier twentieth century.

71. Abdoulaye Bathily, an historian of precolonial Galam, has estimated that during
the eighteenth century annual averages of 2,500 slaves were sold to the Bidan and 2,500
slaves were shipped into the Atlantic trade from along and below the southeastern frontier. His argument is weakened by the fact that he does not make explicit how he arrived
at his estimate of the number of slaves sold to the desert traders, and he incorrectly
assumes that these desert slaves were destined for use in the gum trade, centered in the
Gibla (and thus there is no estimate of the trans-Saharan slave trade). Bathily has also
proposed that the mortality of slaves in passage to the coast for sale into the Atlantic slave
trade was greatly in excess of the mortality of slaves shipped north for sale to desert
traders, although again he does not make explicit how he arrived at this comparison.
In the absence of empirical data, one might as easily argue that the mortality of slaves
in passage into the desert or across the Sahara was higher that the mortality of slaves
in passage to the coast (see Abdoulaye Bathily, *Les portes de l'or. Le royaume de Galam*

[Sénégal] de l'ère musulmane au temps des négriers [VIIe–XVIIIe siècle] [Paris, 1989], 266–271).

72. Colombani, "Le Guidimaka," 412.

Chapter 4. The Horse and Slave Trade

1. Many authors have assumed, probably correctly, that the principal threat to the imported horses was trypanosomiasis. There were, however, other equine diseases of the savanna, including tetanus, piroplasmosis, typho-malaria, glanders, and lymphangitis, which contributed to the decimation of this horse stock. Surprisingly, even for the indigenous, self-reproducing horse populations of the upper Senegal–Niger basin, in the early twentieth century the average lifespan was a mere eight years. For a discussion of the various maladies which struck horses in the late nineteenth and early twentieth centuries, see Pierre, *L'élevage dans l'A.O.F.*, 235–255; and Meniaud, *Le Haut–Sénégal–Niger*, tome 2, 122–133.

2. The early evidence suggesting trypanosomiasis is as follows. Cadamosto reported that horses imported into the Wolof country between the Senegal and Gambia rivers could not survive "because of the great heat" and because they were afflicted with a disease which made them grow "so fat that . . . they are unable to make water and so burst," according to Robin Law, a description which suggests symptoms caused by *Trypanosoma brucei* (Law, *Horse*, 78).

Inferential evidence may be adduced from climatic change. Over time increasing aridity caused the southward extension of the desert edge. Drier climate meant less underbrush and thus far less favorable conditions for the propagation of the tse-tse fly.

3. Some early writers drew distinctions between Arab and Barbary breeds. Students of the biology of the horse draw no such distinctions, arguing that the Arab and Barbary are one and the same. In this chapter, the terms "Arab" and "Barbary" are used interchangeably. The direct evidence on horse mortality in West Africa before the twentieth century for other than pure Barbary horses is fragmentary and vague (Law, *Horse*, 76–82).

4. See, for example, Carrère and Holle, *De la Sénégambie française*, 74.

5. Robin Law argued that horse breeding was established in Senegambia by the end of the sixteenth century, but he based this argument solely on the fact that the Portuguese stopped importing horses at this time (Law, *Horse*, 29–30 and 49–53).

6. Curtin, *Economic Change*, vol. 1, 222. Curtin noted that high prices were occasionally paid for exceptional animals and likened this to European and American patterns of horse ownership.

7. Among the most influential views has been that of Boubacar Barry, expressed in his study of Waalo before French conquest and in his more recent synthesis of Senegambian history. According to Barry, the trade in horses and in slaves from the Sahara and North Africa was in some measure in competition with the Atlantic trade for slaves until the last quarter of the seventeenth century, when it was eclipsed by the failure of the jihad of Nasir al-Din. For Barry, the failed jihad represented the victory of the desert warriors over the desert clerics. It disrupted the flow of trans-Saharan trade and allowed slaves produced in warfare and in pillage to be funnelled toward entrepôts on the Atlantic coast rather than north to the Maghrib (Barry, *Waalo*, 157–158; and Barry, *La Sénégambie du XVe au XIXe siècle*, passim. See also Jean Suret-Canale, "The

Western Atlantic Coast 1600–1800," in J. F. A. Ajayi and Michael Crowder (eds.), *History of West Africa* [New York, 1972], vol. 1, 387–440; Charles Becker and Victor Martin, "Kayor et Baol: Royaumes sénégalais et traite des esclaves au XVIIIe siècle," *Revue française d'histoire d'Outre-Mer* 62, nos. 226–227 [1975], 270–300).

8. Doutressoule, *L'élevage en A.O.F.*, 238–239.

9. Law, *Horse*, 6–7.

10. Humphrey J. Fisher, " 'He Swalloweth the Ground with Fierceness and Rage': The Horse in the Central Sudan, I. Its Introduction," *JAH* 13 (1972), 369–388, and ". . . II. Its Use," *JAH* 14 (1973), 355–379; Law, *Horse*, passim.

11. Fernandes, *Description*, 71, cited by Boulègue, *Grand Jolof*, 88.

12. Moore, *Travels*, "Translations from Writers," 64, a reproduction of Leo Africanus, *Africa* (London, 1660), Book 6: *Of Numidia*. The English translation is at considerable variance with the more authoritative French translation; compare with Jean-Léon L'Africain, *Description de l'Afrique*, trans. from the Italian by A. Épaulard and annotated by A. Épaulard, Th. Monod, H. Lhote, and R. Mauny (Paris, 1956), tome 2, 433.

13. See the text by Sidi Abdallah b. al-Hajj Ibrahim in H. T. Norris, "The History of Shinqīt, According to the Idaw ʿAlī Tradition," *Bull. IFAN*, série B, 24 (1962), 399.

14. Mission catholique de Saint Joseph de Ngazobil (ed.), *Guide de conversation français-wolof* (reprint: Paris, 1987), 63.

15. Fernandes, *Description*, 71.

16. Crone, *The Voyages of Cadamosto*, 78.

17. Ivana Elbl, "The Horse in Fifteenth Century Senegambia," *IJAHS*, 24, no. 1 (1991), 98–99.

18. Crone, *The Voyages of Cadamosto*, 30, 33, cited in Law, *Horse*, 52–53.

19. Elbl, "Horse," 93.

20. Fernandes, "Description," 7; and Pereira, *Esmeraldo de Situ Orbis*, 51, cited by Law, *Horse*, 11, 52–53. Evidence for the scarcity of horses in the desert itself in the fourteenth century can be found in Ibn Khaldun's *Histoire des Berbères* (Paris, 1968–69), 331–332. In discussing the Berbers of the western Sahara, Ibn Khaldun remarks, "Only a few horses are to be seen amongst them." A passage from this work by Ibn Khaldun appears in Norris, *Arab Conquest*, 28–29. Jean Boulègue has suggested that the figures may refer to larger the Wolof region (see his *Grand Jolof*, 48 and 72–73).

21. Pierre, *L'élevage dans l'A.O.F.*, 56–57. Pierre indicated that there were three types of stirrup found in French West Africa: the Arab stirrup, the Hausa stirrup, and a stirrup used by the horsemen of Macina, which resembled the French military issue. On the introduction of the stirrup to West Africa, see Law, *Horse*, 91.

22. The argument that the large horse cavalries noted by early sixteenth-century Portuguese observers must have been supplied by desert traders first appeared in Webb, "Shifting Sands," 88–91. During the late fifteenth century, Portuguese traders established themselves along the Saharan and Senegambian coasts. These traders were closer to the Atlantic provinces than to the metropolitan center of the empire, and over the course of the century, the local elite traded slaves and local produce to the Portuguese in return for the horses that the Portuguese stabled aboard their ships, and this trade may have helped strengthen the military position of the coastal provinces in relation to the core of the empire (Boulègue, *Grand Jolof*, 155–173). Recently, Ivana Elbl has

argued that this horse trade could not have been decisive in the shift of political power taking place in fifteenth-century Senegambia (Elbl, "Horse," 99–103).

23. Soh, *Chroniques du Fouta sénégalais*, 26.

24. Boulègue, *Grand Jolof*, 155–173, esp. 156–162.

25. Doutressoule, *L'élevage en A.O.F.*, 253, 260.

26. Paul Dubie, "L'élevage en Mauritanie," mémoire no. 561, 17, janvier 1937, CHEAM, Paris. In Dubie's system of categorization the horse of Fuuta was the Mbayar. Pierre identified eight principal "families" of the river horses (Pierre, *L'élevage dans A.O.F.*, 30).

27. A. Cligny, "Faune du Sénégal et de la Casamance," in Dr. Lasnet, A. Cligny, Aug. Chevalier, and Pierre Rambaud, *Une mission au Sénégal* (Paris, 1900), 278–280.

28. Doutressoule, *L'élevage en A.O.F.*, 240. The categorization of the pony herds of Senegambia as discrete from those of western Mali is somewhat contested. Elbl follows Hellmut Epstein's argument in his two-volume work *The Origin of the Domestic Animals of Africa* (New York, 1971) that all the small horses in the western savanna came from the same stock. Epstein in his accomplished survey was, however, simply synthesizing more detailed studies, and for Senegambia and the French Soudan the sources cited are the works of Doutressoule and Pierre, who held that the horse stocks of the Senegambian corridor and the Malian savanna were distinct.

29. ANFSOM, Sénégal II, dossier 2, Notes sur le fleuve et la Colonie du Sénégal recueillies en 1817 et 1818, M. Laplace.

30. Both desert and savanna peoples attached great prestige to the ownership of horses. In the desert, this was most evident in the sale of prized horses. It was common at these sales to record the horses' pedigrees, figured matrilineally, in the bill of sale, and the better horses were so expensive that negotiable shares of ownership rather than the horse itself were sold. Partial ownership might entitle the purchaser to ride the horse into battle or in a raid, and to partial ownership of any ensuing foal. For exceptional horses, a share of one-quarter or one-eighth could sell for as much as 100 milch camels (interviews with Muhammad Ahmad Wuld Mshiykh, 22 February 1981, at Nouakchott, 3–4; and with Mokhtar Wuld Hamidun, 19 December 1980, at Nouakchott, 4; Law, *Horse*, 46). At these prices, the best horses were clearly a luxury and an emblem of nobility. But in principle, even at exhorbitant prices, the skillful warrior could recoup his investment in one or more successful raids.

31. Pierre, *L'élevage dans A.O.F.*, 35; Doutressoule, *L'élevage en A.O.F.*, 243. By the twentieth century, the Moors of the Hawd were selling colts to the Black African communities in the upper river region. Farther east, the pattern was reversed. Sedentary communities sold horses to the Twareg, Tukulor, and Fuulbe, who raised few horses of their own (Doutressoule, *L'élevage au Soudan français*, 220).

32. Marcel Leger and L. Teppaz, "Le 'Horse-Sickness' au Sénégal et au Soudan français," *BCEHSAOF* 5 (1922), 219–240.

33. Pierre, *L'élevage dans A.O.F.*, 80, 84.

34. Moore, *Travels*, 63. Horses from the Cape Verde Islands were exported to Senegambia from the late fifteenth century into the first half of the eighteenth century (see Brooks, *Landlords and Strangers*, chapter 10). But there is little or no evidence of the number of horses exported from the islands, and the trade was apparently a minor

one (see T. Bentley Duncan, *Atlantic Islands. Madeira, the Azores, and the Cape Verdes in Seventeenth-Century Commerce and Navigation* [Chicago, 1972]).

35. Curtin, *Economic Change*, vol. 1, 222; Brooks, *Western Africa to c. 1860 A.D.*, 82–83. In fact, Moore's account does not indicate if it was almost exclusively stallions that desert suppliers provided for the southern trades, only that the Wolof supplied stallions to their clients to the south.

36. Mission catholique, *Guide de la conversation*, 63.

37. In the mid-twentieth century, Doutressoule noted that, among sedentary peoples in French West Africa, stallions were reserved principally for the chiefs (Doutressoule, *L'élevage en A.O.F.*, 65).

38. Chambonneau in Ritchie, "Deux textes," 332–333; Barbot, *A Description of the Coasts of North and South Guinea*, 38, 57–58; La Courbe, *Premier voiage*, 126; Labat, *Nouvelle relation*, vol. 3, 68, 235.

39. Interview with Mokhtar Wuld Hamidun, 19 December 1980, at Nouakchott, 4. Harry T. Norris, summarizing the account of Muhammad al-Yadali, also writes that, during Shurbubba, both zwaya and hassani rode on horseback (*Arab Conquest*, 36).

40. Stone, "The Journey of Cornelius Hodges," 93.

41. La Courbe, *Premier voiage*, 146: "Ceux cy [the desert people] portent les cheveux longs et tressez par derrière, s'habillent a la mainiere des negres, vont toujours teste nuë et sont armez de longues piques et de sagayes; ils sont grand maquignons et nourissent beaucoup de chevaux qu'ils troquent avec les negres contre les captifs qu'ils vont apres vendre bien loing dans les terres."

42. Chambonneau, in Ritchie, "Deux textes," 332.

43. Labat, *Nouvelle relation*, vol. 3, 234–235. Gaspard Théodore Mollien noted that the royal stable of the damel of Kajoor was stocked with pure Arab horses at the time of his travels in 1818 (Mollien, *L'Afrique occidentale en 1818* [reprint: Paris, 1967], 40–41).

44. Barbot, *A Description of the Coasts of North and South Guinea*, 39. Somewhat surprisingly, the substitute for the horse in use in Jolof was the camel, also imported from the desert. Unfortunately, Europeans rarely commented upon this trade in camels.

45. " 'Brak' est des plus puissants du pays, il peut avoir 4 à 5000 hommes capables de porter les armes dont près de la moitié en cavalerie," Bibliothèque Nationale (Paris), Fonds français, MS 9557, 30 novembre 1762, Mémoire sur les mines de Bambouc, cited by Barry, *Waalo*, 202. This was, of course, near the end of Waalo's regional military presence. Additional confirmation of the rise of regional military capability of the state of Kajoor may be found in a British document from the early nineteenth century. In 1811 Lieutenant Colonel Maxwell, the lieutenant governor of Senegal, related to a commission of inquiry that the present damel was not as powerful as his predecessors, but that the damel could still field 5,000 or 6,000 men in an emergency. One of the damel's predecessors was said to have brought 5,000 cavalrymen to bear upon a rebellion in Kajoor, presumably in the eighteenth century, although no date was mentioned (PRO, CO 267/29, 1 January 1811, Answers to the Questions proposed to Lt. Colonel Maxwell, Lieutenant Governor of Senegal and Goree by his Majesty's Commissioner for Investigating the Forts and Settlements in Africa).

46. Bibliothèque Nationale (Paris), Fonds français, MS 9557, 30 novembre 1762, Mémoire sur les mines de Bambouc.

47. Park, *Travels*, 119–120.

48. Park, *Travels*, 102.

49. "Besides the cattle, which constitute the chief wealth of the Foulahs, they possess some excellent horses, the breed of which seems to be a mixture of the Arabian with the original African" (Park, *Travels*, 46).

50. Park, *Travels*, 79.

51. Chambonneau, "Relation du Sieur Chambonneau," 309. The trading relationship between the desert and savanna peoples was symbolized by the ritual exchange of a horse for a slave that took place between the Trarza emir and the brak of Waalo (La Courbe, *Premier voiage*, 154–155).

52. "A French ship, that happened to be then in the road of Porto Dali, on board which was Caseneuve [John Casseneuve, a former shipmate of Barbot], who gave this account, bought 80 slaves of the prisoners of war. The rest of the prisoners the usurper sent towards the country of the Moors, to be exchanged for horses, to mount his cavalry" (Barbot, *Description of the Coasts of North and South Guinea*, 425). For further evidence on this conflict between Bawol and Kajoor not mentioned in oral tradition, see Victor Martin and Charles Becker, "Les Teeñ du Baol: Essai de chronologie," *Bull. IFAN*, série B, 38 (1976), 479.

53. ANF C^6 11, Rapport du 14 juin 1736, David Langlois de la Bord. (?—name only marginally legible): "Il s'en fait peu de Captifs en Riviere cette année, Brak a fait 5 a 6 efforts qui n'ont *rien* produit, la plus part a passé entre les mains des Maures pour leur chevaux; nous voulons tenter cette haute saison le Commerce des Chevaux avec St. Yago et pour peu qu'il apporte de profit, nous le continuerons pour le partager après des Roys negres avec les Maures." The French company aborted this initiative, fearing that it was simply a means to increase opportunities for private trade. French traders, however, were bringing at least a few horses from the Cape Verde Islands into southern Senegambia destined for the damel and teeñ at this time (see ANF C^6 10, lettre de avril 1731, Comptoir d'Albreda).

54. By way of negative evidence, Doumet makes no mention of any horse breeding by the damel. His description of the damel's military force for state warfare indicates that a military draft in Kajoor would produce a diverse group of poorly armed conscripts on foot and that the damel, by contrast, would be looked after by his cavalry, with himself at the head (although the cavalry stayed at the rear of aggressive actions) (Doumet, "Mémoire," 39).

55. This route was used annually by the Idaw al-Hajj (who were known to the Europeans as the Darmankour), the zwaya grouping which dominated the trade in gum arabic. According to an account of the 1780s, the Idaw al-Hajj moved north to the Atlas Mountains from August to December or January. Gum arabic moved north on these caravans, which likely indicates that it was a ballast trade; the slaves who made the trans-Saharan journey did so on foot (see ANFSOM, DFC Sénégal, carton 82, no. 75, Mémoire sur la traite de la gomme au Sénégal, août 1783, M. Eyries). The author of this mémoire reported that the marabouts (Darmankour) went to the mountains of Morocco each year after the gum trade. Another report of yearly expeditions to Marrakech by the Darmankour, as well as their detailed coastal route, was published by

M. le Baron Roger, in "Résultat des questions adressés au nommé MBouia, marabout maure, de Tischit, et à un nègre de Walet, qui l'accompagnait," *Recueil des voyages et de mémoires de la Société de géographie de Paris* 2 (1825), 60–61. An anonymous author of a French mémoire dated 1803 indicates that a desert route from Senegal to Morocco was open and in frequent use (ANFSOM, DFC Sénégal, carton 83, no. 105, Des peuples qui habitent les Côtes du Sénégal et les bords de ce Fleuve, Des Royaumes sur la côte de Gorée, Cayor, Baol, Sin et Salum). Further evidence of a coastal route from Wad Nun south to Senegal may be adduced from Auguste Beaumier, "Le choléra au Maroc, sa marche au Sahara jusqu'au Sénégal, en 1868," *BSG*, 6e série, 3 (1872), 303–304; for evidence of a route from Wad Nun down the Atlantic coast and across the desert frontier, see the account of the Moroccan merchant Sidi Hamet in Riley, *Authentic Narrative*, 160–163.

    56. Doumet, "Mémoire," 44.

    57. James F. Searing has estimated that in the period 1760–90 approximately 200–300 slaves per annum were exported from the region of the lower Senegal, through Saint-Louis and Gorée. The lower Senegal, for Searing, would include Waalo, Kajoor, and Bawol (Searing, *West African Slavery*, chapter 2). The estimate of 100–200 slaves exported per annum from Kajoor is my own, based on Searing's figures.

    58. Doumet, "Mémoire," 44. According to a mid-nineteenth-century account, the damel received two-thirds of the plunder from pillaging, but only half of that which was gathered in warfare (Carrère and Holle, *De la Sénégambie française*, 72).

    59. As the French administrator Jean-Gabriel Pelletan observed: "The blacks value highly the horses of the Moors. I have seen black Princes give up to ten or twelve slaves for a horse, and make a raid expressly for the purpose of paying for the horse" (Jean-Gabriel Pelletan, *Mémoire sur la colonie française du Sénégal et ses dépendances* [Paris, An IX], 55, footnote 11).

    Thus through political violence, guns and horses found their way into the hands of slave warriors and nobles throughout Kajoor. According to a mid-nineteenth-century account, the damel exercised a sovereign control over the supply of gunpowder, doling it out to his subordinates just before political violence was to be initiated (Carrère and Holle, *De la Sénégambie française*, 71–72).

    60. Interviews with Mokhtar Wuld Hamidun, 11 April 1981, at Nouakchott, 1–2; and with Ahmad Baba Wuld Shaykh, March 1982, at Nouakchott, 17–18; Marty, *L'émirat des Trarzas*, 80. The period of years during which this right to pillage (with the accord of the damel) was in force is not known.

    61. See, for example, Lamiral, *L'Affrique*, 237–265; ANFSOM, DFC Sénégal, carton 82, no. 82, Côtes d'Afrique, Traite des noires, Par M. de la Jaille, 2 juin 1784, folios 27–28.

    62. "Ils sont marchands; ils exécutent de très-grands voyages dans le Zaarha qu'ils traversent dans toutes les directions; ils font des pillages d'esclaves sur les bords du Sénégal et du Niger, et ils vont les vendre sur les rivages de la mer Méditerranée . . ." (Golberry, *Fragmens d'un voyage*, 301–302).

    63. "Le Roy Dámel me dit un Jour Chez Luy a Chajort [Kajoor]. Je Luy disois tu ne fais plus autant de Captifs que Les autres fois, il me fit repondre Je Vais t'Expliquer pourquoy; C'est qu'apresent Je reçois pour un ceque Je reçevois autrefois pour Cinq. . . il me fit entrevoir que nous Etions des duppes de payer les Captifs 120 Barres

qui est le prix actuel Toutes ces raisons se Passerent Chez Luy Dans Un Voyage que je fit en 1775. Lieu situé a 60 Lieues Du Bord de La Mer" (ANF C⁶ 17, 12 mai 1781, Capitaine Guiof). A similar view of the behavior of the damel can be found in ANF, C⁶ 18, Remarques, Etat et aperçu des esclaves qui peuvent retirer les Nations de l'Europe de la Côte Occidentale d'Afrique, 1783 (unsigned): ". . . celui de Cayor ne se déterminant à faire des pillages que quand il en a de grands besoins."

64. Pruneau de Pommegorge, *Description de la Nigritie*, 16–17.

65. As the brak of Waalo wrote plaintively to the French governor Schmaltz: "aidez nous à acheter des chevaux dont nous avons grand besoin pour repousser les attaques de l'enemi, car vous devez le savoir, il nous est impossible de rien faire sans chevaux" (see the letter from the brak to Schmaltz quoted in ANFSOM, Sénégal II, dossier 2, Mémoire Sur l'Etat de la Colonie du Sénégal jusqu'au dix septembre 1819, P. Valentin, habitant de St. Louis [Sénégal]).

66. PRO, CO 267/29, Answers to the Questions proposed to Lieutenant Colonel Maxwell, . . . 1 January 1811.

67. Mollien noted that, when he visited Ganjool, the town had the appearance of having been recently pillaged. The huts were burned and much of the population had fled. The damel of Kajoor had come demanding that the village offer up 83 slaves to him (Mollien, *L'Afrique occidentale en 1818*, 39–40, 48, and for the quoted and translated text, 76).

68. Mollien, *L'Afrique occidentale en 1818*, 75; ANFSOM, DFC Sénégal, carton 83, no. 147, Rapport de M. de Mackou, . . . 16 mars 1820.

69. ANFSOM, Sénégal XIII, dossier 32, P. Bancal et al., "Deuxième pétition adressée à M. le Gouverneur du Sénégal," Saint-Louis, 11 février 1854, 6. Even by the mid-nineteenth century, full-sized horses, used by the chiefs, continued to be led into Kajoor by desert traders (Carrère and Holle, *De la Sénégambie française*, 74).

70. According to this account, ". . . the people of El Giblah [Gibla] sometimes go far to the southward . . . whence the Arabs obtain black slaves, in the proportion of 3 or 4 slaves for each horse. These slaves are sold again at Wadnoon [Wad Nun]" (Major Rennell, "An Account of the Captivity of Alexander Scott among the Wandering Arabs of the Great African Desert," *Edinburgh Philosophical Journal* 4, no. 8 [1821], 229).

71. Faidherbe, "Renseignements géographiques sur la partie du Sahara," 146–147. The other 75 horses were likely also sold for Black slaves, but these slaves do not figure in the calculations which follow.

72. Louis Faidherbe, "Les Berbères et les Arabes des bords du Sénégal," *BSG*, 4e série (fév. 1854), 109. Although beyond the scope of the present chapter, it is important to note that religious teachings were sometimes exported south along with the horses, and at least on one occasion the horse and slave trade was linked to the establishment of a religious center in Senegambia. In one celebrated instance Shaykh Bu Naama, the father of Shaykh Bu Kunta, went to Kajoor in the early nineteenth century to sell horses on the order of Shaykh Sidi Lamin, a disciple of Shaykh Sidi al-Mokhtar al-Kunti. According to Kunta tradition, Shaykh Bu Naama was shocked at the spiritual condition of the people of Kajoor and received permission to settle there. And thus the desert horse trade figured in the establishment of the Bu Kunta settlement near Thiès

in southern Kajoor (see Paul Marty, "Le groupement de Bou Kounta," *RMM* 31 [1915–16], 415).

73. See chapter 5 below.

74. Louis Faidherbe, "Renseignements géographiques sur la partie du Sahara," 143–144: "Les Marabouts du Tiris, de l'Adrar et des Trarzas viennent acheter des esclaves dans le Cayor en échange de leurs chevaux et les emmènent au Maroc. Cette immigration, qui tend à dépeupler notre colonie, cessera bientôt, grâce à notre situation au Sénégal."

75. ANFSOM, Sénégal II, dossier 4, La Colonie du Sénégal et des dépendances, A. Vallon, 12 août 1861.

76. Doutressoule, *L'élevage au Soudan français*, 220; Doutressoule, *L'élevage en A.O.F.*, 64, 245.

77. Robinson, *Chiefs and Clerics*, 122.

78. ANS 1 G 310, Kayes, Renseignements historiques, géographiques, et économiques sur le cercle de Kayes, 30 mars 1904. I would like to thank François Manchuelle for communicating this reference to me.

79. Pierre, *L'élevage dans A.O.F.*, 79–80.

Chapter 5. The Trade in Gum Arabic

1. For early map examples, see "Carte de la Coste de l'Afrique depuis le cap Blanc jusques a la Riviere de Gambie, presenté a Mon. de Pontchartrain ministre et secretaire destat, controlleur general des finances" (no cartographer attributed, n.d. [c. 1690s]); "Carte très détaillée des Païs compris puis le Cap Blanc jusqua la Rivière de Sierelione" (no cartographer attributed, n.d. [c. 1692]); "Partie Occidentale de l'Afrique ou se trouve La Barbarie . . ." by N. de Fer (n.d.); and "Partie de l'Afrique Françoise ou Du Senegal" by Martin Jean (1729), all in the collection of the Bibliothèque Nationale, Paris. By the 1740s, the gum groves were no longer depicted close to the St. John River. See, for example, "La Guinee de meme que la plus grande Partie du Pais des Negres . . ." by Heritiers d'Homan (1743).

By the late eighteenth century, European observers regularly wrote about three distinct "forests" of gum trees: Sahel, Fatack, and Hiebar, which were supposed to be exploited by the Trarza, Brakna, and Idaw al-Hajj, respectively (see for example, Golberry, *Fragmens d'un voyage*, 193).

2. For a chronology of the possession of Arguin as a trading post by various European powers, see Oßwald, *Handelsstädte*, 470–471.

At least by the second decade of the nineteenth century, trade to Portendick would carry the risk of the loss of the entire gum caravans when they tried to traverse the sand desert (ANS 2 B 4, Note en réponse à deux dépêches Ministerielles de l'19 et 29 septembre 1819 Sur un Article du Journal le Pilote concernant l'ouverture de communication par terre avec l'interieur de l'Afrique et Sur l'Assertion que des tentatives sont projetées par les Anglais pour le transport de leurs marchandises à Tombouctou par l'intermediaire des Maures qui habitent les environs du Sénégal). The view that climatic change had rendered the regions of Arguin and Portendick uninhabitable was also shared by the British governor of the Gambia (NAG 1:4, Governor Randall to the governor of Senegal and dependencies, 12 August 1834).

3. By the end of the twentieth century, many of the gum groves of the southern Sahara have succumbed to drought. For a technical study which surveys the status of the gum trees and explores possibilities for their regeneration, see Bureau Courtoy, *Étude de régénération des gommeraies mauritaniennes. Rapport final* (Bruxelles, 1981).

4. United Nations Sudano-Sahelian Office, *The Gum Arabic Market and the Development of Production* (Geneva and New York, 1983), 16–17.

5. Shoberl, *World in Miniature*, vol. 1, 60–62; Ogilby, *Africa*, 308.

6. Interview with Mokhtar Wuld Hamidun, 25 June 1981, at Nouakchott, 6.

7. For information on the harvesting of gum arabic, see James L. A. Webb, Jr., "The Trade in Gum Arabic: Prelude to French Conquest in Senegal," *JAH* 26 (1985), 153–155. But note that the arboreal-yield figure of 800 grams of gum proposed by Gaston Donnet in the late nineteenth century and cited in this passage is unrealistically high (Webb, "Trade in Gum Arabic," 155, note 17). A mid-twentieth-century study of gum arabic in Mauritania indicated that productive trees yielded on the order of 100 grams of gum per year and that truly productive trees made up only 25 percent or so of the arboreal population; per-hectare yields fluctuated between one and three kilograms (Mohammed Salem Ould M'Khaitirat, "La gomme en Mauritanie," ENFOM mémoire no. 109 [1952], 24, 29).

8. Ould M'Khaitirat, "La gomme en Mauritanie," 65–71; Ould Hamidoun, *Précis sur la Mauritanie*, 14–15; Shoberl, *World in Miniature*, vol. 1, 76.

9. Vitorino Magalhães Godinho, *L'économie de l'empire portugais au XVe et XVIe siècles* (Paris, 1969), 102.

10. P. Bellouard, "La gomme arabique en A.O.F.," *Bois et fôrets des tropiques* 1, no. 9 (1947), 3–18; Curtin, *Economic Change*, vol. 1, 215–216; Golberry, *Travels in Africa*, vol. 1, 144; L'Abbé Demanet, *Nouvelle histoire de l'Afrique française* (Paris, 1767), 54; Wolf-Dieter Seiwert, *Maurische Chronik* (Munich, 1988), 76–77; Carson I. A. Ritchie, "Impressions of Senegal in the Seventeenth Century," *African Studies* 26, no. 2 (1967), 68.

There were other minor uses of gum arabic: for example, Europeans in Saint-Louis du Sénégal used gum arabic as a fumigant. As Pierre Labarthe explained, "Pour purifier l'air pendant la mauvaise saison au Sénégal, on brûle de la gomme arabique dans les casernes et les hôpitaux. Trois onces suffisent par fumigation; mais il est nécessaire que la gomme soit pulvérisée et qu'elle brûle sur un feu très vif. Il faut que les portes et fenêtres de chaque chambre soient fermées jusqu'à ce que la gomme soit tout-à-fait consumée" (Pierre Labarthe, *Voyage au Sénégal pendant les années 1784 et 1785, d'après les memoires de Lajaille* [Paris, 1802], 176).

11. Great Britain, House of Commons, "Report from the Select Committees respecting the importation of gum senega," dated 18 February 1752 in *Journals of the House of Commons*, vol. 26, 441–444. The colors red, purple, blue, yellow were mentioned.

12. The first references to calico printing works are in 1648 in Marseilles. In 1676, the first clear mention of a calico printing industry in both London and Amsterdam appears.

The new engraved copper plates allowed for patterns of up to more than one meter square (S. D. Chapman and S. Chassagne, *European Textile Printers in the Eighteenth*

Century [London, 1981], 6–7, 13. I would like to thank Richard Roberts for bringing this reference to my attention).

13. The data for Table 5.2 were communicated to me directly by Marion Johnson. She was of the opinion that gum sandrake came exclusively from North Africa, and that perhaps the gum arabic did too (personal communication, 5 January 1984). Some gun arabic came from the gum groves in the Gibla, and some came from the sahelian region near Timbuktu. Some gum exported from North Africa was thus brought by caravan across the western Sahara. Gum sandrake does appear to have been North African in origin. For an introduction to the data set, see Marion Johnson, *Anglo-African Trade in the Eighteenth Century*, ed. J. T. Lindblad and Robert Ross, Intercontinenta no. 15 (Centre for the History of European Expansion: Leiden, 1990).

Additional data on "Senegal gum" for the period 1833–38 have been published (see Great Britain, House of Commons, "An Account of All Senegal Gum Imported into Great Britain from 1833–1838," *Sessional Papers*, 1839 (218) XLVI, 389).

14. This periodization of growth in gum exports is based primarily upon Curtin, *Economic Change*, vol. 1, 216–217, but differs with regard to the timing of the first doubling. Curtin locates the first doubling of exports in the 1820s on the basis of export figures from Saint-Louis (compiled in *Economic Change*, vol. 2, 64–65). The period before 1820 is problematic in any case because data are scarce, but the earlier doubling of exports (in the 1780s) is supported directly in ANFSOM, DFC Sénégal, carton 82, no. 70, Traite de la gomme, Rivière du Sénégal, mars 1783, M. Eyries, which includes an estimate of the annual gum trade at 1,200 tons, and indirectly by two estimates c. 1803 of annual European gum consumption at 1,000 tons, in ANFSOM, DFC Sénégal, carton 83, no. 105, Des peuples qui habitent les cotes du Sénégal et les bords de ce fleuve, Des royaumes sur la cote de Gorée, Cayor, Baol, Sin, et Salum, 1803 (unsigned); and P. Herbin de Halle (ed.), *Statistique générale et particulière de la France et de ses colonies*, vol. 7 (Paris, An XII), 98.

During the French occupation of Saint-Louis (1800–1808), exports from the mouth of the Senegal averaged 894 tons per year (excluding trade from the coastal ports) but dropped off considerably during the British occupation from 1809 to 1816 (ANFSOM, DFC Sénégal, carton 83, no. 115, Rapport sur les établissements français d'Afrique, 8 juillet 1817, M. Schmaltz). An estimate of 1,000 tons annual production is found in PRO, CO 267/29, Answers to the Questions proposed to Lieutenant Colonel Maxwell, Lieutenant Governor of Senegal and Goree, by His Majesty's Commissioners for Investigating the Forts and Settlements in Africa, 1 January 1811.

15. ANFSOM, Sénégal XIII, dossier 33, M. le Ministre de la marine et des colonies à M. l'Amiral, 3 decembre 1830. This correspondence summarizes a letter concerning dextrine and gum arabic written by the Comité consultatif des arts et manufactures.

16. See Adel Amin Beshai, *Export Performance and Economic Development in Sudan, 1900–67* (London, 1976), 99–102.

17. ANF C^6 18, Mémoire sur le commerce du Sénégal, février 1783.

18. ANS 2 B 15, Gouverneur au Ministre, 26 juillet 1832; also Marty, "Tentatives commerciales anglaises," 278. This was approximately the same percentage of gum retained for use in France in the 1780s (see above: Table 5.1. European gum consumption).

19. E. Bouët-Willaumez, *Commerce et traite des noirs aux côtes occidentales d'Afrique* (Paris, 1846), 42.

20. For some suggestions about the analysis of the behavior of commodity and other moneys in West Africa, see Webb, "Toward the Comparative Study of Money," 455–466. For a sketch of gum arabic's "peculiar history" in the mercantile system of Great Britain, see Adam Smith, *An Inquiry into the Nature and Causes of the Wealth of Nations*, Modern Library Edition, (New York, 1965), 622.

21. Curtin, *Economic Change*, vol. 2, 96–97, Table A15.5; 98–99, Table A16.5.

22. Golberry characterized the profits of the gum trade as enormous as late as the 1780s (Golberry, *Fragmens d'un voyage*, 254).

23. On the gum wars, see Delcourt, *La France et les établissements français*.

24. Golberry estimated the value of the slave trade at 2,640,000 francs and the gum trade at 3,000,000 francs (Golberry, *Travels in Africa*, vol. 2, 25). J. A. Le Brasseur estimated the annual value of the gum trade (in the 1770s) at 6,000,000 pounds sterling. (J. A. Le Brasseur, "Détails historiques," 89).

25. Bidan nobles cultivate obesity in their women and find it erotic. At one level, obesity can be understood as conspicuous consumption, an expression of the nobles' power to command food resources in the scarcity-stricken desert environment. Although detrimental to the health of Bidan women, obesity may have helped to secure a stable source of nourishment for their young children, in the limited sense that malnourished women cannot lactate properly and that obesity was insurance against malnourishment. Obesity is also thought to induce menses at an early age.

26. Ahmad Baba Wuld Shaykh has suggested that the Europeans encountered by Al-Amin at Gibraltar may have been English (interview with Ahmad Baba Wuld Shaykh, March 1982, at Nouakchott, 1). F. Y. Gaby makes mention of an island in the Senegal River known as the island of the English, indicating an early English presence in the river trade (see his *Relation de la négritie* [Paris, 1689], 82; cited by P. Cultru in his edited publication of La Courbe's *Premier voiage*, 24, note 1).

27. This is likely an anachronism which refers to *nvadha*: the ceremonial firing of guns for an emir or important personage. The first execution of the salute is not known. I have not discovered any archival evidence that nvadha was performed for the Idaw al-Hajj.

28. Interviews with Ahmad Baba Wuld Shaykh, March 1982, at Nouakchott, 1–2. An abbreviated telling of the story of the beginning of the gum trade appears in Ould Hamidoun, *Précis sur la Mauritanie*, 14–15.

The integrity of this oral tradition, collected in the 1980s, is supported by the oral tradition of the beginnings of the gum trade, which is mentioned, if only briefly, in a French translation of a letter from the shamsh Muhammad Aghrabat to the king of France in 1819. Therein, the shamsh notes that it was the Darmankour who began the gum trade with the Europeans, and that the chief at that time was Eliman Ould Nagib (Al-Amin Wuld Najib) and that he, Muhammad Aghrabat, had succeeded Ould Najib (see ANFSOM, Sénégal IV, dossier 16, no. G, Lettre de Schems Mohamed Karabat à Louis 18, 1819).

29. See Seiwert, *Maurische Chronik*, 76–77.

30. This title was also variously rendered as chamchi, chamchy, chems, chemchi, chemchy, sems, schems, or shams by the Europeans. The direct descendants of

Mokhtar Wuld al-Amin Wuld Najib exercised this position of authority until the military invasion by the French in the early twentieth century, which altered the balance of powers in the Trarza.

31. La Courbe, *Premier voiage*, 127.

32. La Courbe, *Premier voiage*, 175; Barry, *Waalo*, 170.

33. "Extrait de la traitte de gomme, de captifs et autres marchandises, faitte à l'Escale du Désert par le Sieur Jean DEMION, commis, depuis le 3 avril jusqu'au 1724," published by Delcourt in his *La France et les établissements français*, 382–387. See also Labat, *Nouvelle relation*, vol. 3, 122–123.

34. ANFSOM, DFC Sénégal, carton 82, no. 70, Traite de la gomme, Rivière du Sénégal, mars 1783, M. Eyries; and ANFSOM, DFC Sénégal, carton 82, no. 75, Mémoire sur la traite de la gomme au Sénégal, août 1783, M. Eyries.

35. By at least the 1780s the Idaw al-Hajj not only dominated the gum markets in the lower Senegal but were active in the coastal trade at Portendick as well (Norris, "Znaga Islam," 499; ANFSOM, DFC Sénégal, carton 82, no. 75, Mémoire sur la traite de la gomme au Sénégal, août 1783, M. Eyries).

36. Herbin de Halle, *Statistique générale et particulière*, 112–113.

37. ANF C⁶ 20, Le Citoyen Jacques Louis Lecuyer, vous présentes différentes Opérations qui peuvent être intéressantes à la République, et qui peuvent faire beaucoup de mal au commerce de nos Ennemies, 1791; ANF C⁶ 20, Sénégal, Bureau des Ports, M. Eyries, 1791.

38. Sometimes these northern warriors penetrated into the Trarza region and disrupted the gum harvest itself. In 1741, for example, zwaya were attacked in their gum forests; their goods were stolen, their camels were stolen, and some of them were killed (ANF C⁶ 12, Rapport au Senegal, 30 juillet 1741).

39. ANF C⁶ 13, lettre de 24 février 1752, de la Brüe et al. The authors of this document also noted that the poor and the marabouts of all the Moor tribes had been roughed up and beaten by the more powerful of the nation because the chief was a weak man. This had discouraged those who used to work the gum groves. See also ANF C⁶ 14, Mémoire, 3 mai 1754 (n.a.).

40. Pruneau de Pommegorge, for example, judged that the British presence at Portendick caused the price of gum arabic to increase by 1,200–1,500 percent (Pruneau de Pommegorge, *Description de la Nigritie*, 267).

41. The desert traders also offered to open up a trade in gold (ANF C⁶ 15, lettre de 6 juin 1765, Saluigny (?—name only marginally legible); ANF C⁶ 15, Voyage fait chez Damel Roy des Cayors Sur les Ordres de N. Le Chev. Des Mesnages, 1765.

42. ANF C⁶ 16, Observations sur l'isle de Gorée Données par Monsieur de Rocheblave Gouverneur à Monsieur de Boniface son successeur, 1773.

43. ANF C⁶ 16, Copie de la Lettre de Cidy Moctar Roy More au gouvernement de Gorée, Reponses des M. de Boniface au Roy More.

44. ANF C⁶ 17, Lettre de 23 juin 1778, M. Armeny de Paradis.

45. ANF C⁶ 16, Gorée, on a rendu compte a monsieur de tout ce que M. Boniface a ecrit au sujet de la traite de l'abbé Demanet on va mettre sous les yeux de Mgr le détail dans le quel cet ecclesiastique est entré a ce sujet; PRO, CO 268/4, Governor O'Hara to the secretary of state, 24 January 1774.

46. ANFSOM, DFC Sénégal, carton 82, no. 82, Côtes d'Afrique, Traite des noirs, M. de la Jaille, 2 juin 1784, folios 14–17.

47. Georges Hardy, *La mise en valeur du Sénégal de 1817 à 1854* (Paris, 1921); Barry, *Waalo*, esp. 237–258.

48. Bouët-Willaumez, *Commerce et traite*, 12–13.

49. Bouët-Willaumez, *Commerce et traite*, 12–13; ANFSOM, Sénégal XIII, dossier 25, État des batiments en traite de gomme aux trois escales de 1829 à 1839 inclusivement"; ANS 2 B 17, Gouverneur au Ministre, 12 août 1839; Dezert, "Du commerce de la gomme au Sénégal en 1841," *Annales maritimes et coloniales* 75, 2e série, 1 (partie non-officielle) (1841), 944.

50. On laptots, see John Malcolm Thompson, "In Dubious Service: The Recruitment and Stabilization of West African Maritime Labor by the French Colonial Military, 1659–1900" (unpublished Ph.D. dissertation, University of Minnesota, 1989); and Edouard François Manchuelle, "Background to Black African Emigration to France: The Labor Migrations of the Soninke, 1848–1987" (unpublished Ph.D. dissertation, University of California, Santa Barbara, 1987). For a general social history of Saint-Louis, see Michael David Marcson, "European-African Interaction in the Precolonial Period: Saint Louis, Senegal, 1758–1854" (unpublished Ph.D. dissertation, Princeton University, 1976); see also Curtin, *Economic Change*, vol. 1, 112–121, 195–196. For a discussion of the problems which resulted from the abolition of slavery in Senegal, see François Renault, *L'abolition de l'esclavage au Sénégal* (Paris, 1972).

51. Anne Raffenel, *Nouveau voyage dans les pays des nègres* (Paris, 1856), tome 2, 173.

52. Curtin, *Economic Change*, vol. 1, 132.

53. ANS Q 18, Du commerce en général et de la traite en particulier, point vital de la colonie du Sénégal, L'agent du service de l'interieur De Monguers, found attached to a letter dated 2 octobre 1838 from De Monguers to the French governor; ANS Q 19, Marchands à M. le Gouverneur, 17 mars 1842; ANFSOM, Sénégal XIII, dossier 24, Conseil privé, Proçès-verbal de la séance, 3 septembre 1833.

54. ANS Q 22, Rapport à Monsieur le Gouverneur du Sénégal et dépendances, sur la traite de la gomme à l'escale du Coq en 1851; ANS Q 22, Ed. Dudra, Le directeur des affaires exterieures, au Gouverneur, 12 octobre 1850; ANS Q 22, M. Valantin, Maire de Saint-Louis, au Gouverneur, 30 novembre 1850, "Considerations générales sur le commerce au Sénégal."

55. The petite traite varied from year to year with a low of perhaps 12–15 tons and a high of 400 tons (M. Caillé, "Tableau statistique du fleuve Sénégal, dressé, en 1843, par M. le Commandant Caillé," *RC*, 2e série, 6 [1851], 8; ANS 2 B 18, Gouverneur au Ministre, 15 avril 1841).

56. ANS Q 22, Rapport à M. le Gouverneur du Sénégal et dépendances, sur la traite de la gomme à l'escale du Coq en 1851; ANS Q 2, Copie des titres constitutifs des avances de coutumes anterieurs à la promulgation de l'ordonnance royale du 15 novembre 1842, folios 1–6.

57. ANS Q 2, Traité conclu entre Chems, chef des Darmancours et . . . le Gouverneur du Sénégal, 1 mars 1847.

58. ANS Q 2, Copie des titres constitutifs . . . , folios 1–6.

59. The prices of gum at the escales present problems for several reasons. The price of gum at a given escale fluctuated considerably in the course of a gum season—at times up to 100 percent—and no series of figures were kept indicating the quantity of gum sold at a given price. In addition, the very nature of the gum trade, with its hidden expenses and gifts, makes the estimation of prices a tricky business. For these reasons the figures assembled by M. Marcson in his doctoral dissertation ("European-African Interaction in the Precolonial Period," Table 1. Gum-Guinée Exchange Rates and Volume in Metric Tons, 159–160) cannot be accepted as anything other than suggestive of prices at the escales and may contain substantial error. Marcson assumes erroneously that the traitants' transportation and maintenance costs were negligible.

60. ANS 2 B 15, Gouverneur au Ministre, 3 septembre 1832. The governor reported in 1832 that a compromise was passed each year but that the traitants violated the agreement at the escales. A compromise was in effect for a good part of the gum season, although not necessarily at all three escales, in 1833, 1837, 1838, 1839, and 1841.

61. ANS Q 18, Traitants au Gouverneur, 1 mai 1837, Escale du Désert; ANS Q 18, Rapport à M. le Gouverneur du Sénégal, par l'officier commandant de l'escale des Darmankours, sur le service des escales, 19 août 1841; ANS 2 B 22, Gouverneur au Ministre, 12 août 1843.

62. ANS 2 B 4, Note en réponse à deux dépêches ministerielles du 19 et 29 septembre 1819 Sur un Article du Journal Le Pilote concernant l'ouverture de communication par terre avec l'interieur de l'Afrique . . . , 5 janvier 1820; ANFSOM, DFC Sénégal, carton 83, no. 147, Rapport de M. Mackau sur les établissements du Sénégal, 16 mars 1820; NAG 1:4, Governor Randall to the governor of Senegal and dependencies, 12 August 1834; Anonymous, "The Gum-trade Renewed at Portendick, with the Moors of the Desert Sahaara," *Royal Gazette; and Sierra Leone Advertiser* 3, no. 155 (19 May 1821), and 3, no. 156 (26 May 1821).

63. John M. Gray, *A History of the Gambia* (Cambridge, 1940), 406–410.

64. ANS 2 B 6, Gouverneur au Ministre, 8 août 1821.

65. Marty, "Tentatives commerciales anglaises," 293.

66. For early views of this crisis, see ANS Q 18, Traitants au Gouverneur, 1 mai 1837; ANS 2 B 17, Gouverneur au Ministre, 20 mars 1837.

67. ANS Q 18, Du commerce en général et de la traite. . .

68. ANS 2 B 17, Gouverneur au Ministre, 26 août 1839.

69. Dezert, "Du commerce de la gomme," 942; Raffenel, *Nouveau voyage*, tome 2, 93.

70. ANS 2 B 18, Gouverneur au Ministre, 9 août 1840.

71. ANS Q 18, Statuts d'un société projetée sous le titre de Société commerciale de la traite de la gomme, 1840; ANS 2 B 18, Gouverneur au Ministre, 11 septembre 1841; ANS 2 B 20, Gouverneur au Ministre, 15 juin 1842.

The idea of the privileged gum association had been proposed earlier, in 1834. It was basically an effort to limit competition between traitants at the escales while maintaining a price floor for guinée, thereby protecting the traitants from the market power of the zwaya and ensuring the négociants' profits. Warfare between the French and the Trarza in 1834 prevented the idea from being implemented, but the following year the Société pour la traite de la gomme was established. The society was to trade collectively, using only 20 boats (10 to stay anchored at the escales and 10 to haul gum from the escales to Saint-Louis), and it was to be liquidated one month after the end of the gum season. Records are inadequate to trace whatever success (if any) this association enjoyed in 1835. It was not proposed again in 1836.

In 1841, the gum merchants were reluctant to sell their gum because of rumors that the compromise would be repealed. When it became apparent that this would not happen, gum flowed to the escales, but it was too late in the season to trade it all (ANS Q 18, Rapport à M. le Gouverneur du Sénégal, par l'officier Commandant l'escale des Darmankours, sur le service des escales, 19 août 1841).

72. Négociants, patented merchants, and traitants bought shares at 5,000 francs each (a number of individuals could purchase collectively a single share) and subscribed shares on behalf of debtor traitants. Creditors were to have access to 75 percent of any profits realized by the traitant debtors, and those who subscribed shares for traitant debtors were to have the right of first claim on up to 50 percent of any profits realized by their subscribed debtors (ANS Q 19, Ministère de la marine et des colonies, Projet d'arret, Pour instituer à Saint Louis une société pour la traite de la gomme [1842]).

73. Anne Raffenel, "De la colonie du Sénégal. Études historiques et commerciales," *RC*, 2e série, 5 (1850), 235; ANS Q 2, Service des escales, Traite en 1843.

An attempt was made during the 1840 trade season to collect the outstanding debt of the Bidan, but the zwaya seem to have circumvented this initiative without difficulty (ANS Q 1, Extrait de l'arrêt du 23 decembre 1840).

74. ANS 2 B 26, Gouverneur au Ministre, 4 février 1847; ANFSOM, Sénégal XIII, dossier 26, V. Dep. au Gouverneur du Sénégal, no. 442, 22 novembre 1847.

75. See Table 5.9 below.

76. ANFSOM, Sénégal XIII, dossier 28, Marine et colonies, Commission syndicale, Traite des gommes au Sénégal pendant l'année 1848; ANFSOM, Sénégal XIII, dossier 28, Marine et colonies, Sénégal et dépendances, Résultat de la traite des gommes pour l'année 1847.

77. ANS Q 1, Arrêt du 9 mai 1849, Fait au palais de l'Elysée national. This liberalization of trade was a consequence of the Revolution of 1848.

78. ANS Q 22, Considérations générales sur le commerce du Sénégal, 30 novembre 1850, M. Valantin; ANS Q 22, Rapport à M. le Gouverneur du Sénégal et dépendances sur la traite de la gomme à l'escale du Coq en 1851 (unsigned); ANS Q 22, Traitants au Gouverneur, no. 94, 24 janvier 1853.

79. ANS Q 1, Arrêt de 22 janvier 1853. The intent of the order may not have been to unloose the commercial houses for direct competition with the traitants, but this was its effect. The important phrase in this order was the following: ". . . sans préjudice du droit reservé aux dites négociants ou marchands de se rendre et de séjourner aux escales, ou d'envoyer et d'y faire séjourner leurs commis pendant la durée de la traite."

80. Manchuelle, "Background to Black African Emigration to France," 99–100.

81. Interview with Muhammad Salim Wuld Baggah, 28 December 1980, at Mederdhra, 8; ANS Q 22, Procès-verbal, Séance du 4 juillet 1858; Anonymous, "Sénégal. Affaires politiques, militaires, et commerciales," 414, 424.

82. This tax was proposed in 1854 (ANS Q 1, Arrêt du 27 mai 1854). For more on the relations between the merchants and the colonial administration, see Leland C. Barrows, "The Merchants and General Faidherbe: Aspects of French Expansion in Senegal in the 1850s," *Revue française d'histoire d'outre-mer* 61 (1974), 247–249.

83. Margaret O. McLane, "Commercial Rivalries and French Policy on the Senegal River, 1831–1858," *African Economic History* 15 (1986), 60, endnote 17; France, Ministère des colonies, *Statistiques coloniales* (1832–).

References

Archival and Library Collections

For this book I have consulted primary documents authored by travellers, merchants, and administrators which survive in the Archives Nationales de France (Paris), the Archives Nationales de France, Section Outre-Mer (Aix-en-Provence), the Bibliothèque Nationale (Paris), the Archives Nationales du Sénégal (Dakar), the Public Record Office (London), and the National Archives of the Gambia (Banjul). Below is a listing of the most important series. Citations of individual documents are made in the notes to the text.

ANF: Archives Nationales de France (Paris).

    Séries Coloniales, C^6. Dossiers 1–35.

ANFSOM: Archives Nationales de France, Section Outre-Mer (Aix-en-Provence).

    Dépôt de Fortifications des Colonies. Sénégal cartons 82–84.

    Dépôt de Fortifications des Colonies. Gorée cartons 75–76.

    Sénégal et dépendances II. Dossiers 2–4.

    Sénégal et dépendances IV. Dossiers 14, 16, 19, and 45.

    Sénégal et dépendances IX. Dossier 26.

    Sénégal et dépendances XIII. Dossiers 24–33, 40.

    Sénégal et dépendances XVI. Dossier 41.

ANS: Archives Nationales du Sénégal (Dakar).

    Sous-série B. Correspondance du départ du Gouverneur au Ministre de la Marine.

        Dossiers 2 B 1–32.

    Sous-série Q. Traite de la gomme et économie du Sénégal. Dossiers 1, 2, 15, 16, 18–23.

Bibliothèque Nationale (Paris).

    Manuscript Collection.

NAG: National Archives of the Gambia (Banjul).

    Reference I. Dossiers 1, 2, 4, 7–9.

PRO: Public Record Office (London).

    Colonial Office Series.

        267: Dossiers 1–6, 8, 10–16, 18, 29, 33, 45.

        268: Dossiers 4, 7.

    Treasury Series.

        64: Dossier 376 B.

        70: Dossier 37.

Historical maps were consulted at the Royal Geographical Society and the British Museum Library in London, the Library of Congress in Washington, D.C., and the Bibliothèque Nationale in Paris.

Oral Interviews

All interviews were tape-recorded in Hassaniyya and later transcribed in French unless otherwise noted. Tribal affiliation of the individual is noted in parentheses. Interviews and the French transcriptions dated from December 1980 to June 1981 were accomplished with the assistance of Muhammad al-Mami Wuld al-Mokhtar (Ulad Barikallah); those dated from December 1981 to May 1982 were accomplished with the assistance of Muhammad Wuld Muhammad Fall Wuld Emir (Tendgha). In the end notes, the number located at the end of each interview citation refers to the page number of its transcript.

Abdallahi Wuld Yaya Buya (Idaw al-Hajj). Interviewed on 24 April 1981 at Wadan.

Ahmad Abd al-Rahman (Laghlal). Interviewed on 19–20 January 1981 at Shinqiti.

Ahmad Baba Wuld Shaykh (Idaw al-Hajj). Interviewed during March 1982 at Nouakchott (not taped).

Allahi Wuld Ba Hamid (Shorfa). Interviewed on 19 December 1981 at Nema.

Ali Wuld Mumin (Limhajib). Interviewed on 18 December 1981 at Nema.

Baba Hamad Wuld Hama Lamin (Kunta). Interviewed on 14 February 1982 at Rashid.

Bati Wuld Mbuya (Limhajib). Interviewed on 20 December 1981 at Walata.

Bay Wuld Shaykhna Muhammadi (Shorfa). Interviewed on 20 December 1981 at Walata.

Dhabi Wuld Zaydan (Shorfa). Interviewed on 25 April 1981 at Wadan.

Didi Wuld Dahan (Kunta). Interviewed on 14 February 1982 at Rashid.

Hadrami Wuld Ubayd (Smassid). Interviewed on 23 January 1981 at Atar.

Khalifa Wuld Jarullah (Ahl Shaykh Wuld Maynu). Interviewed on 9 February 1982 at Mudjeria.

Mohamdi Wuld Dahud (Idaw Ali). Interviewed on 17 February 1982 at Tidjikja.

Mokhtar Wuld Hamidun (Ulad Dayman), a former researcher at the Institut Mauritanien de Recherche Scientifique at Nouakchott and the author of historical works in both French and Arabic. Interviewed from December 1980 through May 1982 at Nouakchott.

Muhammad Abdallahi Wuld Askar (Lagtal). Interviewed on 6 January 1981 in the region of Keur Macène in the lower Trarza.

Muhammad Ahmad Wuld Mshiykh (Ulad Daylim). Interviewed on 22 February 1981 at Nouakchott.

Muhammad Laghdaf Wuld Sidi Muhammad (Ulad Mbarak). Interviewed on 19 December 1981 at Nema.

Muhammad Lamin Wuld Hallah (Laghlal). Interviewed on 19 January 1981 at Shinqiti.

Muhammad Salim Wuld Baggah (Idawdinyucub), the author of a history of the Trarza emirate ("Kitabu tarikhi biladi trarza" [manuscript]). Interviewed on 28–29 December 1980 at Medherdhra.

Muhammad Wuld Imam Wuld Abd al-Qadir (Idaw Ali). Interviewed on 12 February 1982 at Tidjikja.

Shaykh Brahim Wuld Biddah (Idagjmolla). Interviewed on 26 February 1981 at Kaédi.

Shaykh Wuld Banda, a Wolof tributary of the Ahl Tunsi (Ulad Daman), was chief of the village of Keur Macène. Interviewed on 6 January 1981 in the village of Keur Macène.

Sidi Abdallah Wuld Zayn (Idaw Ali). Interviewed on 11 February 1982 at Tidjikja.

Sidina Wuld Hamid Zayn, a freed slave of the Kunta of Rashid. Interviewed on 14 February 1982 at Rashid.

Theses, Dissertations, and Unpublished Manuscripts

Baṭrān, ʿAbdal-ʿAziz ʿAbdallah. "Sidi al-Mukhtar al Kunti and the Recrudescence of Islam in the Western Sahara and the Middle Niger, c. 1750–1811." Unpublished Ph.D. thesis, University of Birmingham, England, 1971.

Boulègue, Jean. "La traite, l'état, l'Islam. Les royaumes Wolof du quinzième aux dix-huitième siècle." Unpublished doctorat d'État, Université de Paris I, 1986.

Brown, William Allen. "The Caliphate of Hamdullahi, ca. 1818–1864; a Study in African History and Tradition." Unpublished Ph.D. dissertation, University of Wisconsin, 1969.

Colvin, Lucie Ann Gallistel. "Kajor and Its Diplomatic Relations with Saint-Louis du Senegal, 1763–1861." Unpublished Ph.D. dissertation, Columbia University, 1972.

d'Arbaumont, Capitaine. "Le sel en Mauritanie et au Soudan." Mémoire no. 1246, 22 juillet 1949. CHEAM, Paris.

Dubie, Paul. "L'élevage en Mauritanie." Mémoire no. 561, janvier 1937. CHEAM, Paris.

Elbl, Ivana. "Portuguese Trade with West Africa, 1440–1520." Unpublished Ph.D. dissertation, University of Toronto, 1986.

Hanson, John Henry. "Umarian Karta (West Africa) in the Late Nineteenth Century." Unpublished Ph.D. dissertation, Michigan State University, 1989.

Hodgkin, Elizabeth. "Social and Political Relations on the Niger Bend in the Seventeenth Century." Unpublished Ph.D. thesis, Centre for West African Studies, University of Birmingham, 1987.

Johnson, James Philip. "The Almamate of Futa Toro, 1770–1836: A Political History." Unpublished Ph.D. dissertation, University of Michigan, 1974.

Kane, Mouhamed Moustapha. "A History of Fuuta Tooro, 1890–1920s: Senegal under Colonial Rule. The Protectorate." Unpublished Ph.D. dissertation, Michigan State University, 1987.

McDougall, Elizabeth Ann. "The Ijil Salt Industry: Its Role in the Precolonial Economy of the Western Sudan." Unpublished Ph.D. thesis, University of Birmingham, England, 1980.

Manchuelle, Edouard François. "Background to Black African Emigration to France: The Labor Migrations of the Soninke, 1848–1987." Unpublished Ph.D. dissertation, University of California, Santa Barbara, 1987.

Marcson, Michael David. "European-African Interaction in the Precolonial Period: Saint Louis, Senegal, 1758–1854." Unpublished Ph.D. dissertation, Princeton University, 1976.

Nicholson, Sharon Elaine. "A Climatic Chronology for Africa: Synthesis of Geological, Historical, and Meteorological Information and Data." Unpublished Ph.D. dissertation, University of Wisconsin, Madison, 1976.

Ould Ahmedou, Mohamed Saïd. "L'insertion bidhane dans le commerce sénégalais: l'exemple des Idaou el-Hajj." Unpublished mémoire de D.E.A., Université de Dakar, 1985-86.

Ould Ahmedou, Mohamed Saïd. "Le Trarza, et ses relations commerciales avec la colonie du Sénégal de 1858 à 1904." Unpublished mémoire de maitrise, Université de Dakar, 1984-85.

Ould Cheikh, Abd el Wedoud. "Nomadisme, Islam et pouvoir politique dans la société maure précoloniale (XI-XIXe siècles)." Unpublished thèse de doctorat de sociologie, Université de Paris V, 1985.

Ould Khalifa, Abdallah Ould Youba. "Les aspects économiques et sociaux de l'Oued Tijigja: De la fondation du ksar à l'indépendance." Unpublished thèse de doctorat, Université de Paris I, 1990-91.

Ould Mohamed El Abd, El-Keihil. "Colonisation française et mutations sociales en Mauritanie: Cas de l'esclavage en milieu maure 1900-1960." Unpublished mémoire de maitrise, Université de Nouakchott, 1986-87.

Ould M'Khaitirat, Mohamed Salem. "La gomme en Mauritanie." ENFOM mémoire no. 109, 1952.

Palmier, Sous Lieutenant. "Les Idouaich." 1956. Filed with the colonial political documents in the Mauritanian government archives.

Sall, Ibrahima Abou. "Les relations entre les Haal-Pulaaren et les Braknas, 1850-1903." Unpublished mémoire de maitrise, Université de Dakar, 1977-78.

Sy, Hammady Samba. "Secheresses et famines en Mauritanie de 1900 à nos jours (1984)." Unpublished thèse de troisième cycle, Université de Rouen, 1986-87.

Thompson, John Malcolm. "In Dubious Service: The Recruitment and Stabilization of West African Maritime Labor by the French Colonial Military, 1659-1900." Unpublished Ph.D. dissertation, University of Minnesota, 1989.

Webb, Alison Jones. "Nineteenth Century Slavery in the Mauritanian Sahara." Unpublished M.A. thesis, The Johns Hopkins University, 1984.

Webb, James L. A., Jr. "Shifting Sands: An Economic History of the Mauritanian Sahara, 1500-1850." Unpublished Ph.D. dissertation, The Johns Hopkins University, 1984.

Bibliographies

Becker, Charles, and Mamadou Diouf. "Une bibliographie des travaux universitaires. Histoire de la Sénégambie." *Journal des africanistes* 58, no. 2 (1988), 163-209.

Brasseur, Paule. *Bibliographie générale du Mali.* Dakar, 1964.

Calderini, Simonetta, Delia Cortese, and James L. A. Webb, Jr. *Mauritania.* World Bibliographical Series no. 141. Oxford, 1992.

Funck-Bretano, C. "Bibliographie du Sahara occidental." *Hespéris* 11 (1930), 203-296.

Joucla, E., and G. Grandidier. *Bibliographie de l'Afrique occidentale française.* Paris, 1937.

Lebel, A. Roland. *L'Afrique occidentale dans la littérature française (depuis 1870)*. Paris, 1925.

Porges, Laurence. *Bibliographie des régions du Sénégal*. Dakar, 1957.

Toupet, Charles. "Orientation bibliographique sur la Mauritanie." *Bull. IFAN*, série B, 21 (1959), 201–239, and série B, 24 (1962), 594–613.

Books and Articles

Abitbol, Michel. "Le Maroc et le commerce trans-saharien du XVII siècle au début du XIX siècle." *Revue de l'occident musulman et de la Méditerranée* 30 (1980), 5–19.

Abitbol, Michel. *Tombouctou au milieu du XVIIIe siècle d'après la Chronique de Mawlāy al-Qāsim B. Mawlāy Sulaymān*. Paris, 1982.

Abitbol, Michel. *Tombouctou et les Arma*. Paris, 1979.

Abun-Nasr, Jamil M. *History of the Maghrib*. Cambridge, 1975.

Adams, Robert. *The Narrative of Robert Adams*. Boston, 1817.

Adanson, Michel. *Histoire naturelle du Sénégal. Coquillages. Avec la relation abrégée d'un voyage fait en ce pays, pendant les années 1749, 50, 51, 52 & 53*. Paris, 1757.

Adanson, Michel. "Mémoires d'Adanson sur le Sénégal et l'île de Gorée." Presented and commented upon by Charles Becker and V. Martin in *Bull. IFAN*, série B, 42 (1980), 722–779.

Adanson, Michel. "Sur les gommiers du Sénégal . . ." In *Mémoire de l'académie des sciences*, 9–10, 20–25. Paris, 1778.

Adanson, Michel. "Sur le gommier rouge . . ." In *Mémoire de l'académie des sciences*, 36–38. Paris, 1773.

Adanson, Michel. "A Voyage to Senegal, the Isle of Goree, and the River Gambia." In John Pinkerton (ed.), *A General Collection of the Best and Most Interesting Voyages and Travels in All Parts of the World*, vol. 16, 598–673. London, 1814.

Ahmed Ennasiri Esslaoui [Es Slawi]. *Kitab Elistiqsa* [Kitab al-Istiqsa], trans. Eugène Fumey in *Archives marocaines*, tomes 9 and 10. Paris, 1906.

Al-Bakrī, Abū ʿUbayd ʿAbd Allāh ibn ʿAbd al-ʿAzīz. *Description de l'Afrique septentrionale*, trans. Mac Guckin de Slane. Paris, 1965.

Albert, P. "Les tribus du sahel atlantique: Sous, Tazeroualt, Dra, Oued Noun, Seguiet el Hamra." *Bulletin de la Société de géographie et archaeologie d'Oran* (avr.–juin 1906), 116–132.

Al-Chennāfī, Muhammad, and H. T. Norris. "How the Hassaniyya Vernacular of Mauritania Supplanted Zenaga." *Maghreb Review* 6, nos. 5–6 (Sept.–Dec. 1981), 77–78.

Al-Ifrānī, Muḥammad al-Saghīr ibn Muḥammad. *Nozhet-Elhâdi. Histoire de la Dynastie Saadienne au Maroc (1511–1670)*, ed. and trans. O. Houdas. Paris, 1889.

Allan, J. A. (ed.), *The Sahara. Ecological Change and Early Economic History.* London, 1981.

Almada, André Álvares de. *Brief Treatise on the Rivers of Guinea*, trans. P. E. H. Hair, with notes by P. E. H. Hair and Jean Boulègue. 2 vols. Department of History, University of Liverpool, 1984.

Alpern, Stanley B. "The Introduction of Crops into West Africa in Precolonial Times." *History in Africa* 19 (1992), 13–43.

Al-Tilimsani, ᶜAbd Allah ibn Qasim. "Itineraire de Tlemcen à Timbectou donné par Abdallah ben Cassem de Tlemcen et suivi par lui jusqu'à Saglia Hamra; communiqué par M. Ch. Courault." *Revue de l'orient*, nouvelle série, 4 (1856), 331–333.

Al-Zayānī, Abū al-Ḳāsim Ahmad ibn ᶜAli ibn Ibrāhim. *Le Maroc de 1631 à 1812*, ed. and trans. O. Houdas. Paris, 1886.

Amilhat, Pierre. "Petite chronique des Id ou Aich, heritiers guerriers des Almoravides sahariens." *Revue des études islamiques* 11 (1937), 41–130.

Ancelle, Jean (ed.). *Les explorations au Sénégal et dans les contrées voisines depuis l'antiquité jusqu'au nos jours*. Paris, 1886.

Anderson, Alexander. *An Authentic Narrative of the Loss of the American Brig Commerce*. New York, 1817.

Anonymous. *Deuxième petition adressé à M. le Gouverneur du Sénégal*. Bordeaux, 1854.

Anonymous. "The Gum-Trade Renewed at Portendic, with the Moors of the Desert Sahaara [sic]." *Royal Gazette; and Sierra Leone Advertiser* 3, no. 155 (19 May 1821) and 3, no. 156 (26 May 1821).

Anonymous. *Mémoire adressé à M. le Ministre de la marine et des colonies par les négociants, marchands, détaillants et habitants indigènes de Saint-Louis*. Bordeaux, 1842.

Anonymous. *Petition adressé à M. le Gouverneur du Sénégal*. Bordeaux, 1852.

Anonymous. "Sénégal. Affaires politiques." *RC*, 2e série, 18 (1857), 123–139.

Anonymous. "Sénégal. Affaires politiques du fleuve." *RC*, 2e série, 19 (1858), 410–448, and 20 (1858), 235–248, 406–409, 665–679.

Anonymous. "Sénégal. Affaires politiques et militaires." *RC*, 2e série, 15 (1856), 194–195, 413–424, 568–578, and 16 (1856), 171–173, 342–354.

Anonymous. *Le Sénégal et les guinées de Pondicherry. Note presenté à la commission superièure des colonies par les négociants sénégalais*. Bordeaux, 1879.

Anonymous. "Sénégal. Situation politique de cette colonie." *RC*, 2e série, 17 (1857), 168–174.

Anonymous. "Statistique coloniale. Traite des gommes au Sénégal." *RC*, 1e série, 3 (1844), 238–242.

Anonymous. "Traite des gommes au Sénégal en 1845." *RC*, 1e série, 8 (1846), 116–119.

Anthonioz, Raphaelle. "Les Imraguen, pecheurs nomades de Mauritanie, II." *Bull. IFAN*, série B, 30 (1968), 751–768.

Astley, Thomas. *A New General Collection of Voyages and Travels*. 4 vols. London, 1745.

Aubinieres, Lieut. "Notes sur le sahel mauritanien," *BCEHSAOF* 18 (1935), 381–392.

Audibert. "Rapport adressé à la commission de l'exposition universelle réunie à Saint-Louis (Sénégal)." *RC*, 2e série, 20 (1855), 117–211.

Austen, Ralph A. *African Economic History*. New York, 1987.

Austen, Ralph. "The Mediterranean Islamic Slave Trade Out of Africa: A Tentative Census." In Elizabeth Savage (ed.), *The Human Commodity. Perspectives on the Trans-Saharan Slave Trade*, 214–248. London, 1992.

Austen, Ralph A. "The Trans-Saharan Slave Trade: A Tentative Census." In Henry A. Gemery and Jan S. Hogendorn (eds.), *The Uncommon Market: Essays in the Economic History of the Atlantic Slave Trade*, 23–72. New York, 1979.

Azan, H. "Notice sur le Oualo." *Revue maritime et coloniale* 10 (1864), 327–360 and 466–498.

Ba, Ahmadou Mahmadou. "Chronologie de l'Adrar." *BCEHSAOF, Renseignements coloniaux* 43 (1933), 36–38.

Ba, Ahmadou Mahmadou. "Contribution à l'histoire des Regueibat." *BCEHSAOF, Renseignements coloniaux* 43 (1933), 333–359.

Ba, Ahmadou Mahmadou. "L'émirat de l'Adrar mauritanien de 1872 à 1908." *Bulletin de la Société de géographie et d'archaeologie d'Oran*, 55e année, 53 (mars 1932), 85–119, and (juin 1932), 263–298.

Ba, Oumar. "Des sites historiques au Brakna (Mauritanie)." *Notes africaines*, no. 118 (1968), 60–62.

Ba, Oumar. "Des sites historiques au Tagant (Mauritanie)," *Journal de la Société des africanistes* 17, no. 2 (1973), 245–246.

Ba, Oumar. "Des sites historiques au Tagant (Mauritanie)," *Notes africaines*, no. 138 (1973), 40–41.

Ba, Oumar (ed.). *La pénétration française au Cayor*, vol. 1. Dakar, 1976.

Baesjou, René. "The Historical Evidence in Old Maps and Charts of Africa with Special Reference to West Africa." *History in Africa* 15 (1988), 1–83.

Baier, Stephen. "Long Term Structural Change in the Economy of Central Niger." In B. K. Swartz and Raymond A. Dumett (eds.), *West African Culture Dynamics*, 587–602. The Hague, 1980.

Baillaud, E. *Sur les routes du Soudan.* Toulouse, 1902.

Barbot, Jean. *A Description of the Coasts of North and South Guinea.* London, 1732.

Barrows, Leland C. "The Merchants and General Faidherbe: Aspects of French Expansion in Senegal in the 1850s." *Revue française d'histoire d'outre-mer* 61 (1974), 236–283.

Barrows, Leland C. "Some Paradoxes of Pacification: Senegal and France in the 1850s and 1860s." In B. K. Swartz and Raymond A. Dumett (eds.), *West African Culture Dynamics*, 515–544. The Hague, 1980.

Barry, Boubacar. *Le royaume du Waalo.* Paris, 1972.

Barry, Boubacar. *La Sénégambie du XVe au XIXe siècle. Traite négrière, islam, et conquête coloniale.* Paris, 1988.

Barth, Fredrik. "A General Perspective on Nomad-Sedentary Relations in the Middle East." In Cynthia Nelson (ed.), *The Desert and the Sown*, 11–22. Berkeley, 1973.

Barth, Heinrich. *Travels and Discoveries in North and Central Africa.* 5 vols. London, 1857–58.

Basset, René. *Mission au Sénégal.* 3 tomes. Paris, 1909.

Bathily, Abdoulaye. *Les portes de l'or. Le royaume de Galam (Sénégal) de l'ère musulmane au temps des négriers (VIIIe-XVIIIe siècle).* Paris, 1989.

Bathily, Abdoulaye. "La traite atlantique des esclaves et ses effets économiques et sociaux en Afrique: Le cas du Galam, royaume de l'hinterland senegambien au dix-huitième siècle." *JAH* 27 (1986), 269–293.

Batran, A. A. "The Kunta, Sidi al-Mukhtar al-Kunti, and the Office of Shaykh al-Tariqa'l-Qadiriyya." In John Ralph Willis (ed.), *Studies in West African History. Vol. 1. The Cultivators of Islam*, 113–146. London, 1979.

Bazin, Jean. "État guerrier et guerres d'État." In Jean Bazin and Emmanuel Terray (eds.), *Guerres de lignages et guerres d'États en Afrique*, 319–374. Paris, 1982.

Beaumier, Auguste. "Le choléra au Maroc, sa marche au Sahara jusqu'au Sénégal en 1868." *BSG*, 6e série, 3 (1872), 287–305.

Becker, Charles. "Conditions écologiques, crises de subsistence et histoire de la population à l'époque de la traite des esclaves en Sénégambie (17e–18e siècles)." *Canadian Journal of African Studies* 20 (1986), 357–376.

Becker, Charles. "Histoire de la Sénégambie du XVe au XVIIIe siècle: Un bilan." *Cahiers d'études africaines* 98, 25-2 (1985), 213–242.

Becker, Charles. "Notes sur les conditions écologiques en Sénégambie aux 17e et 18e siècles." *African Economic History* 14 (1985), 167–216.

Becker, Charles, and Victor Martin. "Kayor et Baol: Royaume sénégalais et traite des esclaves au XVIIIe siècle." *Revue française d'histoire d'outre-mer* 62, nos. 226–227 (1975), 270–300.

Becker, Charles, and Victor Martin. "Journal historique et suite du journal historique (1729–1731)." *Bull. IFAN*, série B, 39 (1977), 223–289.

Bellouard, P. "La gomme arabique en A.O.F." *Bois et forêts des tropiques* 1, no. 9 (1947), 3–18.

Berenger-Feraud, Laurent-Jean-Baptiste. *Les peuplades de la Sénégambie*. Paris, 1879.

Beshai, Abdel Amin. *Export Performance and Economic Development in Sudan, 1900–67*. London, 1967.

Beyries, J. "Evolution sociale et culturelle des collectivités nomades en Mauritanie." *BCEHSAOF* 20 (1937), 465–481.

Beyries, J. "Proverbes et dictons mauritaniens." *Revue des études islamiques* 4 (1930), 1–51.

Boahen, A. Adu. *Britain, the Sahara, and the Western Sudan, 1788–1861*. Oxford, 1964.

Boilat, P. D. *Esquisses sénégalaises*. Paris, 1853.

Bomba, Victoria. "Traditions about Ndianiane Ndiaye, First Buurba Djolof." *Bull. IFAN*, série B, 39 (1977), 1–35.

Bonafos, V. "Les Idaa ou Ali chorfa tidiania de Mauritanie." *RMM* 31 (1915–16), 223–272.

Bonte, Pierre. "Une agriculture saharienne. Les grāyr de l'Adrar mauritanien." *Revue de l'occident musulman et de la Méditerranée*, nos. 41–42 (1986), 378–396.

Bonte, Pierre. "La constitution de l'émirat de l'Adrar: Quelques hypothèses provisoires." *Revue de l'occident musulman et de la Méditerranée* 32 (1981-82), 37–51.

Bonte, Pierre. "The Constitution of the Emirate and the Transformations of Systems of Production in the Adrar (Mauritania)." *Production pastorale et société*, no. 16 (printemps 1985), 33–53.

Bonte, Pierre. "Tribus, factions et état. Les conflits de succession dans l'émirat de l'Adrar." *Cahiers d'études africaines* 22-3-4 (1987-88), 489–516.

Borgne, Capitaine. "Vocabulaire technique du chameau en Mauritanie (dialecte hassaniya)." *Bull. IFAN*, série B, 15 (1953), 292–380.

Borius, A. *Recherches sur le climat du Sénégal*. Paris, 1875.

Bosman, William. *A New and Accurate Description of the Coast of Guinea*. London, 1705.

Boucard, Claude. "Relation de Bambouc (1729)," with an introduction and annotations by Philip D. Curtin and with the collaboration of Jean Boulègue. *Bull. IFAN*, série B, 36 (1974), 246–275.

Bou el-Moghdad. "Voyage par terre entre le Sénégal et le Maroc." *Revue maritime et coloniale* (mai 1861), 477–494.

Bouet, Ed. "Journal de marche de la colonne mobile à travers le Ghiambour-Cayor, le Wallo, et le désert, en avril 1843." *RC*, 1e série, 1 (1843), 219–232.

Bouët-Willaumez, E. *Commerce et traite des noirs aux côtes occidentales d'Afrique.* Paris, 1848.

Bou Haqq. "Noirs et blancs au confins du désert." *BCEHSAOF* 21 (1938), 480–488.

Boulègue, Jean. "Un empire peul dans le Soudan occidental au début du XVIIe siècle." In *La parole, le sol, l'écrit: 2000 ans d'histoire africaine*, tome 1, 699–706. Paris, 1981.

Boulègue, Jean. *Le Grand Jolof.* Paris, 1987.

Boulègue, Jean. "La participation possible des centres de Pir et de Ndogal à la revolution islamique sénégambienne de 1673." In Jean Boulègue (ed.), *Contributions à l'histoire du Sénégal*, 119–125. Paris, 1987.

Bourrel, M. "Voyage dans le pays des maures brakna (rive droite du Sénégal, juin–oct. 1861). *Revue maritime et coloniale* (sept. 1861), 511–545, and (oct. 1861), 18–77.

Boutillier, J. L., P. Cantrelle, J. Causse, C. Laurent, and Th. N'Doye. *La moyenne vallée du Sénégal.* Paris, 1962.

Bovill, E. W. *The Golden Trade of the Moors.* Oxford, 1978.

Boyer, Gaston. *Un peuple de l'ouest soudanais. Les diawara.* Dakar, 1953.

Bradford, G. E., and H. A. Fitzhugh. "Hair Sheep: A General Description." In H. A. Fitzhugh and G. E. Bradford (eds.), *Hair Sheep of Western Africa and the Americas*, 3–22. Boulder, 1983.

Braudel, Fernand. *The Structures of Everyday Life.* New York, 1981.

Brooks, George E. *Landlords and Strangers: Ecology, Society, and Trade in Western Africa, 1000–1630.* Boulder, 1993.

Brooks, George. "Peanuts and Colonialism: The Consequences of the Commercialization of Peanuts in West Africa, 1830–1870." *JAH* 16 (1975), 29–54.

Brooks, George E. "A Provisional Historical Schema for Western Africa Based on Seven Climate Periods (ca. 9000 B.C. to the 19th Century)." *Cahiers d'études africaines* 101–102, 26-1-2 (1986), 43–62.

Brooks, George E. *Western Africa to c. 1860 A.D., a Provisional Historical Schema Based on Climate Periods.* Bloomington, 1985.

Brosset, Capitaine Diego. "Les Nemadi, monographie d'une tribu artificielle des confins sud du Sahara occidental." *BCEHSAOF, Renseignements coloniaux*, no. 9 (sept. 1932), 337–346.

Brosset, Capitaine Diego. "La saline d'Idjil." *BCEHSAOF* 43 (1931), 259–265.

Bryson, Reid A., and Thomas J. Murray. *Climates of Hunger: Mankind and the World's Changing Weather.* Madison, 1977.

Bulliet, Richard W. *The Camel and the Wheel.* Cambridge, Mass., 1975.

Bureau Courtoy. *Étude de régénération des gommiers mauritaniennes. Rapport final.* Bruxelles, 1981.

Butel. "Notes sur les peuplades qui occupent les bords du Sénégal." *RC*, 2e série, 14 (1855), 752–759.

Caille. "Notes sur les peuples de la Mauritanie et de la négritie, riveraine du Sénégal." *RC*, le série, 10 (septembre 1846), 1–10.

Caille, M. le Commandant. "Tableau statistique du fleuve Sénégal, dressé, en 1843, par M. le Commandant Caille." *RC,* 2e série, 6 (1851), 5–19.

Caillié, René. *Travels through Central Africa to Timbuctoo and across the Great Desert to Morocco, performed in the years 1824–1828.* 2 vols., trans. from the French. London, 1830.

Carbonnel, Jean-Pierre. "Analysis of the Recent Climatic Evolution in Burkino Faso (Upper Volta)." *Natural Resources Forum* 9 (1985), 53–64.

Carrère, Frédéric, and Paul Holle. *De la Sénégambie française.* Paris, 1855.

Castries, H. de (ed.). *Les sources inédites de l'histoire du Maroc. Séries I. Dynastie saadienne. Archives et bibliothèques d'Angleterre.* 3 tomes. Paris, 1918.

Chambonneau. "Relation du Sieur Chambonneau, commis de la compagnie de Sénégal, du voyage par luy fait en remontant le Niger (juillet 1688)." *Bulletin de géographie historique et descriptive* 2 (1898), 308–321.

Chapelle, Jean. *Les nomades noirs du Sahara.* Paris, 1958.

Chapman, S. D., and S. Chassagne. *European Textile Printers in the Eighteenth Century.* London, 1981.

Charles, Eunice A. *Precolonial Senegal: The Jolof Kingdom 1800 to 1890.* Boston, 1977.

Chassey, Francis de. *L'étrier, la houe, et le livre.* Paris, 1977.

Chassey, Francis de. *Mauritanie, 1900–1975.* Paris, 1979.

Chastanet, Monique. *Les crises de subsistances dans les villages soninké du cercle de Bakel de 1858 à 1945.* Office de la recherche scientifique et technique outremer. Dakar-Hann, 1982.

Chenier, Louis de. *The Present State of the Empire of Morocco.* Reprint: New York, 1967.

Chenier, Louis de. *Recherches historiques sur les maures.* Reprint: Paris, 1972.

Chevalier, Aug. "Sur la production de la gomme arabique en Afrique occidentale française." *Revue de botanique appliquée et d'agriculture coloniale,* no. 32 (30 avr. 1932), 256–265.

Cissoko, Sékéné-Mody. "Famines et épidémies à Tombouctou et dans la boucle du Niger du XVIe au XVIIIe siècle." *Bull. IFAN* 30 (1968), 806–821.

Cissoko, Sénéké-Mody. *Tombouctou et l'empire songhay.* Dakar, 1975.

Cligny, A. "Faune du Sénégal et de la Casamance." In Dr. Lasnet, A. Cligny, Aug. Chevalier, and Pierre Rambaud, *Une mission au Sénégal,* 276–321. Paris, 1900.

Cochelet, Charles. *Narrative of the Shipwreck of the Sophia.* 2 vols. London, 1822.

Colombani, F.-M. "Le Guidimaka. Étude géographique, historique, et religieuse." *BCEHSAOF* 14 (1931), 365–432.

Colvin, Lucie Gallistel. *Historical Dictionary of Senegal.* Metuchen, N.J., 1981.

Colvin, Lucie Gallistel. "Islam and the State of Kajor: A Case of Successful Resistance to Jihad." *JAH* 15 (1974), 587–606.

Colas, A. "Renseignements géographiques sur l'Afrique centrale et occidentale." *Bulletin de la Société de géographie de Marseille* 3 (1879), 327–358, and 4 (1880), 8–40.

Constantin, Le Frère. "Observatoire du Saint-Louis du Sénégal (École Secondaire). Observations météorologiques. Moyennes conclus de 23 années d'observations." *BCEHSAOF* 13 (1901), 437–473.

Crone, Gerald Roe (ed. and trans.). *The Voyages of Cadamosto and Other Documents on Western Africa in the Second Half of the Fifteenth Century.* London, 1937.

Cultru, Pierre. *Les origines de l'Afrique occidentale: Histoire du Sénégal du XVe siècle à 1870.* Paris, 1910.

Curtin, Philip D. *Cross-Cultural Trade in World History.* Cambridge, 1984.

Curtin, Philip D. *Economic Change in Precolonial Africa: Senegambia in the Era of the Slave Trade,* 2 vols. Madison, 1975.

Curtin, Philip D. "Jihad in West Africa: Early Phases and Interrelations in Mauritania and Senegal." *JAH* 12 (1971), 11–24.

Curtin, Philip D. "Nutrition in African History." *Journal of Interdisciplinary History* 14 (1983), 71–82.

Curtin, Philip D. *The Rise and Fall of the Plantation Complex: Essays in Atlantic History.* Cambridge, 1990.

Damberger, Christian F. *Travels through the Interior of Africa, from the Cape of Good Hope to Morocco.* Boston, 1801.

Daveau, S. "La découverte du climat d'Afrique tropicale au cours des navigations portugaises (XVe siècle au début du XVIe siècle)." *Bull. IFAN,* série B, 31 (1969), 953–988.

David, Pierre. *Journal d'un voiage fait en Bambouc en 1744,* ed. André Delcourt. Paris, 1974.

Davidson, John. *Notes Taken during Travels in Africa.* Published privately by J. L. Cox and Sons, London, 1839.

Delafosse, Maurice, and Henri Gaden. "Chroniques du Fouta sénégalais." *RMM* 24 (1913), 1–114 and 25 (1913), 165–235.

Delaporte, A. "Extrait d'une lettre de Tanger du 14 avril 1826 adressé à M. Jomard (sur la trajet à chameau du Tafilalt à Tombouctou)." *BSG* 13 (jan.–fév. 1827), 82–83.

Delaporte, A., and M. le Baron Roger. "Documents relatifs à un prince noir de l'intérieur de l'Afrique occidentale et au pays de Ouadan." *BSG* 19, no. 1 (1833), 343–356.

Delcourt, André. "L'apport de la collection des journeaux de bord du service hydrographique de la marine (Archives nationales, Paris, Marine 4 JJ). A la connaissance du passé mauritanien." *Annales de l'Institut mauritanien de recherche scientifique,* no. 1 (1975), 44–86.

Delcourt, A. *La France et les établissements français au Sénégal entre 1712 et 1763.* Dakar, 1952.

Demanet, L'Abbé. *Nouvelle histoire de l'Afrique française.* Paris, 1767.

Denis, P. "À propos des salines et des pistes caravanieres du Sahara occidental." *Bulletin de liaison saharienne* 3 (oct. 1952), 26–32.

Désiré-Vuillemin, Geneviève. "Un commerce qui meurt: La traite de la gomme dans les escales du Sénégal." *Cahiers outre-mer* 17 (jan.–mars 1952), 90–94.

Désiré-Vuillemin, Geneviève. *Contribution à l'histoire de la Mauritanie, 1900–1934.* Dakar, 1962.

Désiré-Vuillemin, Geneviève. *Essai sur le gommier et le commerce de gomme dans les escales du Sénégal.* Dakar, 1963.

Désiré-Vuillemin, Geneviève. *Histoire de la Mauritanie.* Nouakchott, 1964.

Devisse, Jean. "Routes de commerce et échanges en Afrique occidentale en relation avec la Méditerranée. *Revue d'histoire économique et sociale* 50 (1972), 357-397.

Dezert. "Du commerce de la gomme au Sénégal en 1841." *Annales maritimes et coloniales* 2e série, 75, tome 1 (partie non-officielle) (1841), 939-948.

Diawara, Mamadou. *La graine de la parole.* Stuttgart, 1990.

Diop, Abdoulaye-Bara. *La société wolof.* Paris, 1981.

Diop, Amadou Bamba. "Lat Dior et le problème musulman." *Bull. IFAN*, série B, 28 (1966), 493-539.

Diouf, Mamadou. *Le Kajoor au XIXe siècle.* Paris, 1990.

Donelha, André. *Descrição da Serra Leoa e dos rios de Guiné do Cabo Verde*, ed., trans., and annotated by Avelino Teixeira da Mota and P. E. H. Hair. Lisbon, 1977.

Donnet, Gaston. *En Sahara. À travers le pays des maures nomades.* Paris, 1898.

Donnet, Gaston. *Une mission au Sahara occidental.* Paris, 1896.

Douls, Camille. "Cinq mois chez les maures nomades du Sahara occidental." *Le tour du monde* 55 (1888), 177-224.

Douls, Camille. "Voyage d'exploration à travers le Sahara occidental et le sud marocain." *BSG* 9 (1888), 437-479.

Doumet. "Mémoire inédit de Doumet (1769). Le Kayor et les pays voisins au cours de la seconde moitié du XVIIIe siècle." Presented and commented upon by Charles Becker and V. Martin. *Bull. IFAN*, série B, 36 (1974), 25-97.

Doutressoule, Georges. *L'élevage au Soudan français.* Paris, 1948.

Doutressoule, Georges. *L'élevage en Afrique occidentale française.* Paris, 1947.

Dubie, Paul. "L'îlot berberophone de Mauritanie." *Bull. IFAN* 2 (1940), 316-325.

Dubie, Paul. "La vie materielle des maures." In *Mélanges ethnologiques*, 111-256. Dakar, 1953.

Duboc, Général. *Mauritanie.* Paris, 1935.

Dubost, Capitaine. "Étude sur le palmier dattier dans le cercle du Tagant." *BCEHSAOF* 9 (1924), 455-468.

Duby, Georges. *Guerriers et paysans.* Paris, 1973.

Du Casse, Sieur. "Mémoire ou relation du Sr Du Casse sur son voyage de Guynée avec 'La Tempeste' en 1687 et 1688." In Paul Roussier (ed.), *L'établissement d'Issiny 1687-1702*, 3-47. Paris, 1935.

Duncan, T. Bentley. *Atlantic Islands. Madeira, the Azores, and the Cape Verdes in Seventeenth-Century Commerce and Navigation.* Chicago, 1972.

Duchon-Doris, J. P., Jr. *Commerce des toiles bleues dites guinées.* Paris, 1842.

Durand, Jean Baptiste Léonard. *Voyage au Sénégal.* 2e édition, 2 tomes. Paris, 1807.

Eannes (de Azurara), G. *The Chronicle of the Discovery and Conquest of Guinea*, trans. and ed. C. R. Beazley and E. Prestage. London, 1896.

Ech-Chenguiti, Ahmed Lamine. *El wasīt*, trans. from the Arabic by Mourad Teffahi. Saint-Louis, Senegal, 1953.

Elbl, Ivana. "The Horse in Fifteenth Century Senegambia." *IJAHS* 24 (1991), 85-110.

Emerit, Marcel. "Les liaisons terrestres entre le Soudan et l'Afrique du nord au XVIIIe et au début du XIX siècle." *Travaux de l'Institut de recherches sahariennes* (University of Algers), 2 (1954), 29-47.

Epstein, Hellmut. *The Origin of the Domestic Animals of Africa.* 2 vols. New York, 1971.

d'Escayrac de Lauture, le Comte. *Le désert et le Soudan*. Paris, 1853.

Fabert, Léon. "Voyage dans le pays des trarzas et dans le Sahara occidental." *BSG*, 7e série (1892), 275–392.

Faidherbe, Louis Léon César. "L'avenir du Sahara et du Soudan." *Revue maritime et coloniale* 8 (1863), 221–248.

Faidherbe, Louis Léon César. "Les Berbères et les Arabes des bords du Sénégal." *BSG*, 4e série (fév. 1854), 89–112.

Faidherbe, Louis Léon César. "Notice historique sur le Cayor." *BSG* (1883), 527–564.

Faidherbe, Louis Léon César. "Notice sur la colonie du Sénégal et sur les pays qui sont en relation avec elle." *Nouvelles annales des voyages de la géographie, de l'histoire, et de l'archaeologie*, 6e série, 5e année, 1 (1859), 5–99.

Faidherbe, Louis Léon César. "Renseignements géographiques sur la partie du Sahara comprise entre l'Oued Noun et le Soudan." *Nouvelles annales des voyages*, 6e série, 5e année (août 1859), 129–156.

Faidherbe, Louis Léon César. *Le Sénégal. La France dans l'Afrique occidentale*. Paris, 1889.

Fall, Tanor Latsukabé. "Recueil sur la vie des Damel (1955)." *Bull. IFAN*, série B, 36 (1974), 98–148.

Fernandes, Valentim. *Description de la côte d'Afrique de Ceuta au Sénégal (1506–1507)*, ed. and trans. P. de Cenival and Théodore Monod. Paris, 1938.

Fisher, Allan G. B., and Humphrey J. Fisher. *Slavery and Muslim Society in Africa*. Garden City, N.Y., 1971.

Fisher, Humphrey J. " 'He Swalloweth the Ground with Fierceness and Rage': The Horse in the Central Sudan, I. Its Introduction." *JAH* 13 (1972), 369–388.

Fisher, Humphrey J. " 'He Swalloweth the Ground with Fierceness and Rage': The Horse in the Central Sudan, II. Its Use." *JAH* 14 (1973), 355–379.

Flize, L. "Le Ndiambour et le Gadiaga." *RC*, 2e série, 17 (1857), 390–398.

Flize, L. "Le Oualo (Sénégal)." *RC*, 2e série, 16 (1856), 299–305.

Follie, M. *Voyage dans les déserts du Sahara, par M. Follie, administrateur des colonies*. Paris, 1792.

Forest, J. *Commerce et industrie. Production des plumes d'autruche de Barbarie. Le sel gemme saharien*. Paris, 1875.

France, Ministère des colonies. *Statistiques coloniales*. Paris, 1832–.

Frejus, Sieur Roland. *The Relation of a Voyage Made into Mauritania, in Africk. . .* Printed by W. Godbid, London, 1671.

Fulcrand, C. "Exploration de la baie d'Arguin." *Revue maritime et coloniale* (May 1861), 495–510.

Gaby, F. Y. *Relation de la négritie*. Paris, 1689.

Gaden, Henri. "La gomme en Mauritanie." *Annales de l'académie des sciences coloniales* 7 (1929), 219–228.

Gaden, Henri. "Légendes et coutumes sénégalaises; cahiers de Yoro Dyâo." *Revue d'ethnographie et de sociologie* (mars/avr. 1912), 119–137, and (mai/août 1912), 191–202.

Gallieni, J. S. *Voyage au Soudan français, 1879–81*. Paris, 1884.

Garcia, J. M. (ed.). *As Viagens dos Descubrimentos*. Lisbon, 1983.

Gellner, Ernest, and Charles Micaud (eds.). *Arabs and Berbers: From Tribe to Nation in North Africa*. London, 1973.

Geneviere, J. "Les Kountas et leur activités commerciales." *Bull. IFAN*, série B, 12 (1950), 1111-1125.

Geoffrey de Villeneuve, R. *L'Afrique ou histoire, moeurs, usages, et coutumes des africains*. Paris, 1814.

Gerteiny, Alfred G. *Historical Dictionary of Mauritania*. Metuchen, N.J., 1981.

Gerteiny, Alfred G. *Mauritania*. New York, 1967.

Golberry, Silv. Meinrad Xavier. *Fragmens d'un voyage en Afrique*. 2 tomes. Paris, 1802.

Golberry, Silv. Meinrad Xavier. *Travels in Africa*, 2 vols. London, 1802.

Goudie, Andrew. *The Human Impact. Man's Role in Environmental Change*. Cambridge, Mass., 1982.

Goudie, Andrew, and John Wilkinson. *The Warm Desert Environment*. Cambridge, 1977.

Grace, Edward. *Letters of a West African Trader. Edward Grace 1767-70*. London, 1950.

Gray, John M. *A History of the Gambia*. Cambridge, 1940.

Gray, William. *Travels in Western Africa in the Years 1818, 1820, and 21*. London, 1825.

Great Britain. House of Commons. "An Account of All Senegal Gum Imported into Great Britain from 1833-1836." *Sessional Papers*, 1839 (218) XLVI, 389.

Great Britain. House of Commons. "Convention between Her Majesty and the Emperor of the French, Relative to Portendick and Albreda; Signed at London, March 7, 1857." *Accounts and Papers* 43 (1857), 547.

Great Britain. House of Commons. "Correspondence between the Portendic Claimants and Her Majesty's Government." *Accounts and Papers* 58 (1847-48), 159-225.

Great Britain. House of Commons. "Correspondence on the subject of a Convention Recently Entered into between Her Majesty and the Emperor of the French, Relative to Portendic and Albreda." *Accounts and Papers* 60 (1857-58), 215-230.

Great Britain. House of Commons. "Papers Relative to the Arbitration of His Majesty the King of Prussia," *Sessional Papers* 51 (1845), paper 626, 75-503.

Great Britain. House of Commons. "Report from the Select Committee Respecting the Importation of Gum Senega." Dated 18 February 1752 in *Journals of the House of Commons*, vol. 26, 441-444.

Gritzner, Jeffrey A. *The West African Sahel: Human Agency and Environmental Change*. Chicago, 1988.

Grosbellet, Bernard. *Le moniteur du Sénégal et dépendances comme source de l'histoire du Sénégal pendant le premier gouvernement de Faidherbe (1856-61)*. Dakar, 1967.

Grosset, E., and Aliou Ibra Ba et al. (eds.). *Analyse de situation de la région du Tagant (R.I.M.) avec attention particulière aux aspects socio-économiques*. Berlin, 1979-80.

Grove, A. T. "The Climate of the Sahara in the Period of Meteorological Trends." In J. A. Allan (ed.), *The Sahara. Ecological Change and Early Economic History*, 61-69. London, 1981.

Gruvel, A., and R. Chudeau. *À travers la Mauritanie occidentale (de Saint-Louis à Port Étienne)*. Paris, 1909.

Guillard, Xavier. "Un commerce introuvable: l'or dans les transactions sénégambiennes du XVIe au XVIIIe siècle." In *Contributions à l'histoire du Sénégal*. Cahiers du Centre de recherches africaines no. 5, 31–75. Paris, 1987.

Hair, P. E. H. "A Note on Jean Barbot (1655–1713)." *Proceedings of the Huguenot Society of London* 23, no. 5 (1981), 295–308.

Hamès, Constant. "L'évolution des émirats maures sous l'effet du capitalisme marchand européen." In Équipe écologie et anthropologie des sociétés pastorales (ed.), *Pastoral Production and Society*, 375–398. Cambridge, 1979.

Hamès, Constant. "La société maure ou le système des castes hors de l'Inde." *Cahiers internationaux de sociologie* 46 (1969), 163–177.

Hamès, Constant. "Statuts et rapports sociaux en Mauritanie précoloniale." *Études sur les sociétés de pasteurs nomades*. Cahiers du centre d'études et de recherches marxistes no. 133 (1977), 10–21.

Hamet, Ismaël. "Les Kountas." *RMM* 15 (1911), 302–318.

Hamet, Ismaël (ed. and trans.). *Chroniques de la Mauritanie sénégalaise*. Paris, 1911.

Hardy, Georges. *La mise en valeur du Sénégal de 1817 à 1854*. Paris, 1921.

Hayward, Derek F., and Julius S. Oguntoyinbo. *Climatology of West Africa*. London, 1987.

Haywood, A. H. *Through Timbuctoo and Across the Great Sahara*. London, 1912.

Herbin de Halle, P. (ed.). *Statistique générale et particulière de la France et de ses colonies,* vol. 7. Paris, An XII.

Héricé. "Note sur le commerce des boeufs du Sénégal avec les antilles françaises." *RC*, 2e série, 11 (1853), 467–473.

Hogendorn, Jan, and Marion Johnson. *The Shell Money of the Slave Trade*. Cambridge, 1985.

Hopkins, Anthony G. *An Economic History of West Africa*. New York, 1973.

Hunkarin, Louis. "L'esclavage en Mauritanie." *Études dahoméenes* (1964), 33–49.

Hunwick, John O. "Notes on a late fifteenth century document concerning 'al-Takrur.' " In Christopher Allen and R. W. Johnson (eds.), *African Perspectives*, 7–33. Cambridge, 1970.

Hunwick, John O. (ed. and trans.). *Sharīʿa in Songhay: The Replies of al-Maghīlī to to the Questions of Askia al-Ḥājj Muhammad*. Oxford, 1985.

Hutchinson, Peter. *Rainfall Variations in the Gambia since 1886*. Republic of the Gambia: Ministry of Water Resources and Environment, Department of Water Resources, 1982.

Ibn Abī Zayd al-Qayrawānī, ʿAbd Allāh ibn ʿAbd al-Raḥmān. *La risala; ou, Épître sur les éléments du dogme et de la loi de l'Islâm selon le rite mâlikite*, ed. and trans. Léon Bercher. Algers, 1968.

Ibn Batuta. *Travels in Asia and Africa*, trans. H. A. R. Gibb. New York, 1929.

Ibn Khaldun. *Histoire des Berbères*. Paris, 1968–69.

Ibn Khaldun. *The Muqaddimah. An Introduction to History*, trans. Franz Rosenthal. Princeton, 1967.

Jackson, J. F. *An Account of the Empire of Morocco*. London, 1811.

Jacob de Cordemoy, Hubert. *Gommes, resines d'origine exotique et vegetaux qui les produisent*. Paris, 1900.

Jacob de Cordemoy, Hubert. *Les plantes à gommes et à resines*. Paris, 1911.

Jannequin, Claude. *Voyage de Libye au royaume de Sénégal le long de Niger.* Reprint: Geneva, 1980.

Johnson, Marion. *Anglo-African Trade in the Eighteenth Century*, ed. J. T. Lindblad and Robert Ross. Intercontinenta no. 15. Centre for the History of European Expansion. Leiden, 1990.

Johnson, Marion. "The Cowrie Currencies of West Africa." *JAH* 11 (1970), 17–49 and 331–353.

Johnson, Marion. "The Nineteenth Century Gold 'Mithqal' in West and North Africa." *JAH* 9 (1968), 547–569.

Johnson, Marion. "The Ounce in Eighteenth-Century West African Trade." *JAH* 7 (1966), 197–214.

Jones, Adam. *Brandenburg Sources for West African History 1680–1700.* Weisbaden, 1985.

Julien, Charles-André. *History of North Africa from the Arab Conquest to 1830*, trans. John Petrie. New York, 1970.

Kane, Moustapha, and David Robinson. *The Islamic Regime of Fuuta Tooro.* East Lansing, 1984.

Kane, Oumar. "Les maures et le Futa Toro au XVIIIe siècle." *Cahiers d'études africaines* 54, 16-2 (1974), 237–252.

Kane, Oumar. "Les maures et le Futa-Toro au XVIIIe siècle." *Afrika Zamani*, no. 2 (1974), 79–104.

Kanya-Forstner, A. *The Conquest of the Western Sudan. A Study in French Military Imperialism.* Cambridge, 1969.

Kiple, Kenneth F. *The Caribbean Slave: A Biological History.* Cambridge, 1984.

Klein, Martin. "The Demography of Slavery in Western Soudan." In Dennis D. Cordell and Joel W. Gregory (eds.), *African Population and Capitalism: Historical Perspectives*, 50–61. Boulder, 1987, rpt. Madison, 1994.

Klein, Martin. "The Impact of the Atlantic Slave Trade on the Societies of the Western Sudan." *Social Science History* 14 (1990), 231–253.

Klein, Martin A. "The Slave Trade in the Western Sudan during the Nineteenth Century." In Elizabeth Savage (ed.), *The Human Commodity: Perspectives on the Trans-Saharan Slave Trade*, 39–60. London, 1992.

Klein, Martin A. "Women in Slavery in the Western Soudan." In Claire C. Robertson and Martin A. Klein (eds.), *Women and Slavery in Africa*, 67–92. Madison, 1983.

Klein, Martin, and Paul E. Lovejoy. "Slavery in West Africa." In H. A. Gemery and J. S. Hogendorn (eds.), *The Uncommon Market: Essays in the Economic History of the Atlantic Slave Trade.* New York, 1979.

Kopytoff, Igor. "The Internal African Frontier: The Making of African Political Culture." In Igor Kopytoff (ed.), *The African Frontier: The Reproduction of Traditional African Societies*, 3–84. Bloomington, 1987.

L'Africain, Jean-Léon. *Description de l'Afrique*, trans. from the Italian by A. Épaulard and annotated by A. Épaulard, Th. Monod, H. Lhote, and R. Mauny. 2 tomes. Paris, 1956.

Labarthe, Pierre. *Voyage au Sénégal pendant les années 1784 et 1785, d'après les mémoires de Lajaille.* Paris, 1802.

Labat, Jean Baptiste. *Nouvelle relation de l'Afrique occidentale.* 4 tomes. Paris, 1728.

Labat, Jean Baptiste. *Voyage de Chevalier des Marchais en Guinée et aux îles voisines, et à Cayenne, fait en 1725, 1726, et 1727.* Amsterdam, 1731.

La Chapelle, F. de. "Esquisses d'une histoire du Sahara occidental." *Hespéris* 11 (1930), 35–95.

La Courbe. *Premier voiage du Sieur de La Courbe fait à la coste d'Afrique en 1685,* ed. P. Cultru. Paris, 1913.

LaForgue, Pierre. "Une secte hérésiarque en Mauritanie: les Ghoudf." *BCEHSAOF* 11 (1928), 654–665.

Laing, A. G. *Travels in Western Africa.* London, 1825.

Lamiral, Dominique Harcourt. *L'Affrique et le peuple affricain.* Paris, 1789.

Lanrezac, H. "Le cercle de Nioro." *Bulletin de la Société de géographie commerciale de Paris* 27 (1905), 222–261.

La Porte, Id. de. "Itinéraire de Constantine à Tafilet à Tombouctou. . ." *Bulletin de la société royale de géographie d'Egypte* 13 (1925), 205–250.

Lappé, Frances Moore. *Diet for a Small Planet.* New York, 1975.

Laroui, Abdallah. *The History of the Maghrib: An Interpretative Essay.* Princeton, 1977.

Lartigue, Le commandant de. "Notice géographique sur le région du sahel." *Renseignements coloniaux et documents publiées par le Comité de l'Afrique française,* no. 5, supplément du *Bulletin du Comité de l'Afrique française* (juin 1898), 109–135.

Lartigue, Le commandant de. "Notice historique sur la région du sahel." *Renseignements coloniaux et documents publiées par le Comité de l'Afrique Française,* no. 4, supplément du *Bulletin du Comité de l'Afrique française* (avr. 1898), 69–101.

Lasnet, Dr., Aug. Chevalier, A. Cligny, Pierre Rambaud. *Une mission au Sénégal. Ethnographie-botanique-zoologie-géologie.* Paris, 1900.

Law, Robin. *The Horse in West African History.* Oxford, 1980.

Lawson, George W. (ed.). *Plant Ecology in West Africa. Systems and Processes.* Chichester, 1986.

Leblanc, Capitaine de frégate. "Voyage à Galam en 1820." *Annales maritimes et coloniales,* 2e partie, t. 1 (1822), 133–159.

Le Brasseur, J. A. "Détails historiques et politiques, mémoire inédit (1778) de J. A. Le Brasseur," presented and brought to publication by Charles Becker and Victor Martin. *Bull. IFAN,* série B, 39 (1977), 81–132.

Leger, Marcel, and L. Teppaz. "Le 'Horse-Sickness' au Sénégal et au Soudan français." *BCEHSAOF* 5 (1922), 219–240.

Lejean, Guillaume. "Le Sénégal en 1859 et les routes commerciales du Sahara." *Revue contemporaine* (15 oct. 1859), 369–403.

Lenz, Oscar. *Timbuktu.* Leipzig, 1884; Paris, 1886.

Lenz, Oscar. *Timbouctou, voyage au Maroc, au Sahara et au Soudan.* Paris, 1887.

Lenz, Oscar. "Voyage du Maroc au Sénégal." *BSG* (1881), 199–226.

Leriche, Albert. "Coutumes maures relatives à l'élevage." *Bull. IFAN* 15 (1953), 1316–1320.

Leriche, Albert. "De l'origine du thé au Maroc et au Sahara." *Bull. IFAN* 15 (1953), 731–736.

Leriche, Albert. "L'islam en Mauritanie." *Bull. IFAN* 11 (1949), 458–470.

Leriche, Albert. "Mesures Maures. Note préliminaire." *Bull. IFAN* 13 (1951), 1227–1256.

Leriche, Albert. "Notes pour servir à l'histoire maure." *Bull. IFAN* 15 (1953), 737-750.

Leriche, Albert. "Notes sur les classes sociales et sur quelques tribus de Mauritanie." *Bull. IFAN* 17 (1955), 173-202.

Leriche, Albert. "Petite note pour servir à l'histoire d'Atar." *Bull. IFAN* 14 (1952), 623-626.

Leriche, Albert. *Terminologie géographique maure*. IFAN-Mauritanie. Saint-Louis du Sénégal, 1955.

Leriche, Albert, and Mokhtar Ould Hamidoun. "Notes sur le Trarza: Essai de géographie historique." *Bull. IFAN* 10 (1948), 461-538.

Levtzion, Nehemiah. *Ancient Ghana and Mali*. London, 1973.

Levtzion, Nehemiah, and J. F. P. Hopkins (eds.). *Corpus of Early Arabic Sources for West African History*, trans. J. F. P. Hopkins. Cambridge, 1981.

Lewicki, Tadeusz. "Gannar—le nom Wolof de la Mauritanie." *Paideuma* (Mitteilungen zur Kulturkunde), 35 (1989), 177-179.

Lewicki, Tadeusz. *West African Food in the Middle Ages*. Cambridge, 1974.

Leyden, John. *A Historical and Philosophical Sketch of the Discoveries and Settlements of Europeans on Northern and Western Africa, at the close of the Eighteenth Century*. Edinburgh, 1799.

Lindblom, Karl Gerhard. *The Use of Oxen as Pack and Riding Animals in Africa*. Stockholm, 1931.

Lintingre, Pierre. *Voyages du Sieur de Glicourt à la côte occidentale d'Afrique pendant les années 1778 et 1779*. Dakar, 1966.

Louvet, Alberic. "Sur le mode de production de la gomme arabique dans les forêts de gommiers," *Journal de pharmacie et de chimie* 24 (1876), 405-411, 447-476.

Lovejoy, Paul E. *Salt of the Desert Sun*. Cambridge, 1985.

Lovejoy, Paul E. "The Volume of the Atlantic Slave Trade: A Synthesis." *JAH* 23 (1982), 473-502.

Lovejoy, Paul, and Stephen Baier. "The Desert-side Economy of the Central Sudan." *IJAHS* 8 (1975), 551-581.

Lucas, Dr. A. J. "Considerations sur l'ethnique maure et en particulière sur une race ancienne: Les Bafours." *Bulletin de la société des africanistes* 1 (1931), 151-194.

Lyon, George F. *Narrative of Travels in Northern Africa in the Years 1818, 1819, and 1820*. London, 1821.

McDougall, E. Ann. "Camel Caravans of the Saharan Salt Trade: Traders and Transporters in the Nineteenth Century." In Catherine Coquery-Vidrovitch and Paul E. Lovejoy (eds.), *The Workers of African Trade*, 99-122. Beverly Hills, 1985.

McDougall, E. Ann. "The Economics of Islam in the Southern Sahara: The Rise of the Kunta Clan." *Asian and African Studies* 20 (1986), 45-60.

McDougall, E. Ann. "The Quest for Tarra: Toponomy and Geography in Exploring History." *History in Africa* 18 (1991), 271-289.

McDougall, E. Ann. "The Sahara Reconsidered: Pastoralism, Politics, and Salt from the Ninth through the Twelfth Centuries." *African Economic History* 12 (1983), 263-286.

McDougall, E. Ann. "Salt, Saharans, and the Trans-Saharan Slave Trade: Nineteenth Century Developments." In Elizabeth Savage (ed.), *The Human Commodity. Perspectives on the Trans-Saharan Slave Trade*, 61-88. London, 1992.

McDougall, E. Ann. "Salts of the Western Sahara: Myths, Mysteries, and Historical Significance." *IJAHS* 23 (1990), 231–257.

McDougall, E. Ann. "A Topsy-Turvy World: Slaves and Freed Slaves in the Mauritanian Adrar, 1910–1950." In Suzanne Miers and Richard Roberts (eds.), *The End of Slavery in Africa*, 362–390. Madison, 1988.

McDougall, E. Ann. "The View from Awdaghust: War, Trade and Social Change in the Southwestern Sahara, from the Eighth to the Fifteenth Century." *JAH* 26 (1985), 1–31.

Machat, J. *Documents sur les établissements français de l'Afrique occidentale au xviiie siècle.* Paris, 1906.

McIntosh, Roderick. "Pulse Model: Genesis and Accommodation of Specialization in the Middle Niger." *JAH* 34 (1993), 181–200.

McIntosh, S. K. and R. J. McIntosh. "Current Directions in West African Prehistory." *Annual Review of Anthropology* 12 (1983), 215–258.

McIntosh, S. K., and R. J. McIntosh. "West African Prehistory (from c. 10,000 to A.D. 1000)." *American Scientist* 69 (Nov.–Dec. 1981), 602–613.

McLane, Margaret O. "Commercial Rivalries and French Policy on the Senegal River, 1831–1858." *African Economic History* 15 (1986), 39–67.

Magalhães-Godinho, Vitorino. *L'économie de l'empire portugais aux XVe et XVIe siècles.* Paris, 1969.

Mage, E. "Voyage au Tagant." *Revue algérienne et coloniale* 3 (1860), 1–29.

Mage, E. *Voyage dans le Soudan occidental 1863–1866.* Paris, 1868.

Manchuelle, François. "Slavery, Emancipation and Labour Migration in West Africa: The Case of the Soninke." *JAH* 30 (1989), 89–106.

Mantell, C. L. "The Water Soluble Gums—Their Botany, Sources and Utilization." *Economic Botany* 3, no. 3 (1949), 3–31.

Margoliouth, D. S. "Al-Tidjaniya." In H. A. R. Gibb and J. H. Kramer (eds.), *Shorter Encyclopaedia of Islam*, 593–595. Ithaca, 1953.

Martin, Alfred G. P. *Quatre siècles d'histoire marocaine, au Sahara de 1504 à 1902, au Maroc de 1894 à 1912, d'après archives et documentations indigènes.* Paris, 1923.

Martin, H. "Les tribus du sahal et du Rio de Oro; les Oulad Bou Sba." *Bull. IFAN* 1 (1939), 587–629.

Martin, Victor, and Charles Becker. "Les Teeñ du Baol: Essai de chronologie." *Bull. IFAN*, série B, 38 (1976), 449–505.

Marty, Paul. "Chroniques de Oualata et de Néma." *Revue des études islamiques* (1927), 353–426 and 531–575.

Marty, Paul. *L'émirat des Trarzas.* Paris, 1917–18.

Marty, Paul. *Études sur l'Islam et les tribus du Soudan.* 4 tomes. Paris, 1920–21.

Marty, Paul. *Études sur l'Islam et les tribus maures; les Brakna.* Paris, 1921.

Marty, Paul. "Le groupment de Bou Kounta." *RMM* 31 (1915–16), 411–442.

Marty, Paul. "Poème historique d'Abou Bakr Ibn Hejab, le Dîmani." *BCEHSAOF* 4 (1921), 252–263.

Marty, Paul. "Relations d'un pelerinage à la Mecque par un marabout peul en 1794–1795." *RMM* 43 (1921), 228–235.

Marty, Paul. "Tentatives commerciales anglaises à Portendick et en Mauritanie (1800–1826)." *Revue de l'histoire des colonies françaises*, 1e trimestre (1922), 1–38; 2e trimestre (1922), 265–302.

Marty, Paul (trans.). "Poème de Mohammed al-Yâdali à la louange de l'Émir des Braknas, Ahmad ould Heïba." *BCEHSAOF* 4 (1921), 264–267.

Mathews, Felix A. "Northwest Africa and Timbuctoo." *Journal of the American Geographical Society of New York* 13 (1881), 196–219.

Mathews, Felix A. "Trade of Morocco with Timbuctoo and the Soudan, across the Great Desert." *U.S. Bureau of Manufactures. Reports from the Consuls of the U.S.* 8 (1881), 792–797.

Mauny, Raymond. "L'expedition marocaine d'Ouadane vers 1543–1544." *Bull. IFAN* 11 (1949), 129–140.

Mauny, Raymond. "Un itinéraire transsaharien du moyen âge." *Bulletin de liaison saharienne* 13 (1953), 31–41.

Mauny, Raymond. "Notes d'histoire et d'archaeologie sur Azougui, Chinguitti et Ouadane." *Bull. IFAN* 16 (1955), 142–152.

Mauny, Raymond. *Tableau géographique de l'ouest africain au moyen age.* Dakar, 1961.

Meakin, Budgett. *The Moorish Empire. A Historical Epitome.* London, 1899.

Meakin, Budgett. *The Moors. A Comprehensive Description.* London, 1902.

Meillassoux, Claude. *The Anthropology of Slavery*, trans. Alide Dasnois. Chicago, 1991.

Meillassoux, Claude. "État et conditions des esclaves à Gumbu (Mali) au XIXe siècle." In Claude Meillassoux (ed.), *L'esclavage en Afrique précoloniale*, 221–251. Paris, 1975.

Meillassoux, Claude. "Female Slavery." In Claire Robertson and Martin A. Klein (eds.), *Women and Slavery in Africa*, 49–66. Madison, 1983.

Meniaud, J. *Le Haut–Sénégal–Niger.* 3 tomes. Paris, 1912.

Mercer, John. *Slavery in Mauritania Today.* Human Rights Group. Edinburgh, 1982.

Mercer, John. *Spanish Sahara.* London, 1976.

Meunie, Dj. Jacques. *Cités anciennes de Mauritanie.* Paris, 1961.

Meunie, Dj. Jacques. "Cités caravanières de Mauritanie: Tishitt et Oualata." *Académie des inscriptions et belles-lettres. Comptes rendus des séances* 154 (1954) 217–226.

Meyers, Allan. "Class, Ethnicity, and Slavery: The Origins of the Moroccan ʿAbid." *IJAHS* 10 (1977), 427–442.

Meyers, Allan. "Slave Soldiers and State Politics in Early ʿAlawi Morocco, 1668–1727." *IJAHS* 16 (1983), 39–48.

Miège, Jean Louis. *Le Maroc et l'Europe.* 4 tomes. Paris, 1961.

Miller, Joseph C. "The Significance of Drought, Disease, and Famine in the Agriculturally Marginal Zones of West-Central Africa." *JAH* 23 (1982), 17–61.

Miské, Ahmed-Bāba. "Al-Wasīt (1911). Tableau de la Mauritanie à la fin du XIXe siècle. *Bull. IFAN*, série B, 30 (1968), 117–164.

Miské, Ahmed Baba. "Une tribu maraboutique. Les Ahel Barikallah." *BCEHSAOF* 20 (1937), 482–506.

Miské, Ahmed-Bāba (ed.). *Al-Wasît. Tableau de la Mauritanie au début du XXe siècle.* Paris, 1970.

Mission catholique de Saint Joseph de Ngazobil (ed.). *Guide de la conversation français-wolof.* Reprint: Paris, 1987.

Mitchinson, Alex. Will. *The Expiring Continent: A Narrative of Travel in Senegambia.* London, 1881.

Mocquet, Jean. *Voyages en Afrique, Asie, Indes orientales et occidentales.* Paris, 1617.

Modat, Colonel. "Aperçu sur la société maure de l'Adrar." *BCEHSAOF* 5 (1922), 264–276.

Modat, Colonel. "Portugais, arabes, et français dans l'Adrar mauritanien." *BCEHSAOF* 5 (1922), 550–582.

Modat, Colonel. "La société berbere mauritanienne à la fin du XIe siècle." *BCEHSAOF* 4 (1921), 658–666.

Mollien, Gaspard Théodore. *L'Afrique occidentale en 1818.* Reprint: Paris, 1967.

Monod, Théodore. "Fruits et graines en Mauritanie." *Bulletin du museum national d'histoire naturelle*, Écologie générale 23, no. 273 (1974), 29–115.

Monod, Théodore. *L'isle d'Arguin (Mauritanie). Essai historique.* Lisbon, 1983.

Monod, Théodore. *Majâbat al-Koubra. Contribution à l'étude de l'"Empty Quarter" ouest saharien.* Dakar, 1958.

Monod, Théodore. "Majâbat al-Koubra (supplément)." *Bull. IFAN*, série A, 23 (1961), 591–637.

Monserat. "Mémoire inédit de Monserat sur l'histoire du nord du Sénégal de 1819 à 1839," edited and presented by Boubacar Barry. *Bull. IFAN*, série B, 32 (1970), 1–43.

Monteil, Vincent. "Al-Bakri (Cordoue, 1068) routier de l'Afrique blanche et noire de l'nord ouest." *Bull. IFAN*, série B, 20 (1968), 39–113.

Monteil, Vincent. "Chronique de Tichit." *Bull. IFAN* 1 (1939), 282–312.

Monteil, Vincent. "Chronique du Walo sénégalais, 1186–1855, par Amadu Wade 1886–1961," trans. from Wolof by Bassirou Cissé. Edited and presented by Vincent Monteil in *Esquisses sénégalaises*, 11–69. Dakar, 1966.

Monteil, Vincent. *Contributions à l'étude de la flore du Sahara occidental, I & II.* Notes et documents IV & V. Institut des hautes études marocaines. Paris, 1949 and 1953.

Monteil, Vincent. *Essai sur le chameau du Sahara occidental.* IFAN-Mauritanie. Saint-Louis du Sénégal, 1952.

Monteil, Vincent. *L'Islam noir.* Paris, 1964.

Moore, Francis. *Travels into the Inland Parts of Africa.* London, 1738.

Moraes Farias, P. F. de. "The Almoravids: Some Questions Concerning the Character of the Movement During its Period of Closest Contact with the Western Sudan." *Bull. IFAN*, série B, 39 (1967), 794–878.

Munier, P. *Le palmier-dattier en Mauritanie.* Annales I.F.A.C., no. 12. Paris, 1955.

Munson, Patrick J. "A Late Holocene (c. 4500–2300 BC) Climatic Chronology for the Southwestern Sahara." In J. A. Coetzee and E. M. Van Zinderen Bakker, Sr. (eds.), *Palaeoecology of Africa and the Surrounding Islands*, vol. 13, 53–62. Rotterdam, 1981.

Muterse, A. "Naufrage du brick-polacre La Lucie sur les côtes du désert du Sahara en juillet 1849." *RC*, 2e série, 6 (1851), 137–152.

Naegele, A. "Le ksar d'Atar et sa palmerie en Mauritanie." *La nature* 3267 (mai 1958), 270–276.

National Research Council. Board on Science and Technology for International Development. Commission on International Relations. *Staff Report: Environmental Degredation in Mauritania.* Washington, D.C., 1981.

Nelson, Cynthia. "Women and Power in Nomadic Societies of the Middle East." In Cynthia Nelson (ed.), *The Desert and the Sown: Nomads in the Wider Society,* 43–59. Berkeley, 1973.

Newbury, C. W. "North African and Sudan Trade in the Nineteenth Century." *JAH* 7 (1966), 233–246.

Nicholson, S. E. "Climatic Variations in the Sahel and Other African Regions during the Past Five Centuries." *Journal of Arid Environments* 1 (1978), 3–24.

Nicholson, Sharon E. "The Methodology of Historical Climate Reconstruction and Its Application to Africa." *JAH* 20 (1979), 31–49.

Nicholson, Sharon E. "Saharan Climates in Historical Times." In Martin A. J. Williams and Hugues Faure (eds.), *The Sahara and the Nile,* 173–200. Rotterdam, 1980.

Nicolaisen, Johannes. *Ecology and Culture of the Pastoral Tuareg with Particular Reference to the Tuareg of Ahaggar and Ayr.* Copenhagen, 1963.

Norris, H. T. *The Arab Conquest of the Western Sahara.* Harlow, Essex, 1986.

Norris, H. T. "Future Prospects in Azayr Studies." *African Language Review* 9 (1970–71), 99–109.

Norris, H. T. "The History of Shinqīt, According to the Idaw ᶜAlī Tradition." *Bull. IFAN,* série B, 24 (1962), 393–413.

Norris, H. T. *Saharan Myth and Saga.* Oxford, 1972.

Norris, H. T. *Shinqitī Folk Literature and Song.* Oxford, 1968.

Norris, H. T. "Znaga Islam during the Seventeenth and Eighteenth Centuries." *Bull. SOAS* 32 (1969), 496–526.

Norris, H. T. (trans. and ed.). *The Pilgrimage of Ahmad. Son of the Little Bird of Paradise: An Account of a Nineteenth Century Pilgrimage from Mauritania to Mecca.* Warminster, England, 1977.

Ockley, Simon (ed.) *An Account of South West Barbary . . . Written by a Person Who Has Been a Slave There.* London, 1713.

Office de la Recherche Scientifique et Technique Outre-Mer. *République du Sénégal, Précipitations journalières de l'origine des stations à 1965.* Paris, 1976.

Ogilby, John. *Africa.* 2 vols. London, 1670.

Ojo, Oyediran. *The Climates of West Africa.* London, 1977.

Oßwald, Rainer. *Die Handelsstädte der Westsahara.* Berlin, 1986.

Ould Ahmed Youra, M'Hammed. "Le livre des lettrés renseignés sur l'histoire des puits." *BCEHSAOF* 3 (1920), 311–345.

Ould Bah, Abdellahi. "Les villes anciennes de Mauritanie et leurs rapports avec le commerce au moyen-age." In *L'Histoire du Sahara et des relations transsahariennes entre le Maghreb et l'Ouest Africain du Moyen-Age à la fin de l'époque coloniale,* 115–124. Bergamo, Italy, 1986.

Ould Bah, Mohamd el Moktâr. "Introduction à la poésie mauritanienne (1600–1900)." *Arabica* 18, no. 1 (1971), 1–48.

Ould Cheikh, Abdel Wedoud. "Une 'caidalité' sans 'caid': Petite contribution à une histoire économique du 'tribalism' dans les confins occidentaux du Sahara." *Al-Wasīṭ*, no. 1 (1987), 11–32.

Ould Cheikh, Abdel Wedoud. *Éléments d'histoire de la Mauritanie.* Centre Culturel Français A. de Saint Exupéry. Nouakchott, 1988.

Ould Cheikh, Abdel Wedoud. "Herders, Traders and Clerics: The Impact of Trade, Religion and Warfare on the Evolution of Moorish Society." In John G. Galaty and Pierre Bonte (eds.), *Herders, Warriors, and Traders. Pastoralism in Africa,* 199–218. Boulder, 1991.

Ould Cheikh, Abdel Wedoud. "La tribu dans tous ses états." *Al-Wasīṭ,* no. 1 (1987), 89–98.

Ould Hamidoun, Mokhtar. *Précis sur la Mauritanie.* IFAN-Mauritanie. Saint-Louis du Sénégal, 1952.

Paddock, Judah. *A Narrative of the Shipwreck of the Ship Oswego.* New York and London, 1818.

Panet, Léopold. *Première exploration du Sahara occidental: Relation d'un voyage du Sénégal au Maroc, 1850.* Reprint: Paris, 1968.

Paradis, Venture de. "Itinéraires sur les pays compris entre le Maroc, Tombouctou, et le Sénégal." *BSG* 11 (1849), 100–105.

Park, Mungo. *Travels in the Interior Districts of Africa: Performed under the Direction and Patronage of the African Association, in the Years 1795, 1796, and 1797.* Reprint: London, 1910.

Pasquier, Roger. "Les traitants des comptoirs du Sénégal au milieu du XIXème siècle." In *Actes du Colloque Entreprises et Entrepreneurs en Afrique (XIXème et XXème siècles),* Laboratoire "Connaissance du Tiers-Monde," tome 1, 141–164. Paris, 1983.

Pelletan, Jean-Gabriel. *Mémoire sur la colonie française du Sénégal et ses dépendances.* Paris, An IX.

Pellow, Thomas. *The History of the Long Captivity and Adventures of Thomas Pellow in South Barbary.* Reprint: New York, 1973.

Pereira, Duarte Pacheco. *Esmeraldo de Situ Orbis,* trans. and annotated by Raymond Mauny. Bissau, 1956.

Petoney, Melchior. "A Relation Sent by Melchior Petoney to Nigil de Moura at Lisbon, from the Iland and Castle of Arguin . . ." In Richard Hakluyt (ed.), *The Principal Navigations Voyages Traffiques & Discoveries of the English Nation,* vol. 5, 43–44. London, Toronto, and New York, 1927.

Phillips, Richard (ed.). *A Collection of Modern and Contemporary Voyages and Travels,* vol. 4, Jean Baptiste Léonard Durand, "A Voyage to Senegal," 9–184. London, 1806.

Pierre, C. *L'élevage dans l'Afrique occidentale française.* Paris, 1906.

Poiret, Abbé. *Voyage en Barbarie, ou lettres écrites de l'ancienne Numidie, 1785–1786.* Paris, 1789.

Poulet, Georges. *Les maures de l'Afrique occidentale française.* Paris, 1904.

Pruneau de Pommegorge, A. G. *Description de la Nigritie.* Paris, 1789.

Raffenel, Anne. "De la colonie du Sénégal. Études historiques et commerciales." *RC,* 2e série, 4 (1850), 389–419; 2e série, 5 (1850), 5–44, 225–249, 311–335.

Raffenel, Anne. "Le haut Sénégal et la Gambie en 1843 et 1844." *RC*, le série, 8 (1846), 309–340.

Raffenel, Anne. *Nouveau voyage dans les pays des nègres*. 2 tomes. Paris, 1856.

Raffenel, Anne. *Voyage dans l'Afrique occidentale*. Paris, 1846.

Regnault, M. (ed.). *Résumé des voyages d'exploration faits par l'ordre du Gouverneur du Sénégal en 1859, 1860, et 1861, avec des notes et une carte*. Paris, 1864.

Renault, François. *L'abolition de l'esclavage au Sénégal*. Paris, 1972.

Rennel, Major. "Account of the Captivity of Alexander Scott among the Wandering Arabs of the Great African Desert," *Edinburgh Philosophical Journal* 4, no. 7 (Jan. 1821), 38–54, and no. 8 (Apr. 1821), 225–243.

Revol. "Études sur les fractions d'Imraguen sur la côte mauritanienne." *BCEHSAOF* 20 (1937), 179–224.

Ricard, Robert. "Les portugais et le Sahara atlantique au XVème siècle." *Hespéris* 11 (1930), 97–110.

Richardson, David. "Slave Exports from West and West-Central Africa, 1700–1810: New Estimates of Volume and Distribution." *JAH* 30 (1989), 1–22.

Richardson, James. *Travels in the Great Desert of the Sahara*. 2 vols. London, 1848.

Riley, James. *An Authentic Narrative of the Loss of the American Brig Commerce. . .* New York, 1813.

Ritchie, Carson I. A. "Deux textes sur le Sénégal (1673–1677)." *Bull. IFAN*, série B, 30 (1968), 289–353.

Ritchie, Carson I. A. "Impressions of Senegal in the Seventeenth Century." *African Studies* 26, no. 2 (1967), 59–93.

Robbins, Archibald. *A Journal, Comprising an Account of the Loss of the Brig Commerce of Hartford, Conn.* Hartford, Conn., 1829.

Robert-Chaleix, Denise. "Nouveaux sites médiévaux mauritaniens: Un aperçu sur les régions septentrionales du Bilad as-Soudan." In *L'histoire du Sahara et des relations transsahariennes entre le Maghreb et l'Ouest Africain du Moyen-Age à la fin de l'epoque coloniale*, 46–58. Bergamo, Italy, 1986.

Roberts, Richard L. "Ideology, Slavery, and Social Formation: The Evolution of Maraka Slavery in the Middle Niger Valley." In Paul E. Lovejoy (ed.), *The Ideology of Slavery in Africa*, 170–199. Beverly Hills, 1981.

Roberts, Richard L. "Long Distance Trade and Production: Sinsani in the Nineteenth Century." *JAH* 21 (1980), 169–188.

Roberts, Richard L. "Production and Reproduction of Warrior States: Segu Bambara and Segu Tukulor, c. 1712–1890." *IJAHS* 13 (1980), 389–419.

Roberts, Richard. *Warriors, Merchants, and Slaves: The State and the Economy in the Middle Niger Valley, 1700–1914*. Stanford, 1987.

Robinson, David. *Chiefs and Clerics*. Oxford, 1975.

Robinson, David. *The Holy War of Umar Tal*. Oxford, 1985.

Robinson, David. "The Islamic Revolution of Futa Toro." *IJAHS* 8 (1975), 185–211.

Roger, M. le Baron. *Fables sénégalaises*. Paris, 1828.

Roger, M. le Baron. "Résultat des questions adressés au nommé MBouia, marabout maure, de Tischit, et à un nègre de Walet, qui l'accompagnait." *Recueil des voyages et de mémoires de la Société de géographie de Paris* 2 (1825), 51–62.

Rosevear, D. R. *The Carnivores of West Africa*. London, 1974.

Rotberg, Robert I., and Theodore K. Rabb (eds.). *Climate and History: Studies in Interdisciplinary History.* Princeton, 1981.

Rousseau, R. "Le Sénégal d'autrefois. Étude sur le Cayor. Cahiers de Yoro Dyâo." *BCEHSAOF* 16 (1933), 237–298.

Rousseau, R. "Le Sénégal d'autrefois. Étude sur le Oualo. Cahiers de Yoro Dyâo." *BCEHSAOF* 12 (1929), 133–211.

Rousseau, R. "Le Sénégal d'autrefois. Étude sur le Toubé. Papiers de Rawane Boy." *BCEHSAOF* 14 (1931), 334–365.

Saad, Elias N. *Social History of Timbuktu.* Cambridge, 1983.

Sabatié, A. *Le Sénégal. Sa conquête et son organisation.* Saint-Louis du Sénégal, 1925.

Saᶜdī, ᶜAbd al-Rahmān ibn ᶜAbd Allāh. *Tarikh es-Soudan*, ed. and trans. O. Houdas. Reprint: Paris, 1964.

Saint-Père, J.-H. *Les Sarakollé du Guidimakha.* Paris, 1925.

Sal, Alioun. "Voyage de M. Alioun Sal, sous-lieutenant indigène à l'escadron de spahis du Sénégal (1860)." In Jean Ancelle (ed.), *Les explorations au Sénégal et dans les contrées voisines depuis l'antiquité jusqu'au nos jours*, 197–245. Paris, 1886.

Saugnier and Brisson. *Voyages to the Coast of Africa.* Reprint: New York, 1969.

Saulnier, Eugene. *La compagnie de Galam au Sénégal.* Paris, 1921.

Savigny, J. B., and A. Correard. *Narrative of a Voyage to Senegal in 1816.* Reprint: London, 1968.

Schmidt-Nelson, Knut. *Desert Animals: Physiological Problems of Heat and Water.* Oxford, 1964.

Schmitz, Jean. "L'État géomètre: Les leydi des Peul du Fuuta Tooro (Sénégal) et du Maasina (Mali)." *Cahiers d'études africaines*, 103, 26–3 (1986), 349–394.

Schnapper, B. "La fin du régime de l'exclusif: le commerce étranger dans les possessions françaises d'Afrique tropicale (1817–1870)." *Annales africaines* (1959), 149–200.

Searing, James F. "Aristocrats, Slaves, and Peasants: Power and Dependency in the Wolof States, 1700–1850." *IJAHS* 21 (1988), 475–503.

Searing, James F. *West African Slavery and Atlantic Commerce: The Senegal River Valley, 1700–1860.* Cambridge, 1993.

Seiwert, Wolf-Dieter. *Maurische Chronik.* Munich, 1988.

Shabeeny, El Hage Abd Salem. *An Account of Timbuctoo and Housa: Territories in the Interior of Africa*, ed. and trans. James Grey Jackson. London, 1820.

Shaw, Thomas. "Travels or Observations relating to Barbary." In John Pinkerton (ed.), *A General Collection of the Best and Most Interesting Voyages*, vol. 15, 499–680. London, 1814.

Shoberl, Frederic (ed.). *The World in Miniature. Africa, Containing a Description of the Manners and Customs with Some of the Historical Particulars of the Moors of the Zahara, and of the Negro Nations between the Rivers Senegal and Gambia.* 4 vols. London, 1821–1827.

Silla, Ousmane. "Villes historiques de l'Afrique saharo-soudanaise." *Revue française d'études politiques africaines* 29 (1968), 25–38.

Sinclair, A. R. E., and J. M. Fryxell. "The Sahel of Africa: Ecology of a Disaster." *Canadian Journal of Zoology* 63 (1985), 987–994.

Smith, Adam. *An Inquiry into the Nature and Causes of the Wealth of Nations.* Modern Library Edition. New York, 1965.

Smith, Andrew B. "Domesticated cattle and their introduction into West Africa." In Martin A. J. Williams and Hugue Faures (eds.), *The Sahara and the Nile,* 489–501. Rotterdam, 1980.

Smith, G., MBE. "Climate." In J. L. Cloudsley-Thompson (ed.), *Sahara Desert,* 17–30. Oxford, 1984.

Soh, Siré Abbas. *Chroniques du Fouta sénégalais.* Paris, 1913.

Soller, Ch. "Les caravanes du Soudan occidental et les pecheries d'Arguin." *Bulletin de la Société de géographie commerciale de Paris* 10 (1888), 280–287.

Stenning, D. J. *Savannah Nomads.* London, 1959.

Stewart, Charles C. "Emergent Classes and the Early State: The Southern Sahara." In Donald Crummey and Charles C. Stewart (eds.), *Modes of Production in Africa: The Precolonial Era,* 69–92. Beverly Hills, 1981.

Stewart, Charles C. "Political Authority and Social Stratification in Mauritania." In Ernest Gellner and Charles Micaud (eds.), *Arabs and Berbers: From Tribe to Nation in North Africa,* 375–393. London, 1973.

Stewart, Charles C. "Southern Saharan Scholarship and the 'Bilad al-Sudan'." *JAH* 17 (1976), 73–93.

Stewart, Charles C., with E. K. Stewart. *Islam and Social Order in Mauritania: A Case Study from the Nineteenth Century.* Oxford, 1973.

Stone, Thora G. "The Journey of Cornelius Hodges in Senegambia, 1689–90." *English Historical Review* 39 (1924), 89–95.

Street, Alayne, and Françoise Gasse. "Recent Developments in Research into the Quaternary Climatic History of the Sahara." In J. A. Allen (ed.), *The Sahara. Ecological Change and Early Economic History,* 7–28. Cambridgeshire, England, 1981.

Suret-Canale, Jean. "The Western Atlantic Coast 1600–1800." In J. F. A. Ajayi and Michael Crowder (eds.), *History of West Africa,* vol. 1, 387–440. New York, 1972.

Swidler, W. W. "Adaptive Processes Regulating Nomad-Sedentary Interaction in the Middle East." In Cynthia Nelson (ed.), *The Desert and the Sown,* 23–41. Berkeley, 1973.

Taine-Cheikh, Catherine. "La Mauritanie en noir et blanc. Petite promenade linguistique en hassaniyya." *Revue du monde musulman et de la Méditerranée* 54, no. 4 (1989), 90–105.

Tall, Madina Ly. *Contribution à l'histoire de l'empire du Mali.* Dakar, 1977.

Tamari, Tal. "The Development of Caste Systems in West Africa." *JAH* 32 (1991), 221–250.

Tauzin, Aline. "Le gigot et l'encrier. Maitres et esclaves en Mauritanie à travers la littérature orale." *Revue du monde musulman et de la Méditerranée* 51, no. 1 (1989), 74–90.

Thilmans, G. "Les planches sénégalaises et mauritaniennes des 'Atlas Vingboons' (XVIIe siècle)." *Bull. IFAN,* série B, 37 (1975), 95–116.

Thilmans, G., and J. P. Rossie. "Le 'Flambeau de la Navigation' de Dierick Ruiters." *Bull. IFAN,* série B, 31 (1969), 106–119.

Thomas, Benjamin E. *Trade Routes of Algeria and the Sahara*. Berkeley, 1957.

Thornton, John. *Africa and Africans in the Making of the Atlantic World, 1400–1680*. Cambridge, 1992.

Timbuktī, Mahmūd Kutī ibn Mutawakkil Kutī. *Tarikh el-fettach*, ed. and trans. O. Houdas. Paris, 1913.

Toupet, Charles. "La vallée de la Tamourt en Naaj: problèmes d'aménagement." *Bull. IFAN*, série B, 20 (1958), 68–110.

Toupet, Charles. *La sédentarisation des nomades en Mauritanie centrale sahelienne*. Lille, 1977.

Toupet, Charles. "Le ksar de Tichit." *La nature* 3274 (dec. 1959), 536–539.

Toupet, Charles. "Le rhythme des travaux agricoles en Mauritanie. L'utilité des calendriers agraires." *Notes africaines* 93 (1962), 24–27.

Toupet, Charles. "L'évolution du climat de la Mauritanie du môyen age jusqu'au nos jours." In *La désertification au sud du Sahara*, 56–63. Dakar, 1976. (Colloque de Nouakchott, 17–19 decembre 1973.)

Tristam, H. B. *The Great Sahara: Wanderings South of the Atlas Mountains*. London, 1860.

Tymowski, Michal. "Famines et épidemies à Oualata et à Tichit au XIXe siècle." *Africana Bulletin* (Warsaw), no. 27 (1978), 35–53.

United Nations Sudano-Sahelian Office. *The Gum Arabic Market and the Development of Production*. Geneva and New York, 1983.

Valantin, Durand. *Mémoire redigée à l'occasion de la pétition presentée à l'assemblée nationale par les commerçants européens du Sénégal*. Bordeaux, 1849.

Vene, A. "Relation du combat de M'Bilor et les évenements qui l'ont precedés et suivi." *Le spectateur militaire* 19 (juin 1835), 249–272.

Vergniot, Olivier. "De la distance en histoire. Maroc-Sahara occidental: Les captifs du hasard (XVIIe–XXe siècles)." *Revue du monde musulman et de la Méditeranée* 48–49, nos. 2–3 (1988), 96–125.

Vincent, B. "Acte de vente passé à Tombouctou; manuscrit arabe venue de Tombouctou." *Journal asiatique*, 3e série, 9 (1840), 375–389.

Vincent, Capt. M. "Voyage d'exploration dans l'Adrar." *Revue algérienne et coloniale* (oct. 1860), 445–494.

Vincent, Capt. M. "Voyage et expéditions au Sénégal et dans les contrées voisines. Voyage dans l'Adrar et retour à St.-Louis." *Le tour du monde* (1861), 49–64.

Webb, James L. A., Jr. "Ecological and Economic Change Along the Middle Reaches of the Gambia River, 1945–1985." *African Affairs: The Journal of the Royal African Society* 91 (1992), 543–565.

Webb, James L. A., Jr. *The Gambia in Graphs: A Summary of the National Agricultural Statistics*. Technical Report No. 3, USAID Project No. 625-0012. Dakar, 1986.

Webb, James L. A., Jr. "The Horse and Slave Trade between the Western Sahara and Senegambia." *JAH* 34 (1993), 221–246.

Webb, James L. A., Jr. *Rainfall and Risk in the Gambia River Basin: Implications for Investment Planning*. Technical Report No. 1, USAID Project No. 625-0012. Dakar, 1986.

Webb, James L. A., Jr. "Toward the Comparative Study of Money: A Reconsideration of West African Currencies and Neoclassical Monetary Concepts." *IJAHS* 15 (1982), 455–466.

Webb, James L. A., Jr. "The Trade in Gum Arabic: Prelude to French Conquest in Senegal." *JAH* 26 (1985), 149–168.

Whitcomb, Thomas. "New Evidence on the Origins of the Kunta—1 & 2." *Bull. SOAS* 38 (1975), 103–123 and 403–417.

Willis, John Ralph. "Introduction. Reflections on the Diffusion of Islam in West Africa." In John Ralph Willis (ed.), *Studies in West African History*. Vol. 1. *The Cultivators of Islam*, 1–39. London, 1979.

Willis, John Ralph. "The Western Sudan from the Moroccan Invasion (1591) to the Death of Al-Mukhtar Al-Kunti (1811)." In J. F. A. Ajayi and Michael Crowder (eds.), *History of West Africa*, vol. 1, 512–555. New York, 1976.

Windhus, John. *A Journey to Mequinez*. London, 1725.

Wuld as-Saᶜd, Muhammad al Muḫtar. "Émirats et espace émiral maure. Le cas du Trarza aux XVIIIe–XIXe siècles." *Revue du monde musulman et de la Méditerranée* 54, no. 4 (1989), 53–82.

Zeuner, Frederick E. *A History of Domesticated Animals*. New York, 1963.

Zeys, E. "Esclavage et guerre sainte. Consultation adressé aux gens du Touat par un érudit nègre, cadi de Timbouctou au XVIIème siècle." *Réunion d'études algériennes, Bulletin* 2 (1900), 125–151, 166–189.

Zouber, Mahmoud A. *Ahmad Bābā de Tombouctou (1556–1627). Sa vie et son œuvre*. Paris, 1977.

Index

Abitbol, Michel, 47

Acacia senegal. *See* Gum arabic

Acacia verek. *See* Gum arabic

Adanson, Michel: botanical studies of, 7; observations of, concerning sahelian fires, 7; observation of, of length of rainy season, 9

Adrar: rainfed agriculture in 1600, 10; and Sahelian cattle zone, 11; Bafur settlements in, 15; and Berber populations in seventeenth century, 16; early Tukulor residence in, 17; establishment of warrior emirate in, 18; dispersal and reorganization of Tadjakanet in, 48; emigrations from, due to desertification, 48; emigration of Kunta from, 51; dependence of, on imported food, 52; proximity of, to salt deposits, 56; shift of commercial center of, from Wadan to Shinqiti, 56–57; towns as commercial centers, 57, 58, 60, 133; salt caravans, 58, 60, 61; trade with Maghrib, 61, 62, 95; date production and trade, 62; salt as commodity money in, 62; horse breeding in, 70, 71, 74

Aftut, 163*n20*

Agriculture: rainfed, 3, 10, 14, 132; and changing crop regime as result of ecological change, 8; floodplain and flood recession, along Senegal River, 10, 14; jeeri land, 14; waalo land, 14; and freed slaves, 26; French experimentation at stations of, 27, 44, 115; desert-edge strategies of, in low rainfall years, 53–54. See also Cultivators, Black

Ahl Behenin, 145*n54*

Ahl Gannaar: formation of, 30; religious conversation of, 31; and Wolof cultivators, 31–32; linked to Nasir al-Din's governor of Waalo, 33; and jihad of Nasir al-Din, 34; ethnic transformation of, 36; diminished prestige of, 46; spiritual power of, 151*nl6*

Ahl Nbidnan, 145*n54*

Ahl Sidi Mahmud: formation of, 52; competition of, for the Kunta, 56

Ahl Tunsi, 158*n68*

Ahmad Bin Hayba Bin Nagmash, 43

Ahmadu Shaykhu, 95

Alawite dynasty: deputations from Saharan tribes, 48; invasions of western Sahara by, 48–49; seasonal raids of, on Black villages, 49. *See also* Morocco; Political violence; Raids

Algeria: slave markets in, 65

Ali al-Kori, 42, 151*nl6*

Ali Shandhora: and Moroccan military assistance, 39–40, 156*n56*; defeat of Brakna forces by, 40; and imported Dutch cloth, 98; and cattle trade with Saint-Louis du Sénégal, 153*n36*

Almoravids, 32

Al-Amin Wuld Najib, 110

Amader, 6

Amar Wuld Kumba, 148*n74*

Amar Wuld Mokhtar, 123

Amari Ngone Sobel: ritual bath of enthronement, 29; strikes against northern pressure, 29; and establishment of desert marabouts in Kajoor, 36; foundation of new capital, 151*nl2*. *See also* Damel; Kajoor

Amber, 124, 155*n44*

Amersal, 56

Andriot, 8

Aqqa, 48

Arab nomads: and arabization in fourteenth-seventeenth centuries, 14–15; immigration of, 14–15; and emergence of desert social order, 18; groups of, in Tagant, 18; southward drift of, down Atlantic littoral, 28. *See also* Arabo-Berbers; Ethnic identity

Guns: in European trade, 19, 82; introduced by trans-Saharan caravan, 61; used by Ulad Amar, 81; and slave trade, 89, 93; and gunpowder supply controlled by damel, 175n59
Gurara, 47, 166n42

Hafsa Mint Mahmsidigh, 110
Hamar, 154n39. *See also* Idaw al-Hajj
Hamid Fall: and foundation of Tigumatin, 30; and creation of the Ahl Gannaar, 31; in Wolof tradition, 31
Hamit Shay: and pillage in Kajoor, 160n87
Haratin: and grain production, 14, 46; in Mauritania today, 26; status of, 26; villages of, 26; captives brought to Morocco, 48; and gum trade, 119; of the Trarza emir, 157n57
Hassani: roles of, in western sahel, 18; style of life compared to that of zwaya, 20; need for mobility, 20; extraction by, of surplus from Black farmers, 20; and social/political hierarchy, 20–21, tactical advantage of, in raids, 22; raids on Black villages, 22–24, 64; and Shurbubba, 33, 35; political dominance of, in eighteenth century, 39–44; and Maïsa BiGe, 41; and gum trade, 119, 122; and French authority, 136. *See also* Arab nomads
Hassaniyya: and ethnic identity, 15; as lingua franca, 15; as language zone, 18
Hawd: rainfed agriculture in, 10; herding by, including horses, 13, 14; early Black settlements in, 17; establishment of emirate in, 18; grain tax in, 23–24; slavery in, 25; Soninke rivalry and civil war in, 48–49; progressive domination of desert forces in, 49; salt caravans, 56, 60; livestock-grain trade, 61; political violence in, 64; horses in, 71, 73–74, 95; cavalry in, 81
Hides: exports, 153n33
Hodges, Cornelius, 49, 53, 76
Horse trade: and raids, 24, 82; in horse-and-slave trade, 25, 69, 82, 87–90, 93–95; and jihad of Nasir al-Din, 34; and declining fortunes of Idaw al-Hajj, 46; imports from North Africa, 68; and economy of Senegambia, 69; from Sahara to Mali, 70; and Wolof kingdoms, 75, 82; interpretation of, by Boubacar Barry, 170n7; from

Cape Verde Islands, 172n34. *See also* Horses
Horses: herding of, with other animals, 13; used in raids, 23; mortality of, 68, 69, 72, 74–75, 76; cavalry in savanna states, 68, 69, 71–72, 75, 77–79, 80–82, 94–95; West African pony, 68, 70, 72–73; and immunity to disease, 68, 72; North African, 68, 72, 80; interbreeding, 68, 72–73, 75, 81, 87, 88; Barbary, 68, 73–74, 75, 76, 80, 88; and political violence, 68–69, 71–72, prices, 69, 75–76, 88, 89, 94, 95; saddles, 70; as tribute, 71; Arab stirrup, 71–72, 171n21; and French cavalry, 74–75; Wolof terminology for, 75; desert cavalry, 76, 81; and grain demand, 155n50; average lifespan of, in early twentieth century in upper Senegal-Niger basin, 170n1; pedigrees, 172n30

Ibn Battuta, 143n40
Ibn Khaldun, 171n20
Id Acheghra, 30
Id Agvudya, 30, 110
Idaw al-Hajj: settlement of, in Njambuur, 35–36, 154n38; assimilation of, into Black world, 36; and plantations, 44; reestablishment in the Trarza, 44; under attack from Trarza warriors, 44; diminished fortunes of, 46; migration from Wadan to Trarza, 48, 109; settlement in Tagant, 52; warfare between factions at Wadan, 52; and gum trade, 109–112; negotiations with French, 115; 120, 129; marriage among, 154n39; settlements in Senegal, 154n39; annual trans-Saharan caravan and, 174n55; trade dominance of, at Portendick, 181n35
Idaw Ali: and foundation of Tidjikja, 50; competition of, for the Kunta, 56; and spread of Tidjani Islam, 56
Idaw Ish, 120, 149n5, 164n23
Idewbje, 52
Iggawin, 146n61
Ijil: rock salt deposits at, 56, 57–58; free transportation of salt from, for Kunta, 58; distance of, from caravan towns, 58; identification of, 165n37; estimate of size of salt caravans from, 167n53. *See also* Salt; Salt trade
Imragen, 26
Inchiri: and Sahelian cattle zone, 11; 14; Bafur settlements in, 15

Lovejoy, Paul E., 65
Ludamar. *See* Ulad Amar
Lutaydat, 157*n56*

Maghrib: as northern reaches of great
camel zone, 11; fourteenth-century migrations from, to western Sahara, 14; caste
in, 21; importance of salt exports to, 55;
livestock trade, 61; slave markets in, 63,
65, 67, 88–89, 90, 135; as source of
horses, 72, 75, 82, 95
Maitres de langue, 120, 129
Maize: annual rainfall required to cultivate,
8; cessation of cultivation in Waalo, 8; as
a dominant crop of the late seventeenth
and early eighteenth centuries, 8; introduction by Portuguese, 8; as a minor crop
in Kajoor, 8; reduced yields due to drought,
9; price in late seventeenth century, 37; as
contemporary staple in southern Sene-
gambia, 141*n20*; terminology in Labat
text, 141*n17*
Majabat al-Kubra, 16, 48
Malaria, 3, 14
Mali, 14
Malian empire: importance of horse trade
to, 68
Mambodje Kumba, 42
Al-Mansur Saadi, 30
Manumission, 26
Marchands détaillants, 116
Marigotiers, 117, 118
Marrakech, 88, 174*n55*
Masna: in Tishit, 61; diaspora in western
Mali, 61
Mauritania, Islamic Republic of: slave and
freed populations in, 26, 169*n70*
Mawlay Ishmaïl, 48
Maxwell, Lt. Colonel, 93, 160*n84*
Mazamba Jakhumpa, 115
Mbakoul, 36
Mbayar, 72. *See also* Horses
Mbul, 31, 32, 151*n12*, 152*n17*
Meïsa BiGe, 41
Mérinaghen, 161*n91*
Midlich, 32
Migration: early, as result of desertifica-
tion, 15–17; of warrior groups in Gibla in
fourteenth and fifteenth centuries, 28; and
immigration of Bubbazul, 29; direction of

Arab and Berber, 29, 30; and formation
of Ahl Gannaar, 30; and Idaw al-Hajj, 36;
as result of famine, 41–42; participation in
White, from Adrar to Tagant in seven-
teenth century, 50. *See also* Livestock
herding
Millet: compared to maize, 8; as commodity
money, 62; and marigot gum trade, 119
Mkubul, 166*n39*
Mokhtar Mbay, 36
Al-Mokhtar Wuld al-Amin Wuld Najib, 110
Mollein, Gaspard Théodore, 94
Moore, Francis, 9, 75
Moroccan Raids. *See* Alawite dynasty;
Political violence; Raids
Morocco: raiding by, 24, 49; supply of
North African horses from, 70; slave ex-
ports to, 94; and gum market, 99; inva-
sion of Waalo by, 157*n63*. *See also* Alawite
dynasty; Maghrib; Saadian empire
Mpar, 72. *See also* Horses
Muallimin, 146*n61*
Mudaaf, 63
Muhammad al-Habib, 45, 46
Muhammad Talib Wuld Bajid, 51
Muhammad Wuld Muhammad Shayn,
164*n23*
Muhammad al-Yadali, 33, 34
Muhandh Baba, 45
Mun, 54
Muslaje, 154*n38*. *See also* Idaw al-Hajj

Najib. *See* Al-Amin Wuld Najib
Nasir al-Din: reform movement and conver-
sion of Black states, 32–33; and jihad,
32–35; death of, in battle, 33; interpreta-
tions of reform movement of, 33–35,
152*n28*, 153*n29*; and Atlantic slave trade,
34–35; and use of horses, 76
Ndakhoumpe, 154*n38*, 154*n39*. *See also*
Idaw al-Hajj
Ndara Sghair, 151*n16*
Nder, 36
Négociants, 116, 117, 118, 124, 126, 127
Ngalil, 154*n38*. *See also* Idaw al-Hajj
Ngoumbelle, 154*n38*. *See also* Idaw al-Hajj
Ngurbel, 39, 111
Nicholson, Sharon E., 4
Niger Bend: Moroccan conquest of, 16; as
source of slaves, 64, 66